Revolutionizing Education in the Age of AI and Machine Learning

Maki K Habib
The American University in Cairo, Egypt

A volume in the Advances in Educational Technologies and Instructional Design (AETID) Book Series

IGI Global
DISSEMINATOR OF KNOWLEDGE

Published in the United States of America by
IGI Global
Information Science Reference (an imprint of IGI Global)
701 E. Chocolate Avenue
Hershey PA, USA 17033
Tel: 717-533-8845
Fax: 717-533-8661
E-mail: cust@igi-global.com
Web site: http://www.igi-global.com

Library of Congress Cataloging-in-Publication Data

Names: Habib, Maki K., 1955- editor.
Title: Revolutionizing education in the age of AI and machine learning / editor, Maki K. Habib.
Description: Hershey, PA : Information Science Reference, [2019] | Includes bibliographical references.
Identifiers: LCCN 2018036346| ISBN 9781522577935 (hardcover) | ISBN 9781522577942 (ebook)
Subjects: LCSH: Artificial intelligence--Educational applications.
Classification: LCC LB1028.43 .R484 2019 | DDC 371.33/4--dc23 LC record available at https://lccn.loc.gov/2018036346

This book is published in the IGI Global book series Advances in Educational Technologies and Instructional Design (AETID) (ISSN: 2326-8905; eISSN: 2326-8913)

British Cataloguing in Publication Data
A Cataloguing in Publication record for this book is available from the British Library.

Advances in Educational Technologies and Instructional Design (AETID) Book Series

ISSN:2326-8905
EISSN:2326-8913

Editor-in-Chief: Lawrence A. Tomei, Robert Morris University, USA

MISSION

Education has undergone, and continues to undergo, immense changes in the way it is enacted and distributed to both child and adult learners. In modern education, the traditional classroom learning experience has evolved to include technological resources and to provide online classroom opportunities to students of all ages regardless of their geographical locations. From distance education, Massive-Open-Online-Courses (MOOCs), and electronic tablets in the classroom, technology is now an integral part of learning and is also affecting the way educators communicate information to students.

The **Advances in Educational Technologies & Instructional Design (AETID) Book Series** explores new research and theories for facilitating learning and improving educational performance utilizing technological processes and resources. The series examines technologies that can be integrated into K-12 classrooms to improve skills and learning abilities in all subjects including STEM education and language learning. Additionally, it studies the emergence of fully online classrooms for young and adult learners alike, and the communication and accountability challenges that can arise. Trending topics that are covered include adaptive learning, game-based learning, virtual school environments, and social media effects. School administrators, educators, academicians, researchers, and students will find this series to be an excellent resource for the effective design and implementation of learning technologies in their classes.

COVERAGE

- Virtual School Environments
- Curriculum Development
- Game-Based Learning
- Educational Telecommunications
- Social Media Effects on Education
- Adaptive Learning
- Hybrid Learning
- Web 2.0 and Education
- Online Media in Classrooms
- Digital Divide in Education

The Advances in Educational Technologies and Instructional Design (AETID) Book Series (ISSN 2326-8905) is published by IGI Global, 701 E. Chocolate Avenue, Hershey, PA 17033-1240, USA, www.igi-global.com. This series is composed of titles available for purchase individually; each title is edited to be contextually exclusive from any other title within the series. For pricing and ordering information please visit http://www.igi-global.com/book-series/advances-educational-technologies-instructional-design/73678. Postmaster: Send all address changes to above address.

Titles in this Series

For a list of additional titles in this series, please visit:
https://www.igi-global.com/book-series/advances-educational-technologies-instructional-design/73678

The Roles of Technology and Globalization in Educational Transformation
Blessing F. Adeoye (Walden University, USA) and Gladys Arome (Marian University, USA)
Information Science Reference • copyright 2020 • 259pp • H/C (ISBN: 9781522597469) • US $195.00 (our price)

Utilizing Educational Data Mining Techniques for Improved Learning Emerging Research and Opportunities
Chintan Bhatt (Charotar University of Science and Technology, India) Priti Srinivas Sajja (Sardar Patel University, India) and Sidath Liyanage (University of Kelaniya, Sri Lanka)
Information Science Reference • copyright 2020 • 166pp • H/C (ISBN: 9781799800101) • US $165.00 (our price)

Claiming Identity Through Redefined Teaching in Construction Programs
Sherif Mostafa (Griffith University, Australia) and Payam Rahnamayiezekavat (Western Sydney University, Australia)
Information Science Reference • copyright 2020 • 259pp • H/C (ISBN: 9781522584520) • US $185.00 (our price)

Global Perspectives on Teaching and Learning Paths in Islamic Education
Miftachul Huda (Universiti Pendidikan Sultan Idris Malaysia, Malaysia) Jimaain Safar (Universiti Teknologi Malaysia, Malaysia) Ahmad Kilani Mohamed (Universiti Teknologi Malaysia, Malaysia) Kamarul Azmi Jasmi (Universiti Teknologi Malaysia, Malaysia) and Bushrah Basiron (Universiti Teknologi Malaysia, Malaysia)
Information Science Reference • copyright 2020 • 341pp • H/C (ISBN: 9781522585282) • US $195.00 (our price)

Social Justice and Putting Theory Into Practice in Schools and Communities
Susan Trostle Brand (University of Rhode Island, USA) and Lori E. Ciccomascolo (University of Rhode Island, USA)

For an entire list of titles in this series, please visit:
https://www.igi-global.com/book-series/advances-educational-technologies-instructional-design/73678

IGI Global
DISSEMINATOR OF KNOWLEDGE

701 East Chocolate Avenue, Hershey, PA 17033, USA
Tel: 717-533-8845 x100 • Fax: 717-533-8661
E-Mail: cust@igi-global.com • www.igi-global.com

Table of Contents

Detailed Table of Contents

Artificial intelligence (AI) is ubiquitous in our lives and is progressing at an accelerated rate in the past 60 years. AI application is diverse and AI technology continues to grow. It enables a machine to think like human beings and has opened a new horizon for industries, businesses, transportation, hospitals, and schools. How is AI applied to educational settings? How will the emergence of AI technology assist teachers' teaching and improve students' learning? Will the implementation of AI technology in education replace schoolteachers? What would be the ethical concerns of AI technology? What role do teachers play with AI in education? The purpose of this chapter is to explore the roles that teachers play in the innovation and evolution of AI and to seek approaches teachers should take in coping with AI technology. Issues and problems of teaching with AI will be discussed; solutions will be recommended.

The development of AI technologies in recent years has opened the doors to a wide array of application domains. One field of study in particular has great potential to use this knowledge: physical education and sport. New devices and software have made their way into the field of physical activity, motivating the investigation of AI-driven technologies as a tool in developing a new type of educational system. The general scope of this chapter is to analyze the use of AI individualized education in one major field of study: physical education and sport. The use of AI technologies

Robotics e-learning environment that facilitates tailored learning for individual students studying robotics is developed. The developed collaborative and distributed intelligent environment (CoDIE) enables multi-users to access simultaneously remote and integrated mixed reality facilities through the web. The developed system constitutes a robotic center to help in transferring theoretical knowledge enhanced by simulation and practical experience. It enables realistic interaction by immersing users in a shared 3D CoDIE. The system enables users to do programming, simulations, experiments, manipulating data and objects, diagnostics and analyses, control and monitor actions. Also, users can receive feedback from the system or instructors. The developed system has been implemented and tested using two real manipulators and virtual robots supporting real-time tracking and simulation. Three modes of operations have been implemented, individual robot training mode through virtual robot models, multi-user mode working together, and individual or group-based training by instructor.

The fast-growing field of technology allows for the development, design, and implementation of smart solutions to several industries such as smart grid, manufacturing, automotive, and robotics. Trends in smart solutions are based on providing a certain degree of intelligence to the process and products through intelligent artificial and machine learning algorithms. It also involves further use of devices based on power electronics elements, fast microcontrollers, intelligent algorithms, and processing of information via local or cloud. Hence, a new workforce that possesses multidisciplinary skills (i.e., dealing with different fields of knowledge in order to find solutions to complex problems) is required. Recently, virtual laboratories have emerged so as to aid in the improvement of forming engineers. In this chapter, a virtual co-simulation laboratory is proposed to deal with the lack of engineers with multidisciplinary skills in mind; additionally, a new framework based in co-simulation, co-modeling, and co-design is proposed in order to maximize the use of the laboratory proposed.

Learning is the main feature that is connected to education. Education increases the power of visualization and to differentiate between the right and wrong. Education in these days has become expensive for the poor guardians. Education indeed helps to know the real values in relation to social and cultural behavior so that one can become a decent person in nature in society. The role of technology in modern education helps to lookout the current trends and to solve the problems using artificial intelligence in education. AI tools play a vital role in research and help to access the literature worldwide. AI can also provide the solution to social challenges like diversity in nature, security, and privacy of the person. Apart from education, AI has made an impact in other fields like social media, communication, and technology.

Intelligent tutoring systems (ITS) research is not a new field of study. Despite its pedagogical value, very few ITS are developed intended for Filipino learners. The dearth of ITS research in a local setting discounted the fact Filipino learners might need a different learning approach. This chapter presented the state of ITS research in the Philippines. Readers would be informed that there is a need for multidisciplinary studies relating to Filipino learners that could serve basis for the development of culturally-related ITS. It also described Filipino learners in terms of culture, and it will attempt to link these descriptions as design considerations for the development of ITS. Finally, it provided insights and directions on how to develop an ITS for Filipino learners.

E-learning or learning management systems (LMS) are broadly used in higher education systems. They've become a necessity to help the participants (instructors, students, and administrators) in their daily use. Learning analytics presents an auspicious approach. This chapter aims to examine the acceptance of analytics and use of an LMS at Jordanian universities. It also focuses on the factors influencing acceptance of analytics in LMS at Jordanian universities. Therefore, the chapter presents a new model for acceptance of analytics in learning management systems at Jordanian universities. It calls Jordanian learning management system (JLMS). This chapter is based on the most recent and related literature explaining various scenarios where learning management systems address learning issues in the digital environment in a way that was not possible in the previous confines of print logics.

The present blistering modernization, epitomized by artificial intelligence, demands engineering graduates to address holistic, fast-changing, and even unknown problems. Thus, skills development, such as self-learning, is gaining importance against the traditional educational approach. To this regard, the wit-learning methodology was designed to stimulate the research skills during a course, supported on the similitude of the research endeavor with the desired engineers' profile. It stands out from other proposed alternatives targeting the students' capabilities that do not focus on research skills or misses their quantitative evaluation. In this chapter, the wit-learning methodology is presented together with its assessment regarding research skills acquisition, using direct and indirect measurements. Notably, it was verified to help improve the research skills through three criteria: the improvement of the students' research reports, the increased students' agreement to researchers while evaluating research reports, and their understanding of the research goals and processes.

Preface

Advances in artificial intelligence (AI) and computer technologies along with the development of machine learning techniques are helping to open the way dealing with big data, facilitate effective techniques to analyze data with some level of inference capabilities to support decision making. In addition, applications of machine learning are impacting every aspect of life such as, customer services, retails, education, health diagnosis, intelligent cars, robotics, industrial automation, object identification and computer vision, understanding natural languages and more. Furthermore, the advancement in the development of many virtual agent tools has contributed to the interaction experience of users.

AI serves as a catalyst for transformation in the field of digital teaching and learning that introduces novel solutions to revolutionize all dimensions of the educational process leading to tailored individualize learning experience and to change the role of teachers more into mentoring and recommendations, and automate all administrative processes linked to education. AI and machine learning are already contributing and expect to highly expand to improve the quality of the educational process by bringing advantages to the teaching, learning and administration, such as, personalized and interactive tutoring with the ability to adjust the content and the learning pace of each individual student while assessing their performance and gives feedback; support adaptive and interdisciplinary learning path using each student's performance feedback and help to assess the collected and accumulated information to restructure student's learning path using AI technologies and based on individual creative skills; the use of virtual and augmented technologies based on AI supporting 3D interactive animations and play as a virtual assistant role; help to resolve challenges facing students with learning disabilities by adapting the teaching style using cognition systems to fulfil their needs, while it helps educators to recognize students with learning disabilities; have adaptive curriculum development; effective grading and advising process; enhance collaborative learning; support formation of global educational social network in different dimensions of the education process.

These shifts in the educational paradigm have a profound impact on the quality and the way we live, interact with each other, and define our values. Thus, there is a need for an earnest inquiry into the cultural repercussions of this phenomenon that extends beyond superficial analyses of AI-based applications in education.

This book *Revolutionizing Education in the Age of AI and Machine Learning* addresses the need for a scholarly exploration of the cultural and social impacts of the rapid expansion of artificial intelligence in the field of education including potential consequences these impacts could have on culture, social relations, and values. The content within this publication covers such topics AI and tutoring, role of teachers, physical education and sports, interactive E-learning and virtual laboratories, adaptive curricula development, support critical thinking, and augmented intelligence and it is designed for educators, academicians, administrators, researchers, and professionals.

This new book aims to capture the state-of-art of research developments in the subject area of revolutionizing education in the era of AI and machine learning and to provide the latest practical and theoretical knowledge in the field. This handbook includes 10 chapters:

Chapter 1: The Changing Roles of Teachers With AI by Libi Shen and Anchi Su aiming to explore the roles that teachers play in the innovation and evolution of AI and to seek approaches teachers should take in coping with AI technology.

Chapter 2: AI and Individualized Education in Phys Ed and Sport by Adrian Patrascu and Monica Patrascu. This chapter focuses on analyzing the use of AI individualized education in physical education and sports, and investigate AI-driven technologies as a tool in developing such technologies.

Chapter 3: Revolution by Evolution: How Intelligent Tutoring Systems Are Changing the Education by Stefka Tzanova discusses the development of intelligent tutoring systems (ITSs) for education in the last decade and traces the challenges they meet by examining its social and cultural impacts.

Chapter 4: Concerning the Integration of Machine Learning Contents in Mechatronics Curricula by Jörg Frochte, Markus Lemmen, and Marco Schmidt provides an analysis of how machine learning can be integrated as a mandatory part of the curriculum of mechatronic degree courses while considering the required minimal changes in fundamental courses, and how traditional subjects like robotics, automation and automotive engineering can profit most of this approach.

Chapter 5: Robotics E-Learning Supported by Collaborative and Distributed Intelligent Environment by Maki K. Habib introduces the development of Robotics E-Learning environment that facilitates tailored learning for individual students studying Robotics. This is supported by the development of collaborative and distributed intelligent environment (CoDIE) that enables multi users to access simultaneously remote and integrated mixed reality facilities through the Web.

Chapter 6: Virtual Laboratory to Face New Challenges in the Industry: Virtual Laboratory as Part of New Education Age by Arturo Soriano, Pedro Ponce, and Arturo Molina proposes a virtual co-simulation laboratory to deal with the lack of engineers with multidisciplinary skills in mind; In addition, a new framework based in co-simulation, co-modeling, and co-design is proposed in order to maximize the use of the laboratory proposed.

Chapter 7: Impact of Social and Cultural Challenges in the Education Using AI by Kapil Sethi, Ajay Sharma, Shweta Chauhan, and Varun Jaiswal presents how the impact of using AI in education on the real values in relation to social and cultural behavior.

Chapter 8: Intelligent Tutoring Systems for Filipino Learners: Current Research, Gaps, and Opportunities by Rex Bringula introduces the state of Intelligent Tutoring Systems (ITS) research in the Philippines and the needs.

Chapter 9: A New Paradigm for Acceptance of Analytics in Learning Management Systems at Jordanian Universities (JLMS) by Abdeleh Al Amoush and Kamaljeet Sandhu aims to present a new model for acceptance of analytics in learning management systems at Jordanian universities, it calls Jordanian Learning Management System (JLMS).

Chapter 10: The Wit-Learning Methodology as a Means for Research Skills Acquisition: A Longitudinal Assessment by Luis Ibarra, Arturo Soriano, Pedro Ponce, and Arturo Molina presents wit-learning methodology together with its assessment regarding research skills acquisition, using direct and indirect measurements. This work was verified to help improve the research skills through three criteria: the improvement of the students' research reports, the increased students' agreement to researchers while evaluating research reports, and their understanding of the research goals and processes.

The development and advancement of the field of revolutionizing education in the era of AI and machine learning helps to motivate educators, academicians, researchers and professionals who are looking to broaden their knowledge and expertise to develop innovative, intelligent, and sustainable ideas, and techniques supporting the development and applications of AI and machine learning in education with focus on today's and future's most pressing challenges.

Maki K. Habib
The American University in Cairo, Egypt

Chapter 1
The Changing Roles of Teachers With AI

Libi Shen
University of Phoenix, USA

Anchi Su
UCLA, USA

ABSTRACT

Artificial intelligence (AI) is ubiquitous in our lives and is progressing at an accelerated rate in the past 60 years. AI application is diverse and AI technology continues to grow. It enables a machine to think like human beings and has opened a new horizon for industries, businesses, transportation, hospitals, and schools. How is AI applied to educational settings? How will the emergence of AI technology assist teachers' teaching and improve students' learning? Will the implementation of AI technology in education replace schoolteachers? What would be the ethical concerns of AI technology? What role do teachers play with AI in education? The purpose of this chapter is to explore the roles that teachers play in the innovation and evolution of AI and to seek approaches teachers should take in coping with AI technology. Issues and problems of teaching with AI will be discussed; solutions will be recommended.

DOI: 10.4018/978-1-5225-7793-5.ch001

INTRODUCTION

Artificial Intelligence (AI) is omnipresent in our lives and is progressing efficiently in modern world. The beginning of AI can be traced to the 1956 Dartmouth summer research project on Artificial Intelligence initiated by John McCarthy, Marvin Minsky, Nathaniel Rochester, and Claude Shannon (McCarthy, Minky, Rochester, & Shannon, 2006). Today, AI work is performed in detecting cancer, reducing the risk of airplane collisions, and developing autonomous vehicles, etc. AI-equipped robots have outperformed human surgeons in sewing up cuts; performing search and rescuing missions; providing care for children, seniors, and hospital patients; assisting credit card companies with fraud detection; and assisting Apple's Siri, Microsoft's Cortana, and Amazon's Alexia to learn users' behaviors to better serve their customers (Etzioni & Etzioni, 2017).

AI technology has been applied to education in the recent two decades. The Intelligent Tutoring Systems (ITS) cover all major AI topics (e.g., knowledge representation, machine learning, natural language, planning, reasoning, explanation), and the systems has formed an interesting test-bed to formalize cognitive theories and to experiment with their operationalization (Andriessen & Sandberg, 1999). AI in education has been applied to various domains, such as physics, programming, writing essays, and reading as well as the development of instructional systems. The most typical AI applications in the educational field involve knowledge representation, intelligent tutoring, natural language processing, and autonomous agents (Drigas & Ioannidou, 2012). AI in education has created powerful learning environments and positive interactive experiences for students over the decades.

Additionally, AI application tools have successfully been applied to solve problems in special education related to physical and sensory impairments, Autistic Spectrum Disorders, reading/writing/spelling difficulties, dyslexia, Attention Deficit Hyperactivity Disorder, difficulties in mathematics, and Attention Deficit Disorder (Drigas & Ioannidou, 2012). The focus of Artificial Intelligence in education is on the development and evaluation of computer software to improve teaching and learning. Woolf (2015) believed that AI is invaluable because it can personalize instruction, enhance student experience, supply data for the development of novel education theory, and teach 21st century skills (i.e., cognitive skills, interpersonal skills, intrapersonal skills). Luckin, Holmes, Griffiths, and Forcier (2016, p.14) pinpointed that "AI scientists are currently building on new approaches in machine learning, computer modeling, and probability statistics to improve financial decision making, and are using decision theory and neuroscience to drive the development of more effective medical diagnostics."

It seems that AI in education is ubiquitous and omnipotent; however, while human teachers can understand students' tones and inflections within a dialogue to provide continual feedback through ongoing dialogue, the "Intelligent Tutoring Systems are still limited in dialogue and feedback" (Woolf, 2015, p.43). AI can make mistakes while making decisions for students (Rieland, 2017). We might ask AI technology becomes more intelligent and capable than teachers, will it replace teachers in the job market in the future? What role should teachers take in the era of AI technology? The purpose of this chapter is to explore the roles of teachers with the amelioration of AI in education (AIEd) and approaches teachers should take in the era of AI technology advancement.

BACKGROUND

New technologies have contributed to the evolution of teaching methods and materials as well as impacting student learning at schools. In the past century, traditional teaching methods have been replaced by newer approaches due to the technological innovation. Seventeen years ago, Smith (2002) indicated that "two influences that shaped reading instruction during the period 1950 and 1965 were expanding knowledge and technological revolution" (p. 287). McArthur, Lewis, and Bishay (2005, p. 42) posited that "new technologies can automate symbol-manipulation algebra and spelling correction, making these skills less important to learn, while increasing the importance of higher-order skills required to do creative mathematics and writing" with ITS. The Intelligent Tutoring Systems (ITS) was the earliest application of Artificial Intelligence (AI) in education. It was developed to implement traditional methods of learning and teaching in the 1980s. Over the years, the Intelligent Tutoring Systems (ITS), the Interactive Learning Environments (ILEs), and the movement from ITS to ILEs and to mixed-initiative systems (a combination of both approaches) in teaching and learning were developed.

ITS consists of four components: a domain model, a student model, a tutor model, and a user interface model (ITS, 2018). ITS is a computer system that provides customized instruction and feedback to students without teacher intervention. The Intelligent Tutoring Systems paradigm has dominated the field of AI in Education for about 20 years (Andriessen & Sandberg, 1999). Since ITS typically tries to "replicate the role of a teacher or a teaching assistant, and increasingly automate pedagogical functions such as problem generation, problem selection, and feedback generation" (ITS, 2018, p.4), it helped to create new methods and to redefine valued educational goals.

Microworlds and ILEs have shifted educational goals and methods to foster a deeper conceptual understanding of ideas (e.g., Boolean networks and chaos, graph theory, and inquiry skills) (McArthur Lewis, & Bishay, 2005). The principles of the Interactive Learning Environments (ILEs) consisted of construction instead of instruction; student control instead of tutor control; individualization determined by the student, not the teacher; and rich feedback generated by the student's interaction with the learning environment not the tutor (McArthur, Lewis, & Bishay, 2005). Microworlds and ILEs supported student-centered learning through inquiry and called for curriculum reform; however, they faced three challenges: cognitive challenges, evaluation challenges, and implementation limitations (McArthur, Lewis, & Bishay, 2005). Thus, AIEd advanced further and shifted from ITS to ILEs due to the progress or breakthrough in AI over the years.

Several questions emerged in the era of AI. What can AI do for teachers, students, and administrators at schools? Will AI replace schoolteachers and staff as it did to factory workers? What would happen if AIEd surpasses human intelligence and dominates education in future? How does the implementation of AI impact pedagogy, students' individual learning, curriculum design, educational policies, and teachers' jobs? What changing role can teachers take? These are important issues for exploration. Popenici and Kerr (2017) pinpointed that,

The rise of AI makes it impossible to ignore a serious debate about its future role of teaching and learning in higher education and what type of choices universities will make in regard to this issue. The fast pace of technology innovation and the associated job displacement, acknowledged widely by experts in the field (source), implies that teaching in higher education requires a reconsideration of teachers' role and pedagogies (p. 10-11).

LITERATURE REVIEW

In the past two decades, many researchers have devoted efforts to exploring AI in education (AIEd). Some researchers focused on the functions, application, and development of AI in education (e.g., Altinay, Karaatmaca, & Altinay, 2019; Andriessen & Sandberg, 1999; Beck, Stern, & Haugsjaa, 2005; Brown & Kauchak, 2013; Faggella, 2017; Gadanidis, 2017; Gose, 2016; Kumar, 2017; Madda, 2017; Popenici & Kerr, 2017; Poth, 2018; Rajasingham, 2009; Rieland, 2017; Rizzotto, 2017; Wagner, 2018; Wollowski, Neller, & Boerkoel, 2017). Others expressed the concerns of ethics in AI (e.g., Burton et. al, 2017; Etzioni & Etzioni, 2017; Lambert, 2018; Lee, 2018; McClure, 2018). Also, educational robotics has brought interest to teachers and researchers in recent years, and many researchers have explored the impact and challenges of educational robotics in teaching and learning (e.g., Alimisis,

2013; Atmatzidou, Demetriadis, & Nika, 2018; Crowe, 2018; Mallawaarachchi, 2017; Oblinger, 2018; Ortiz & Smith, 2015). In the following, the definitions, foundation, categories, evolution, and application of AI will be examined. The advantages and disadvantages of artificial intelligence, intelligent tutoring systems, and models of AI in education will be reviewed; the functions and applications of AI in education will be investigated.

Definitions of Artificial Intelligence (AI)

Professor John McCarthy coined the term "Artificial Intelligence" with Marvin Minsky, Nathaniel Rochester, and Claude Shannon in a proposal on August 31, 1955. McCarthy, Minsky, Rochester, and Shannon (1956) outlined their efforts to find ways machines could use language, form abstractions and concepts, and solve human problems. Andriessen and Sandber (1999) addressed the dynamic aspects of AI, which distinguished it from other technologies. Have the definitions of AI changed in the past six decades? How have the definitions changed over the years?

As shown in **Table 1,** the definitions were developed from "the science of making machines do things that would require intelligent if done by men" (McCarthy, Minsky, Rochester, & Shannon, 1956) to "computing systems that are able to engage in human-like processes such as learning, adapting, synthesizing, self-correction and use of data for complex processing tasks" (Popenici & Kerr, 2017, p.2) and "a field of study that deals with methods to ensure that human intelligence is imitated by the computer" (Altinay, Karaatmaca, & Altinay, 2019, p.330). In 1999, AI was "a modelling science, developing, applying and investigating formalized models of salient aspects pertaining to learning and instruction, allowing reasoning and derivation of new facts, thereby giving the models in use a dynamic flavor" (Andriessen & Sandberg (1999, p.131). In 2009, AI was "the science and engineering of making intelligent machines, especially intelligent computer programs" (McCarthy, 2007, p.2). In 2019, AI was "a field of study that deals with methods to ensure that human intelligence is imitated by the computer" (Altinay, Karaatmaca, & Altinay, 2019). The essence of AI does not change, because AI is using computers to understand human intelligence.

An important breakthrough is that artificial intelligence agents can be either in a physical form such as robots or in software form with intellectual capacity (Drigas & Ioannidou, 2012). Rajaraman (2014) considered AI as computer programs with intelligence, while Lickin, Holmes, Griffiths, and Forcier (2016) regarded it as computer systems designed to interact with the world through capabilities and intelligent behaviors. Today, the focus is on how to create computers and computer software that are capable of intelligent behavior.

Table 1. Definition of Artificial Intelligence

Researchers (Years)	Definitions of Artificial Intelligence
McCarthy, Minsky, Rochester, & Shannon (1956)	The science of making machines do things that would require intelligence if done by men. An attempt will be made to find how to make machines use language, form abstractions and concepts, solve kinds of problems now reserved for humans, and improve themselves.
Andriessen & Sandberg (1999)	A modelling science, developing, applying and investigating formalized models of salient aspects pertaining to learning and instruction, allowing reasoning and derivation of new facts, thereby giving the models in use a dynamic flavor. The dynamic aspect is the most essential feature distinguishing AI from other technologies, e.g. web-based technologies (JAVA applications), hypermedia, multimedia databases, CMC environments (p.131).
McCarthy (2007)	It is the science and engineering of making intelligent machines, especially intelligent computer programs. It is related to the similar task of using computers to understand human intelligence, but AI does not have to confine itself to methods that are biologically observable.
Rajasingham (2009)	As a branch of computer science that seeks to create a device to perform functions that are normally associated with human intelligence, such as reasoning and optimization through experience and factual and heuristic knowledge. AI activity includes expert systems, natural language understanding, speech recognition, vision, and robotics (p.388).
Drigas & Ioannidou (2012)	The study and development of intelligence agents that can perceive their environment and take actions that increase their possibilities of success. Artificial intelligence agents can be either in a physical form of the device (e.g., humanoid robots) or in software form with 'intellectual' capacity (e.g. a virtual avatar) (p.1366).
Whitby (2013)	The study of intelligent behavior (in humans, animals, and machines) and the attempt to find ways in which such behavior could be engineered in any type of artifact. Some intelligent behavior is produced by the right sort of computer software, some by the physically right sort of robot, and some by a combination of the two.
Rajaraman (2014)	Computer programs which seemingly exhibit intelligence, that is, computers perform tasks which when performed by humans require them to be intelligent (p.198).
Saranya & Phil (2016)	Intelligent agents that acts as environment and changes the actions into success. Some of the actions which computers deal with artificial intelligence are learning, reasoning, perception, problem solving, and language-understanding (p.313).
Luckin, Holmes, Griffiths, & Forcier (2016)	Computer systems that have been designed to interact with the world through capabilities (for example, visual perception and speech recognition) and intelligent behaviors (for example, assessing the available information and then taking the most sensible action to achieve a stated goal) that we would think of as essentially human" (p.14).
Pan (2016)	The ability of machines to understand, think, and learn in a similar way to human beings, indicating the possibility of using computers to simulate human intelligence. Since the 1970s, AI has expanded into research fields, including mechanical theorem proving, machine translation, expert systems, game theory, pattern recognition, machine learning, robotics, and intelligent control (p.410).
Etzioni & Etzioni (2017)	Activity devoted to making machines intelligent, and intelligence is that quality that enables an entity to function appropriately and with foresight in its environment. A popular understanding of AI is that it will enable a computer to think like a person.
Gadanidis (2017)	AI is the intelligence evident in machines or software. It is also the name of the academic field of study which studies how to create computers and computer software that are capable of intelligent behavior (p.133).
Saravanan, Sreedevi, & Subhamathi (2017)	Artificial Intelligence is the study of how to make computers do things at which, at the moment, people are better (p.418).
Popenici & Kerr (2017)	Computing systems that are able to engage in human-like processes such as learning, adapting, synthesizing, self-correction and use of data for complex processing tasks (p.2).
Altinay, Karaatmaca, & Altinay (2019)	A field of study that deals with methods to ensure that human intelligence is imitated by the computer (p.330).

In sum, most of the definitions remain indistinguishable, but the functions of AI have proliferated. Has AI changed our lives and roles as teachers? Etzioni and Schoenick (2018) believed that AI is a rapidly emerging technology which can potentially change our daily lives with a scope and speed that human beings have never experienced before. In the following, more detailed information about AI will be examined and AIEd will be discussed.

The Foundation, Categories, Evolution, and Application of AI

To understand what AI can do, a brief overview of the foundation, branches, categories, and application of AI was conducted. Gustafson and Gustafson (2016) described that representation, search, reasoning, and learning are the four **foundations** of AI; samples of research in AI include games (e.g., chess programs), natural language processing (e.g., representation of the syntax and semantics of the language), perception (e.g., vision-perception programs), autonomous mobile robotics (e.g., rovers on Mars, industrial robots, localization), and expert systems (e.g., medical diagnosis program). The **branches** of AI consist of logical AI, search AI, pattern recognition, representation, inference, common sense knowledge and reasoning, learning from experience, planning, epistemology, ontology, heuristics, and genetic programming (McCarthy, 2007). The **types** of Artificial Intelligence Systems can be classified into the following: robotics (e.g., Asimo, Pepper, Spot, Nao, MyKie), expert systems (e.g., Amazon Alexa, Apple Siri, Microsoft Cortana, Google Now), language translators (e.g., Google Translate, IBM Watson), intelligent computer assisted instruction (e.g., Mika from Carnegie's Learning, iTalk2Learn), game playing (e.g., IBM's Deep Blue, Façade, Black and White, Sims, Versu, F.E.A.R.), neural computing (e.g., BrainMaker, NeuralShell Easy, NeuroSolutions, Neural Ware), fuzzy logic (e.g., Massive Software, Vibrobox, Texo Controls), genetic algorithms (Evolver, XpertRule GenAsys), computer vision and scene recognition, natural language processing, and intelligent agents (Saravanan, Sreedevi, & Subhamathi, 2017).

How was AI developed over the decades? The **development** of AI systems can be categorized into six stages: Naïve Solution Stage (1950s), General Method Stage (1970s), Domain Knowledge Stage (1980s), Integration Stage (1990s), Interactive Robots (2000s), and Natural Language Chatbots (2010s) (Saravanan, Sreedevi, & Subhamathi, 2017). Saravanan, Sreedevi, and Subhamathi (2017, p.418) further illustrated that "Intelligent agents, Chat bots, Expert systems and Speech Recognition Systems are some of the facets of Artificial Intelligent systems which are already in gouge. By 2030, Artificial Intelligence is likely to have spread into almost all the fields – Ubiquitous." Some of the **applications** of AI included game playing, speech recognition, understanding natural language, computer vision, expert systems, and heuristic classification (McCarthy, 2007).

How is AI related to education? In higher education, Rajasingham (2009) described the idea of a HyperClass based on HyperReality in which human intelligence and Artificial Intelligence intermesh and interact to provide anyone, anywhere, and anytime learning. Thus, teaching can be done by using *Just in Time Artificially Intelligent Tutors* (JITAITs) and learning can be done by using avatars-online simulacra of themselves to interact as a telepresence in classes from different countries and locations. As a result, higher education, like many other industries, may be in for major change as AI becomes more widespread (Gose, 2016). Intelligent agents including Chatbots (e.g., Amazon's Alexa and Apple's Siri) have become more sophisticated. Gose (2016) predicted that they will eliminate six percent of jobs by 2021 in transportation and customer service. Pan (2016) further emphasized that,

With the current popularization of the Internet, universal existence of sensors, emergence of big data, development of e-commerce, rise of the information community, and interconnection and fusion of data and knowledge in society, physical space, and cyberspace, the information environment surrounding AI development has changed profoundly, leading to a new evolutionary stage: AI 2.0. (p.410).

Advantages and Disadvantages of Artificial Intelligent Systems

Although people's opinions are divided on whether AI will replace human jobs, researchers have witnessed the pros and cons of AI technology. The pros of AI are: machines can do mundane tasks and won't get bored as humans do; AI and cognitive technologies help make faster decisions; AI has the ability of big data processing and machine learning; AI offers error-free processing of data; AI can take the risk doing jobs humans can't do; and AI technology helps achieve better research outcomes (Patrizio, 2016).

The cons of AI, as pointed out by Patrizio (2016), included: AI will cost lesser-skilled people their jobs; AI could mean a lot of power will be in the hands of a few who control it; AI does not have the ability to make judgement calls (Patrizio, 2016). Additionally, Saranya and Phil (2016) provided the following disadvantages with AI: (a) it may lead to destruction if the control of machine drives in the wrong manner; (b) it will lead to unemployment if robots start to replace humans in all fields; (c) it can be changed foremost to mass scale destruction; (d) it can do the opposite of programmed instructions if it malfunctions; (e) it has the efficiency to corrupt the younger generation; and (f) it can function only based on its programing and lacks a human touch. It appears that while AIEd will assist teachers in school work, instruction, assessment as well as helping students learn, it has its limitations. The models of AI in Education should be reviewed for further understanding.

Models of AI in Education

The aforementioned review provided basic information on AI technology. In the following, the models of AI in education (AIEd) will be explored. A decade ago, researchers examined the models of AI systems in education. There are three key models of AIEd: pedagogical (i.e., the knowledge and expertise of teaching), domain (i.e., knowledge of the subject being learned), and learner models (i.e., knowledge of the learner) (Luckin, Holmes, Griffiths, & Forcier, 2016).

Examples of the **pedagogical model** consist of productive failure (allowing students to explore a concept and make mistakes before being shown the right answer); feedback (questions, hints, or haptics) triggered by student actions and is designed to help the student improve their learning; and assessment to inform and measure learning. Examples of the **domain model** include how to add, subtract, or multiply two fractions; Newton's second law (forces); causes of World War I; how to structure an argument; and different approaches to reading a text (e.g., for sense or for detail). Examples of the **learner model** involves the student's previous achievement and difficulties; the student's emotional state; and the student's engagement in learning (e.g., time-on-task) (Luckin, Holmes, Griffiths, & Forcier, 2016, p.19). There three models cover teaching contents, learner's knowledge, context of the courses, assessment, feedback, and learner's emotional state.

Additionally, AIEd researchers have developed models to represent the social, emotional, and metacognitive aspects of learning, which "allows AIEd systems to accommodate the full range of factors that influence learning" (Luckin et al., 2016, p.21). AIEd has focused on the design of digital tutors historically to provide exposition of concepts to be learned and to have the intelligence to respond meaningfully to student behavior (e.g., offering adaptive support, describing student learning styles, or delivering culturally appropriate communication) (Gadanidis, 2017). AIEd has been developed and is making progress continuously and effortlessly. Gadanidis (2017, p.134) emphasized that "AI machines that match and surpass human intelligence may be seen as leading to positive technological advances"; however, "AI singularity may prove disastrous" and as Stephen Hawking told the BBC that "The development of full AI could spell the end of the human race."

Intelligent Tutoring Systems and Education

Intelligent Tutoring Systems have been developed since the 1980s. The components of Intelligent Tutoring Systems (ITS) included the student model, the pedagogical module, the domain knowledge module, the communication module (Woolf, 1992), and the expert model (Beck, Stern, & Haugsjaa, 2005). In 1999, Jerry Andriessen and

Jacobijn Sandberg noted that the following trends decreased reliance on traditional ITS-research: (1) more emphasis on open domains, (2) taking into account the learning environment, (3) collaboration as a didactic strategy, and (4) use of information databases (Andriessen & Sandberg, 1999). Later, ITSs was categorized into two dimensions: abstraction of the learning environment and the knowledge type of the instruction (Beck, Stern, & Haugsjaa, 2005).

Examples of ITS are abundant. There were Algebra Tutor (engaging students in problem solving with modern algebraic tools), SQL-Tutor (teaching students how to retrieve data from databases), COLLECT-UML (supporting pairs of students working collaboratively on UML class diagram and providing feedback), Mathematics Tutor (helping students solve word problems using fractions, decimals and percentages), eTeacher (supporting personalized e-learning assistance), ZOSMAT (addressing all the needs of a real classroom), REALP (enhancing students' reading comprehension by reader-specific lexical practice and personalized practice with authentic materials from the Web), CIRCSIM-Tutor (for medical students to learn about regulating blood pressure), Why2-Atlas (addressing students' writing problems through dialogues and asking them to correct their essays), SmartTutor (supporting the needs of continuing education students), AutoTutor (helping college students in learning computer hardware, operating systems and the Internet), ActiveMath (a web-based adaptive learning environment for mathematics for improving long-distance learning, completing traditional classroom teaching, and supporting individual lifelong learning), and ESC101-ITS (an intelligent tutoring system for introductory programming problems) (ITS, 2018).

However, ITS has its limitations. For instance, ITS is expensive to develop and to implement; its immediate feedback and hint sequences failed to develop deep learning in students; it failed to ask questions of the students to explain their actions; evaluation of an ITS is difficult, time-consuming, and costly (ITS, 2018). ITS has subject competence limitations and restricted knowledge of teaching as well.

The Functions and Applications of AI in Education (AIEd)

What can AIEd offer at the moment? There are three functions for AIEd: an agent function, a heuristic function, and an evaluation function (Saranya & Phil, 2016). Luckin et al. (2016) indicated that AIEd can provide an intelligent, personal tutor for every learner; AIEd can offer intelligent support for collaborative learning; and AIEd's intelligent virtual reality can support learning in authentic environments (Luckin et al., 2016). In other words, with Intelligent Tutoring Systems (ITS), no teacher is needed because "virtual pedagogical agents might also be included, acting as teachers, learning facilitators, or student peers in collaborative learning quests"

(Luckin et al., 2016, p.29). Additionally, those three types of applications can be used to provide assistance to learners with special education needs, and motivate learners who cannot attend school (Luckin et al., 2016).

AIEd will provide just-in-time assessments to shape learning, offer new insights into how learning is progressing, assist us to move beyond 'stop-and-test', embody new insights from the learning sciences, and give us lifelong learning partners (Luckin et al., 2016). The benefits of AIEd are numerous. For example, based on Luckin et al. (2016), AIEd will augment our physical landscape and allow formal classroom content to become the learner's physical reality. AIEd will connect to the Internet of things and permits any network-enabled objects to be interconnected with any other network-enabled machine. AIEd will be attuned to how we feel and how we move.

Faggella (2017) provided more examples of how AI is applied in education. First, the creation of **smart content** from digital guides of textbooks to customizable learning digital interfaces are being introduced from elementary to post-secondary, and within corporate environments (Faggella, 2017). AI was used in Cram 101 to "help disseminate and breakdown textbook content into digestible smart study guide that includes chapters summaries, true-false and multiple-choice practice tests and flashcards (Faggella, 2017). *Nextex Learning* "allows educators to design digital curriculum and content across devices, integrating rich media like video and audio, as well as self- or online-instructor assessment" (Faggella, 2017, p.2). Second, **intelligent tutoring systems**, such as *Mastery Learning*, is a one-on-one tutoring system to support the effectiveness of individualized tutoring and instruction in the classroom. For instance, Carnegie Learning's Mika software uses cognitive science and AI technology to provide personalized tutoring and real-time feedback for post-secondary students. The iTalk2Learn System 16 that has an effect on young students learning fractions, applied a learner model that explicitly included information about an individual's mathematics knowledge, cognitive needs, emotional state, as well as feedback received, and the students' responses in turn. Third, AI brought **virtual facilitators and learning environments**. For example, the University of Southern California (USC) Institute for Creative Technologies created smart virtual environments and applications with AI, 3-D gaming, and computer animation to develop authentic virtual characters and realistic social interactions ((Faggella, 2017, p.4). USC Creative Technologies SimCoach Prototype includes initiatives under development such as virtual facilitators, augmented reality, and intelligent tutor in remote learning and training program. Fourth, AI has paved **new learning pathways** for the coming decade. Education has been dominated by the interaction between teachers and students in the past; therefore, the integration of AI has been slower.

AI has the ability to analyze large amounts of data in real time (e.g., students' performance in a particular skill across subjects over the course of a year) and can automatically provide new content or specific learning parameters to help meet students' needs for continual practice and feedback, as well as allow teachers to better understand students' performance and construct more effective personalized learning plans (Faggella, 2017). Lambert (2018) also provided some examples of AI in smarter classrooms, such as Khan Academy's AI that can identify students' strengths and learning gaps and adjust content accordingly. Software such as McGraw-Hill Connect and Aplia allow teachers to manage coursework for large classes of students at the same time (Lambert, 2018).

The aforementioned review has illustrated general models as well as the functions and applications of AI in Education. Kumar (2017) presented ten roles for Artificial Intelligence in education (AIEd). Those ten roles included: (1) AI can automate basic activities in education like grading; (2) educational software can be adapted to students' needs; (3) AI can point out places where courses need improvement; (4) students can get additional support from AI tutors; (5) AI-driven programs can give students and educators helpful feedback; (6) AI is altering how we find and interact with information; (7) AI could change the role of teachers; (8) AI can make trial-and-error learning less intimidating; (9) Data powered by AI can change how schools find, teach, and support students; and (10) AI may change where students learn, who teaches them, and how they acquire basic skills (Kumar, 2017). Rieland (2017) explained that teachers have to serve as data scientists who understand AI, who monitor data, and who evaluate the data to identify how students are learning.

What roles do teachers play with AI doing so many things at schools? What challenges do teachers face? What should teachers do to cope with the digital revolution in education with AI? In the following, problems and issues along with solutions and recommendations will be discussed.

MAIN FOCUS OF THE CHAPTER

Issues, Controversies, Problems

1. Do Teachers Have Sufficient Technology Skills to Cope with AIEd?

AI technology is reshaping the economy, changing the world, and playing a significant role in providing personalized instruction for all students, while teachers are being slowly pushed away from the front of the classroom to assume the roles of coach and facilitator. AI technology can help with communication, differentiation, personalization, exploration, and assessments in the classroom (Poth, 2018). Some educators perceive it as a threat to their existence and a danger to student-data privacy; others take a positive view and believe that AI technology can free them from mundane tasks like lecturing, grading, and creating abundant opportunities for student improvement, and more meaningful trial-and-error learning.

Since AI will play an essential role in the next phase of education system reform and it will not happen by chance (Luckin et al., 2016), teachers' roles will be changed and transformed. How will teachers cope with the changes? Teachers will need to be central agents in the next phase of AIEd (Luckin et al., 2016). Teachers will need to be equipped with technology literacy, new design skills, and an understanding of AIEd system. As Luckin et al. (2016, p.31) noted, what teachers need are as follows:

- A sophisticated understanding of what AIEd systems can do to enable them to evaluate and make sound value judgements regarding new AIEd products
- To develop research skills which allow them to interpret the data provided by AIEd technologies, to ask the most useful questions from the data, and to walk students through what the data analysis is telling them (for instance, using Open Leaner models).
- New teamworking and management skills as each teacher will likely have AI assistants in addition to their usual human teaching assistants, and they will be responsible for combing and managing these resources most effectively.

The major issue centers on if schoolteachers will have the skills to cope with these challenges. How much work can they do and what technology skills must they have? Teachers are not software engineers or high-tech people. Are they ready to take the changing roles that are thrust upon them with AIEd? Etzioni and Schoenick (2018) believed that AI is "a rapidly emerging technology that has the potential to change our everyday lives with a scope and speed that humankind has never experienced before" (p.28). Three core components of learning are curriculum, learning and teaching, and assessment. The problem is that if AIEd is capable of fulfilling all components while possibly surpassing human intelligence, students will not need teachers. If students can learn with machines, what should teachers and their assistants do? What should school administrators do if AI can do their jobs? What should school districts provide to teachers? How do teachers develop their expertise in AI technology and how do they deal with those challenges?

2. Do Changing Roles Mean Losing Jobs?

When asked if AI aimed at human-level intelligence, McCarthy (2007) responded "yes. The ultimate effort is to make computer programs that can solve problems and achieve goals in the world as well as humans" (p. 5). In 1993, the computer scientist Vernon Vinge publicized the notion of "singularity" in which "an AI-powered computer or robot becomes capable of redesigning and improving itself or of designing AI more advanced than itself" so that AI will exceed human intelligence (Luckin, Holmes, Griffiths, & Forcier, 2016, p.15). Luckin et al. (2016) further cited from Stephen Hawking, Stuart Russell, Max Tegmark, and Frank Wilczek that "the potential downsides of AI becoming too clever" (p. 15).

Artificial Intelligence has significant impact on human beings. While its development has improved people's lives, it also replaces many jobs. As Etzioni and Etzioni (2017, p. 35) noted, cyber revolution with the use of computers and AI "is destroying many jobs: first blue-collar jobs (robots on the assembly line), then white-collar ones (banks reducing their back-office staff) and now professional ones (legal research)." Lee (2018) gave alert to technology companies that they should stop pretending AI won't destroy jobs. "AI will displace a large number of jobs, which will cause social discontent.... It will soon be obvious that half of our job tasks can be done better at almost no cost by AI and robots" (Lee, 2018, para 2). He believed that human beings are not ready for this fast transition (Lee, 2018).

In *"You're Fired," Says the Robot: The Rise of Automation in the Workplace, Technophobes, and Fears of Unemployment*, McClure (2018) addressed that new workplace technologies (e.g., robots, AI) affect some people (e.g., females, non-white minorities) more than others, and they impact anxiety levels. Technophobes are more likely "to report having anxiety-related mental health issues and to fear unemployment and financial insecurity" (McClure, 2018, p.139). He concluded that "an unprecedented number of citizens could lose their jobs to robots and software that can work for cheaper and for longer hours than any human" (McClure, 2018, p.153). In Madda's (2017) interview of eight educators (i.e., superintendents, coaches, and teachers) to determine if AI scares them or if AI makes them live easier, provided mixed results; some educators believed that AI make the world better, but others believed that AI would replace acumen and de-professionalized teachers' roles. Some worried that students would not take ownership of their learning experience without a teacher because of AI, and AI will render the teaching profession obsolete (Madda, 2017).

However, some educators believed that no form of AI technology can care about students and communicate with students in a meaningful way (Madda, 2017). Theoretically, AI cannot build relationships with students and make a difference; therefore, it won't replace teachers. Should teachers worry about that the advancement of AIEd would take over all their jobs so they have nothing to do?

3. What Are the Ethical Consideration for AIEd?

We should consider what might happened and what should be done if AIEd goes wrong. As Whitby (2013) pointed out, there have been no agreed upon criteria regarding who should be held responsible when things go wrong. "There is now international concern about the use of autonomous military robots, with some authorities calling for a moratorium on their deployment. The use of robots in caring applications – for example, in child care – and in "smart homes" for elderly people also raises ethical issues that remain unresolved" (Whitby, 2013, p.7). Mannino et al. (2015, p.1) pointed out that, "progress in AI research makes it possible to replace increasing amounts of human jobs with machines. Many economists assume that this increasing automation could lead to a massive increase in unemployment within even the next 10-20 years." They further specified that "Many AI experts consider it plausible that this century will witness the creation of AIs whose intelligence surpasses that of humans in all respects" (Mannion et al., 2015, p.2). Crowe (2018) also regarded robot ethics as a major challenge. Five major topics concerning the ethical problems are: sensitive tasks that require human supervision could be entirely delegated to robots; human beings will no longer take responsibility for failures; unemployment and de-skilling of the workforce; AI could erode human freedom; and using AI in an unethical way (Crowe, 2018). Additionally, for AI to learn complex tasks on its own with minimal training data is critical.

In fact, AI has already reached or overtaken human levels in some domain areas, such as with a self-learning backgammon program that reached the level of the world's best players in 1994; the computer *Deep Blue* beat the reigning world champion Garry Kasparov at chess in 1997; *Cepheus* solved the first variant of poker *Fixed Limit Holden heads-up* in 2015 (Mannion et al., 2015). "New ethical challenges arise when constructing domain specific AIs capable of taking over cognitive work in social dimensions – work that, until now, has been carried out by humans" (Mannion et al., 2015, p.4). Ethical concerns exist with education data. Who owns the education data? Who can use the data? Who is accountable and responsible? What role should teachers take if AIEd was used as a classroom spy to record and report teachers' performance? Our concern might endanger personal relationships between human beings and machines.

Burton et al. (2017) raised some important ethical questions for AI systems: How should AIs behave in our society? What should we do if jobs are in short supply? Should AI systems be allowed to kill? Should we worry about superintelligence and the singularity? How should we treat AIs? Artificial Intelligence systems are developed by computer software engineers. Should ethical considerations be included in AI courses in universities? Should professors who teach AI courses integrate ethical considerations and how to avoid AI malfunction or destruction in future? If not, these may become problems for human beings.

SOLUTIONS AND RECOMMENDATIONS

Luckin et al. (2016) predicted that in 15 years many new jobs will be more cognitively demanding than those currently available; social skills will be where humans continue to excel; and teachers have to re-skill large parts of the current workforce – in essence, creating a learning society. What should teachers do about it? How does the government or relevant authorities such as Department of Education help?

1. Regulations and Restrictions are Needed.

Are there regulations for the development of AI in education? Etzioni and Etzioni (2017) pointed out that "regulating AI on an international level is highly challenging task" (p. 33). There are four principles to guide the construction of new AIs; AI should be comprehensible; its actions should be basically predictable; it should be impervious to manipulation; and it should have clearly determined responsibilities (Mannion et al., 2015).

Mannino et al (2015) raised nine recommendations (i.e., responsible approach, forward thinking, education, transparency over new measures, information, AI safety, global cooperation and coordination, research, and regulation) to solve the problem. In other words, it is of great importance to ensure that the advantages of AI outweigh the disadvantages; for researchers and decision makers to deal with the consequences of AI research on AI safety and research project funding; to find additional options and to identify the set of measures with maximum effect; to establish research grants for answering the empirical questions; build awareness of the risks associated with AI progress for experts working on AI, investors, and decision-makers; encourage research on AI safety; and improve international coordination and cooperation to maintain the safety of AI; to promote, fund, and coordinate relevant interdisciplinary research projects; to regulate experiments on living test subjects and to carry out under the strict supervision of ethics commissions (Mannino et al., 2015).

Knight (2018) suggested that government should invest more in AI research, prepare for job losses, nurture AI talent experts, prioritize education, guide regulations, and understand AI technology. AI is a complex and a fast-moving field. It is risky if there are no regulations and policies. Knight (2018) pointed out, "the US doesn't necessarily need new rules and regulations for AI, but there may be situations where the government could step in to help apply existing laws" (para 1).

2. Do What AI Cannot Do or Do the Jobs that AI Creates.

Teachers can read students' facial expressions, body languages, and appearance to infer students' emotional status; AI could struggle with analyzing the complex needs appropriately and immediate cues communicated by a classroom full of students (Lambert, 2018). Teachers can use robots with AI as teaching assistants for their classrooms because an AI robot works best when paired with an active human facilitator (Lambert, 2018). We should have a positive outlook regarding technology advancement with AI.

On the one hand, when AI systems become more complicated, some job displacement will occur. On the other hand, three new categories of AI-driven business and technology jobs (i.e., trainers, explainers, and sustainers) will be available (Wilson, Daugherty, & Morini-Bianzino, 2017). Trainers will teach AI systems how they should perform; explainers provide clarity to bridge the gap between business leaders and technologists; sustainers help ensure that AI systems are operating as designed and addressing the unintended consequences appropriately (Wilson, Daugherty, & Morini-Bianzino, 2017). Trainers include customer-language tone and meaning trainer, smart-machine interaction modeler, and worldview trainer; explainers consist of context designer, transparency analyst, and AI usefulness strategist; sustainers involve automation ethicist, automation economist, and machine relations manager (Wilson, Daugherty, & Morini-Bianzino, 2017).

The issue involves how teachers can change their roles from instructors to the trainers, explainers, and sustainers. Problems will be solved if the Department of Education and school districts can provide training, workshops, or certificate programs for schoolteachers so that they can transform from classroom instructors to trainers, explainers, and sustainers. Teacher training is needed in the future to cope with AI development, or teachers will lose jobs eventually.

3. Teachers Should Adapt to Changes with Training.

How should teachers adapt to changes? Faggella (2017) stated that "AI will likely not replace but will serve as an invaluable extension of the human expert, helping teachers to more effectively meet the diverse needs of many students simultaneously" (p.5). Rizzotto (2017) projected that the future of education with AI would be personalized learning (i.e., diverse programs, learning experiences, instructional approaches, and strategies that fit individual student's preferences, interests, inspirations, weaknesses, background), experiential learning (i.e., learning by doing; hands-on experience), and mastery-based learning (i.e., students should move forward with a subject once they've mastered all concepts preceding it since all knowledge is interconnected and cumulative) which could change education forever. Rizzotto (2017) further addressed that "A.I. has been learning about us for the longest time – now it's only a matter of time before it starts teaching us" (p. 28).

AI and immersive technology will reshape teaching and learning soon. "The convergence of big data and immersive education can be combined to give the classroom new every-changing forms" (Rizzotto, 2017, p.28). Therefore, teachers have to get training and change their approaches in instruction to cope with AI. With regular training, teachers will not afraid of unemployment and will survive in AIEd classrooms better. What skills should teachers learn?

Since the innovation of AI promotes the development of AIEd, teachers need to learn technology skills to cope with AI advancement. Luckin et al. (2016) proposed the use of AIEd to effect education system reform. There are three categories (i.e., foundational literacies, competencies, and character qualities) and 16 skills for teachers to learn (Luckin et al., 2016). The skills under foundational literacies include literacy, numeracy, scientific literacy, information communication, technology literacy, financial literacy, and cultural and civic literacy; the skills under competencies include critical thinking, problem-solving, communication, and collaboration; the skills in character qualities involves curiosity, initiative, persistence/grit, adaptability, leadership, and social and cultural awareness (Luckin et al., 2016).

4. Follow the Trends and Support the Blended Learning Environment.

In the New Medium Consortium Horizon Report, Skiba (2017) pinpointed that two long-term trends are deeper learning and advancing cultures of innovation; the mid-term trend involves the measurement of learning and the use of assessment tools; the short-term trend involves blended and collaborative learning. Two solvable challenges are improving digital literacy and integrating formal and informal learning; two difficult challenges are the achievement gap and achieving digital equity; two wicked challenges are managing knowledge obsolescence and rethinking the roles of educators (Skiba, 2017).

For the development of technologies, there are adaptive learning technologies, mobile learning, the Internet of Things (IOT), next generation learning management system (LMS), natural user interfaces, and Artificial Intelligence (Skiba, 2017). "AI needs to recognize when people are more effective on their own – when to get out of the way, when not to help, when not to record, when not to interrupt or distract" (Cheng, 2018). The advance of technologies has reshaped the traditional classroom and built a new online system for teaching and learning. Schoolteachers should learn to teach or monitor students online. Following the trends and updating professional skills are mandatory and essential for teachers.

FUTURE RESEARCH DIRECTIONS

In this chapter, definitions of AI, the development of AI in education, the changing roles of teachers with AI in education were reviewed. Future researchers can conduct a quantitative or a qualitative study to explore the impact of Artificial Intelligence in Education (K-12 or college level). Researchers can also explore the strategies teachers can use to cope with the drastic changes in the classroom with AI technology. Researchers can also scrutinize the needs of AI at schools regarding curriculum design, content of the courses, assessments, and resources.

CONCLUSION

In this chapter, the definitions, functions, evolution, and applications were reviewed. The advantages and disadvantages of AI technology in education were reviewed. How teachers' roles change with AI technology was discussed. Problems and solutions incurred due to the progressive development of AI in education. It is obvious that the innovation of AI technology is persistent and the advance of AI technology in education is swift and incessant. The next generation of AI robots might be smaller, lighter, and less expensive in schools, at homes, in the office, and on the streets in the years to come. Teachers need to recognize these changes and innovate their teaching accordingly. Since AIEd can take over tasks like grading, helping students learn with virtual tutoring, adapting to other aspects of teaching, be programmed to provide expertise, answering students' questions, finding information, and taking the place of teachers for basic course materials, as Kumar (2017) indicated, the roles of teachers should be changed from instructors to facilitators, from tutors to monitors, and from observers to trainers. Teachers will supplement AI lessons, assist students who are struggling, and provide human interaction as well as hands-on experiences for students (Kumar, 2017).

Woolf, Lane, Chaudhri, and Kolodner (2013) described five challenges for AI and education, including "(1) mentors for every learner; (2) learning 21st century skills; (3) interaction data to support learning; (4) universal access to global classrooms; and (5) lifelong and life wide learning" (p.81). Woolf (2015) believed that two future directions for AIEd include personalize teaching (e.g., one-to-one attention, supporting learners with decision-making and reasoning in volatile changing environment, responding to student affect) and teaching 21st Century skills (e.g., cognitive skills, interpersonal skills, and intrapersonal skills). "Two AI techniques that can improve teaching for 21st Century skills are dialogue systems and inquiry learning" (Woolf, 2015, p.43). It takes steps to integrating AI technology at schools, so teachers should follow the trends, accept the challenges, and change their roles to cope with AI.

In fact, we as teachers need to discover jobs that AI can't do. Additionally, school districts should train teachers to survive with AI in education. In the future, the classroom environment will be a combination of teachers and AI systems. Therefore, schools should provide environments to accommodate both creative intelligence of human beings and the analytical intelligence of computers and robots.

Wagner (2018) raised five major shifts of AI technology: (1) from stand and deliver instruction to facilitation and coaching; (2) from developers of content to developers of learning experiences; (3) from siloed classrooms to virtual social networks; (4) from textbooks and set curriculum to blended courses and customized design; (5) from a hierarchical top-down network to lateral virtual global network. We must develop reliable and valid indicators that will allow us to track learner progress on all of the skills and capabilities needed to thrive in the current century and at the level of the individual, the school, the district, and the country. We need a better understanding of what AIEd can do and what teachers can do in new learning contexts with AIEd. To avoid being laid off due to the overdevelopment of AIEd, we need to have the super remote to control AI robots in the classroom.

REFERENCES

Alimisis, D. (2013). Educational robotics: open questions and new challenges. *Themes in Science & Technology Education, 6*(1), 63-71. Retrieved from https://files.eric.ed.gov/fulltext/EJ1130924.pdf

Andriessen, J., & Sandberg, J. (1999). Where is education heading and how about AI? *International Journal of Artificial Intelligence in Education*, *10*, 130–150.

Atmatzidou, D., Demetriadis, S., & Nika, P. (2018). How does the degree of guidance support students' metacognitive and problem-solving skills in educational robotics? *Journal of Science Education and Technology*, *27*(1), 70–85. doi:10.100710956-017-9709-x

Beck, J., Stern, M., & Haugsjaa, E. (2005). *Applications of AI in education*. Retrieved from http://citeseerx.ist.psu.edu/viewdoc/download?doi=10.1.1.87.405&rep=rep1&type=pdf

Brown, L. E., & Kauchak, D. (2013). *Educational advances in Artificial Intelligence*. Association for the Advancement of Artificial Intelligence. doi:10.1609/aimag.v34i4.2508

Burton, E., Goldsmith, J., Koenig, S., Kuipers, B., Mattei, N., & Walsh, T. (2017). Ethical considerations in Artificial Intelligence courses. *AI Magazine*, *38*(2), 22–34. doi:10.1609/aimag.v38i2.2731

Cheng, L. (2018, Jan. 15). Beauty in the machine. *Time Magazine,* 26.

Crowe, S. (2018). *10 biggest challenges in robotics*. Retrieved from https://www.therobotreport.com/10-biggest-challenges-in-robotics/

Drigas, A. S., & Ioannidou, R. (2012). Artificial Intelligence in special education: A decade review. *International Journal of Engineering Education*, *28*(6), 1366–1372.

Etzioni, A., & Etzioni, O. (2017). Should Artificial Intelligence be regulated? *Issues in Science and Technology*, *33*(4), 32–36. Retrieved from https://papers.ssrn.com/sol3/papers.cfm?abstract_id=2993506

Etzioni, O., & Schoenick, C. (2018). Artificial Intelligence: What educators need to know. Two AI researchers lay out what you need to know about Artificial Intelligence. *Education Week*, *37*(16), 28–29. Retrieved from https://www.edweek.org/ew/articles/2018/01/10/artificial-intelligence-what-educators-need-to-know.html

Faggella, D. (2017). *Examples of Artificial Intelligence in education*. Retrieved from https://www.techemergence.com/examples-of-artificial-intelligence-in-education/

Gadanidis, G. (2017). Artificial Intelligence, computational thinking, and mathematics education. *The Information Journal of Information and Learning Technology*, *34*(2), 133–139. doi:10.1108/IJILT-09-2016-0048

Gose, B. (2016). When the teaching assistant is a robot: Faculty members experiment with Artificial Intelligence in the classroom. *The Chronicle of Higher Education*. Retrieved from https://www.chronicle.com/article/When-the-Teaching-Assistant-Is/238114

Gustafson, S. M., & Gustafson, D. A. (2016). *Artificial Intelligence*. Retrieved from https://www.accessscience.com/content/artificial-intelligence/053300

Intelligent Tutoring Systems. (2018). In *Wikipedia*. Retrieved from https://en.wikipedia.org/wiki/Intelligent_tutoring_system#Limitations

Knight, W. (2018). Here's how the U.S. needs to prepare for the age of artificial intelligence. *MIT Technology Review*. Retrieved from https://www.technologyreview.com/s/610379/heres-how-the-us-needs-to-prepare-for-the-age-of-artificial-intelligence/

Kumar, A. (2017). *10 roles for Artificial Intelligence in education*. Retrieved from https://www.linkedin.com/pulse/10-roles-artificial-intelligence-education-anil-kumar

Lambert, K. (2018). Could Artificial Intelligence replace our teachers? *Education World*. Retrieved from http://www.educationworld.com/could-artificial-intelligence-replace-our-teachers

Lee, K. (2018). Tech companies should stop pretending AI won't destroy jobs. *MIT Technology Review*. Retrieved from https://www.technologyreview.com/s/610298/tech-companies-should-stop-pretending-ai-wont-destroy-jobs/

Luckin, R., Holmes, W., Griffiths, M., & Forcier, L. B. (2016). *Intelligence unleashed: An argument for AI in education*. London: Pearson.

Madda, M. J. (2017). *Educators on Artificial Intelligence: Here's the one thing it can't do well*. Retrieved from https://www.edsurge.com/news/2017-11-20-educators-on-artificial-intelligence-here-s-the-one-thing-it-can-t-do-well

Mallawaarachchi, V. (2017). *Living with robots – the good, the bad and the ugly on humanity*. Retrieved from https://becominghuman.ai/living-with-robots-the-good-the-bad-and-the-ugly-on-humanity-1097f524f936

Mannino, A., Althaus, D., Erhardt, J., Gloor, L., Hutter, A., & Metzinger, T. (2015). Artificial Intelligence: Opportunities and risks. *Policy Paper by the Effective Altruism Foundation*, (2), 1-16.

McArthur, D., Lewis, M., & Bishay, M. (2005). The role of Artificial Intelligence in education: Current progress and future prospects. *I-manager's Journal of Educational Technology*, *1*(4), 42–80.

McCarthy, J. (2006). *The philosophy of AI and the AI of philosophy*. Retrieved from http://jmc.stanford.edu/articles/aiphil2.html

McCarthy, J. (2007). *What is Artificial Intelligence?* Retrieved from http://jmc.stanford.edu/artificial-intelligence/index.html

McCarthy, J., Minsky, M. L., Rochester, N., & Shannon, C. E. (2006). A proposal for the Dartmouth summer research project on Artificial Intelligence. *AI Magazine*, *27*(4), 12–14. Retrieved from http://jmc.stanford.edu/articles/dartmouth.html

McClure, P. K. (2018). "You're fired," says the robot: The rise of automation in the workplace, technophobes, and fears of unemployment. *Social Science Computer Review*, *36*(2), 139–156. doi:10.1177/0894439317698637

Oblinger, D. G. (2018). Smart machines and human expertise: Challenges for higher education. *EDUCAUSE Review.* Retrieved from https://er.educause.edu/articles/2018/8/smart-machines-and-human-expertise-challenges-for-higher-education

Ortiz, A. M., & Shaunna, S. (2015). The power of educational robotics as an integrated STEM learning experience in teacher preparation programs. *Journal of College Science Teaching*, *44*(5), 42–47. doi:10.2505/4/jcst15_044_05_42

Pan, Y. (2016). Heading toward Artificial Intelligence 2.0. *Engineering*, *2*(4), 409–413. doi:10.1016/J.ENG.2016.04.018

Patrizio, A. (2016). *Pros and cons of AI.* Retrieved from https://www.datamation.com/applications/pros-and-cons-of-artificial-intelligence.html

Popenici, S. A. D., & Kerr, S. (2017). Exploring the impact of Artificial Intelligence on teaching and learning in higher education. *Research and Practice in Technology Enhanced Learning, 12*(22), 1-13. Retrieved from https://telrp.springeropen.com/articles/10.1186/s41039-017-0062-8

Poth, R. D. (2018). *Artificial Intelligence: Implications for the future of education.* Retrieved from http://www.gettingsmart.com/2018/01/artificial-intelligence-implications-for-the-future-of-education/

Rajaraman, V. (2014). John McCarthy – Father of Artificial Intelligence. *Resonance: Journal of Science Education.* Retrieved from https://www.ias.ac.in/article/fulltext/reso/019/03/0198-0207

Rajasingham, L. (2009). The impact of Artificial Intelligence systems on future university paradigms. *MERLOT Journal of Online Learning and Teaching, 5*(2), 386-394. Retrieved from http://jolt.merlot.org/vol5no2/rajasingham_0609.pdf

Rieland, R. (2017). Is Artificial Intelligence the key to personalized education? *Smithsonian.com.* Retrieved from https://www.smithsonianmag.com/innovation/artificial-intelligence-key-personalized-education-180963172/

Rizzotto, L. (2017). *The future of education: How A.I. and immersive tech will reshape learning forever.* Retrieved from https://tfpodcast.io/2017/08/30/episode-36-the-future-of-education-how-a-i-and-immersive-tech-will-reshape-learning-forever/

Saranya, D., & Phil, M. (2016). A study on Artificial Intelligence and its applications. *International Journal of Advanced Research in Computer and Communication Engineering.*, *5*(4), 313–315.

Saravanan, K., Sreedevi, E., & Subhamathi, V. (2017). A review of Artificial Intelligence systems. *International Journal of Advanced Research in Computer Science*, *8*(9), 418–420. doi:10.26483/ijarcs.v8i9.5095

Skiba, D. J. (2017). Horizon report: Knowledge obsolescence, Artificial Intelligence, and rethinking the education role. *Nursing Education Perspectives*, *38*(3), 165–167. doi:10.1097/01.NEP.0000000000000154

Smith, N. B. (2002). *American reading instruction*. Newark, DE: International Reading Association.

Wagner, K. (2018). *A blended environment: The future of AI and education*. Retrieved from http://www.gettingsmart.com/2018/01/a-blended-environment-the-future-of-ai-and-education/

Whitby, B. (2013). *Artificial Intelligence. In Encyclopedia of philosophy and the social sciences*. Thousand Oaks, CA: SAGE Publications, Inc.

Wilson, H. J., Daugherty, P. R., & Morini-Bianzino, N. (2017). The jobs that Artificial Intelligence will create. *MIT Sloan Management Review*, *58*(4), 14–16. Retrieved from http://ilp.mit.edu/media/news_articles/smr/2017/58416.pdf

Wollowski, M., Neller, T., & Boerkoel, J. (2017). Artificial Intelligence education. Association for the Advancement of Artificial Intelligence. *AI Magazine*.

Woolf, B. P. (2015). AI and education: Celebrating 30 years of marriage. *AIED 2015 Workshop Proceedings, 4*, 38-47.

Woolf, B. P., Lane, H. C., Chaudhri, V. K., & Kolodner, J. I. (2013). AI grand challenges for education. *AI Magazine*. Retrieved from https://www.aaai.org/ojs/index.php/aimagazine/article/view/2490

KEY TERMS AND DEFINITIONS

Artificial Intelligence (AI): The science of making intelligent machine that require human intelligence.

Artificial Intelligence in Education (AIEd): Applying artificial intelligence technology to the field of education and using it in students' learning at schools.

Intelligent Tutoring System (ITS): A computer system that provides customized and immediate instruction and feedback to students without the intervention of a human teacher.

Interactive Learning Environments (ILEs): The settings for a pedagogical approach that incorporates digital technology and virtual communication by students in course design and delivery.

Virtual Facilitators: Online teachers who facilitate virtual classes by using computer software and the Internet to deliver instruction to students.

Chapter 2
AI and Individualized Education in Phys Ed and Sport

Adrian Patrascu
Babeş-Bolyai University, Romania

Monica Patrascu
https://orcid.org/0000-0003-2201-2312
University Politehnica of Bucharest, Romania

ABSTRACT

The development of AI technologies in recent years has opened the doors to a wide array of application domains. One field of study in particular has great potential to use this knowledge: physical education and sport. New devices and software have made their way into the field of physical activity, motivating the investigation of AI-driven technologies as a tool in developing a new type of educational system. The general scope of this chapter is to analyze the use of AI individualized education in one major field of study: physical education and sport. The use of AI technologies in training future teachers is also discussed and analyzed. The implementation of AI software in sport is brought to attention, along with relevant case studies. Limitations and hurdles in constructing intelligent support systems for training were identified. Accessibility of an AI-driven educational system was detailed, pointing out barriers with regard to culture, social environment, and age differences.

DOI: 10.4018/978-1-5225-7793-5.ch002

INTRODUCTION AND CONTEXT

Ever since the industrial revolution of the 18th century, the different educational systems around Europe tried to prepare the population for the new jobs and abilities that the industries required. This was achieved by molding both the body and the mind toward the desired form that best suited effectiveness in the workplace. Over the centuries these desired models of behaviour may have changed but the base objective of the educational system has remained the same: to adapt the individual for the greater (societal) good.

The technological era we live in has allowed the development of artificial intelligence (AI) and, subsequently, its spread into many fields of study. Different industries have explored the use of AI to improve either the effectiveness or safety of production. Even though AI-driven modules, applications, or agents may be used to undertake difficult or complex tasks previously performed by humans, the educational system is still concerned with adapting humans for future jobs. But we have at our disposal the means to adapt the workplace for humans with the use and implementation of AI-based technologies.

To achieve this we must start at the roots, where humans as individuals begin their journey toward becoming useful for society: the educational system. Through AI implementation within the educational system, not only are we able to create a flexible and permanently adapting environment for development, but we can also turn the educational molding of the future worker from a relatively rigid domain toward abilities that allow them to be more flexible at the end of the process.

Even though the educational system is still conceptually rooted in an aging dogma, the modern era has infused its process with a series of principles. These principles are not new, their beginnings can be found in Greek or Roman schools. Nevertheless, they grew in importance due to the need of making the educational process less reliant on subjective progress but more consistent through objective evolution. One of these principles is the individualization of the educational process. It can offer a unique way of molding the teaching process for each individual subject, with the sole purpose of obtaining optimal results. It has the power to transform the form of the educational process so drastically that it may seem a totally different endeavor, but at its core it remains the same. Through individualization it is possible to: make education more effective, to obtain optimum outcomes, to adapt the process to the needs of the individuals, and to reach particularized final objectives of development.

We believe that AI-driven technology can be successfully used in achieving the individualization of the educational process. The flexibility, constant adaptation, and the step by step growth of an intelligent system may be used in the educational process effectively due to the fact that some of these characteristics can be found among the principles of education itself.

The general scope of this chapter is to analyze the use of AI toward individualized education in one major field of study: physical education and sport. We have chosen this field because it offers high diversity in the outcomes of the educational process: forming teachers of physical education, trainers, coaches, researchers, managers of sport related entities, and injury prevention or recovery personnel.

This chapter is primarily a position paper, derived out of two decades of combined experience in teaching in the fields of phys ed & sport and in systems engineering, and designing intelligent systems with applications in both fields. The paradigms of education at the beginning of the new millennium are often found lacking, through the entirety of the new generation's formative years. It is our duty to identify these shortcomings, to fix them for the future of our society; and what better way to start if not by making use of the 'new and shiny' array of tools made available through machine intelligence? This is a first step, a small one, but important nonetheless.

Throughout the chapter we will cover the reasons why AI can be used for the individualization of education concerning four aspects: physical education, sport, general physical performance, and accessibility. Our main objective is to analyze the particularities of these educational processes, to identify areas where improvement is paramount, and to determine opportunities where AI integration can solve some of these problems.

We are going to address several aspects of AI and individualized education in sports. These aspects mostly address problems and issues we've identified through our direct involvement in the educational system regarding physical education and sport. The aspects we'll be covering are:

- AI and physical education.
- AI and sport.

AI AND PHYSICAL EDUCATION

Focusing our attention on the process of forming future physical education teachers, we have discovered that they are offered information in a rigid manner, at least in Eastern Europe. The assimilation of this information has a weak link with developing the adaptation-to-situation of future teachers. Even though this capacity of adaptation to unpredicted situations is still being developed, it is rather earned and chiseled during a more empirical subjective process after the end of the educational process. We believe that the use of AI during the educational process can, on the one hand, help future teachers earn the ability to link their theoretical knowledge with practice, and on the other help them specialize to a particular case or situation regarding different types of students.

The practical experience for a teacher in the field of physical education can, in many cases, weigh more than the theoretical information and know-how. This is due to the chaotic nature of the environment where the activity is performed. Many unknown direct or indirect factors can alter the course of events during physical activities. In these cases the ability of a teacher to act fast and reliably can be the decisive factor between a successful outcome and a failed one.

The link between the information held by future teachers and its practical application can be generated by the use of AI-driven technology. In this section we explore what type of AI applications can achieve this. We also discuss the different methods of designing AI software and their implications over the old educational process of future teachers. Furthermore, we cover the limitations of such apps in the context of the educational process.

There are five major situations where AI-driven technology may improve the educational process of forming a teacher. These situations are aspects of the process itself: the environment where the process takes place, the method being used, the means used to transfer information, the curriculum, and the interactions of social components.

The Environment and AI-Driven Technology

The environment is one of the most flexible aspects of the educational process of both the future teachers and the students they will work with (Ernst, 2004). The use of smart technologies (Aguilar, 2005) can alter it either in small parts or completely in such a way that allows a better control of both the process and of the outcome.

Portable AI applications can be used to alter the environment through the use of graphic representations. The user may be faced with a visual representation of a certain situation. Through their interaction with the software and dependent on their choices the AI may transform the situation. These graphical representations can cover various events: a tactical decision, a progressive modification of biomechanical movement, whether changing patterns or contact-surface type changing. In the end these applications will have an interactive form. A well known form is, for instance, that of an automated chess-playing system, where the inference module can analyze the situation and react accordingly to the decisions or actions of the user.

An educational process using this style can help the future teacher learn to adapt to new situations and to take the right decision depending on the visual information.

The ultimate type of AI-driven software that can alter the environment for the educational process is the one that can incorporate the use of 3D virtual reality (Nilsson, 2004). The ability of a software to take future teachers and transport them in a scenario where they must adapt and react, represents the optimal way to increase their practical experience. Although it can be lacking in some aspects, the endless possibility of scenarios that this type of system offers can help teach future trainers the right decision in difficult events. Moreover, using this type of technology, the user may be faced with aspects of: sports methodology, physiology, systematization, biomechanics, and pedagogy.

A version of virtual reality that uses 2D representation can also be valuable in forming the future teachers. Spatial representation and orientation may be increased with the use of such models, and in some cases they were found to be less distracting (Richards, 2015) than their 3D counterparts. Improving these abilities will help future trainers with abstract representations of different body movements or group dynamics. Furthermore, the ability to understand different scenarios and visualise them from 2D in a cognitive 3D way, may be developed by such a system (Merchant, 2014).

AI-Driven Technology as Methods of Teaching

The use of AI tech can be a good method of teaching due to its properties. The adaptation of an intelligent machine—be it in a software implementation (Van Gogh Museum, 2015) or a robotic system (Ku, 2018)—to the actions of the user can make the whole educational process more fluid. It also allows for a flexible method of teaching that can mold itself to the needs of the user.

The real-time response of some AI-driven applications opens the door for a new way of structuring the overall class. This characteristic ensures the permanent control over both the flow and quantity of information toward students.

Even though the simple use of any AI-driven module is considered a method of teaching, this can be further enhanced by the use of applications that can address a specific part of the class.

An AI application that can offer a real-time analysis (Kim, 2015) of various physiological processes can be used during a class to help future teachers understand the impact of the workout on the body. This way the knowledge earned during theoretical classes can be linked with the real world physical modifications that occur within the students' bodies.

Similarly, data analysis for longer time frames of learning can help future teachers understand the possible mistakes made during a training period. The interaction between the user and such an application can turn a sports methodology class into a hands-on experience. This way future trainers can identify the moment the mistake was made and, if the software allows it, the effects of the mistake.

Besides the physiological parameters an inference-based module can also analyse the performance of the subject from a sports point of view. Different percentages of quantitative data can be interpreted (Baker, 2014) to show the evolution of a student or a team. The ability to link individual or group performance in a sport to the actual content of a training period allows future teachers to understand the importance of planning and scheduling for obtaining top results.

No matter what type of AI is used during a methodology class, such tools are very useful for understanding the link between the content of the workout and the final results or effect.

Another way an AI-driven app can help during classes is by offering a dynamic interaction with any database of information (Galway, 2014). Conducting a theoretical class in this manner helps future trainers to discover the relationship between notions that are either domain specific or that have a cross-domain origin. Moreover, such instruments are often used for evaluation at the end of the course, both of the student and of the teacher (Verma, 2017).

AI Software as Means of the Teaching Process

In the field of physical education the means (Metzler, 2017) are the actual exercise and activity made by students or athletes. Though them, both teaching and physical fitness can be achieved. Considering this, the use of AI technologies as a mean of teaching anything is not only limited to software variations, but also needs to incorporate other (hardware-in-the-loop) components.

First of all, any AI tech in teaching specific sports techniques—from range of motion to proper posture and so on—must have the ability to control a mechanical appendage/component. For example, in teaching field tennis it is required for the AI to be able to control the speed, direction and spin of the ball-throwing mechanism. Moreover, for correcting the actual biomechanical movement, an AI controlled arm can help the user to improve from a neuromuscular point of view. Even though the teaching of techniques can be achieved through these types of systems, its practical value may be limited due to the complex nature (Sheridan, 2016) of the process being controlled.

Second, there are many activities in the field of physical education and sport that can use a system based on AI-driven software (Fister, 2015). Activities like racing, archery, bobsleighing, skiing or cycling, to name a few, may use such types of technology with quite high efficiency. This is due to their individual characteristics such as: simple single plane movements, circular and cyclical biomechanics or having the visual control of the activity as a dominant component. For example, teaching through the use of an AI system that incorporates a display and all the components of a cockpit, can help future teachers understand what it feels like in different situations during the race, all done in a controlled environment that can be repeated as many times as needed (Boril, 2016). Also, the use of such a system makes it possible to recreate older 'legendary' sport events that may help future trainers to learn what the best decision in those situations is.

AI-Driven Curriculum

We have touched, indirectly, this subject in the previous sections. The curriculum sums up all the knowledge a future teacher must have at the end of the studies. Even though the curriculum is set by the direction determined by each country's educational system, there is a possibility to use an AI software that helps complete the knowledge set by the overall curriculum.

An AI application that allows the user to interact with information on the screen is one way to achieve this. A Google (Brabazon, 2016) type of search engine that covers the physical education field of knowledge is such an example. From the machine intelligence side, research is fertile in this area, i.e. the study of knowledge representation, ontologies and related support systems (Toro, 2015). Online repositories are more and more often equipped with relational knowledge-bases, adaptive thesaurus instruments, wiki-type (Jony, 2017) of hyperlink enhanced knowledge delivery, etc. (Zheng, 2015). The technology is not new (Jarke, 1989), but its uses in the classroom (Chu, 2017) are relatively recent. If in such an instrument one can set the starting point, physiology for example, and then branch out in various directions, it can help the future teacher strengthen the link between different aspects of the field. Moreover, the curriculum can be molded to the needs of the user according to their strengths and weaknesses. The virtual world of knowledge environments is waiting for the knowledge itself, in most cases, to be added by experts in their respective fields.

Analysis algorithms with an intelligent inference core can be used to evaluate student conceived (Lancor, 2014) curriculums and determine their consistency. This emerging field of research could help future teachers understand the main aspects that need to be covered by a curriculum and such results will come in handy when the need for a personalized curriculum design arises.

To a lesser extent, these types of application may be used to analyse the content set by each teacher for their group or class of students. In this way, the content of a training period may be changed or not depending on the needs of the group. There are, however, limitations of this method: the know-how of the teacher in using the software (Gao, 2015), quantifying subjective aspects of technique, the dimension of the database used for comparison and the lack of permanent and consistent evaluation of the students.

Social Components Through AI Technology

The social component should be considered at the forefront of physical education due to the simple fact that the job of any teacher involves constant contact and interaction with other people, either small children, teenagers, or adults.

Using AI-based models to simulate (Barmaki, 2015) the interaction with different categories of people will help future teachers understand how these groups react or behave in different situations. Age, sex, cultural, regional or linguistic differences may be used to offer a vast array of combinations for future teachers to interface with. This will be beneficial for the specialization of teachers that will be working in distinct ethnic regions or with people with disabilities (Haber et. al, 2016). The experience gain through this method may, first, reduce the risk of undesired behaviours on the teacher's behalf, and, second, guarantee a higher degree of professionalism in the workplace through a better ability to adapt to different social groups.

The specialization of future teachers aimed at different types of educational institutions (special education schools, adapted curriculum schools, private schools, rural or urban schools) can also be perfected by the use of AI-driven software tools. This can be achieved through the use of an analysis software that can evaluate some of the teacher's characteristics and determine their strengths and weaknesses according to each type of educational institution. One thing that this kind of tool can not do is to easily quantify and interpret the subjective desires and motivations of a future teacher (although there are attempts, especially in the Beliefs-Desires-Intentions (Adam, 2016) approach, the perspective is relatively fresh (Dubois, 2017)). Nevertheless, identifying the strong traits of a teacher and helping self-understanding of these traits may, in the end, conduct to better educational planning and delivery of content, knowledge, etc.

Many of the future teachers may be choosing their workplace according to some personal principles or past events that made them desire a certain job level. This may cause a conflict between the expectations and the reality for these future trainers. The conflict may have a negative effect on the teachers because they are either aiming too high for their possibilities and abilities, or they are overqualified for the chosen level of the job. Both situations are a problem because this is one way of maintaining a high level of teacher motivation: having the proper level of abilities and knowledge for the optimal level of their chosen educational institution.

As mentioned before, the use of an AI analyzer (Abiyev, 2015) can offer an evaluation of this conflict. This analysis can be enhanced by the use of the previously described AI-assisted curriculum development. The combination of these two can help diminish the limitations generated by the subjective aspects. The adaptation of the curriculum combined with the prognosis of the optimal level of the job, can result in a sufficient outcome of the educational process regarding the future teacher's workplace satisfaction.

AI AND SPORT

One area of the massive domain that deals with human physical activities is the study of sport activity. We believe that this area is the most dependent on the individualized (Bartlett, 2017) process of education. If the process is constructed with regard to the differences in the trained subject's characteristics (age, gender, height, weight, etc.), we may have strong reasons to believe that the end result will generate an improvement in the subject's performance.

Physical activity encompasses any type of human activity that is made in a controlled environment, under certain preset rules, with the use of the motor functions of the body and with a clear objective of the end result. It can have a play-like component and may or may not be supervised by a trained person.

Sport, in general, is a subset of the general physical activity with the main goal of improving one's physical abilities for the sole purpose of outperforming others in a competition. In this context, sport performance is the driving force of any training period. There is a constant struggle to push the limits of the athlete so that new levels of physical performance can be achieved. With the evolution of knowledge in the field of sport science, so did the methods and means used to achieve better performance. These new methods or means are sometimes borrowed from other fields of study. AI-driven technologies, mixed with systems engineering, is one aspect of research that has started to offer new ways and methods of conducting a training session in sports.

Data analysis using AI-driven algorithms can already be used in training. These applications (Lang, 2017; Seneviratne, 2017; Malone, 2017) cover anything from physiological data to actions performed in training or during an official competition. The conclusion or interpretations of such software can help a trainer control the effects of the workout, allowing him the ability to intervene and change the content of the training according to the findings. Most of the time the data analysis can be used a tool by the trainer to understand the effects, if any, on the athlete's body. The usefulness of such applications rises from their ability to, if constructed correctly, mimic the rules and guidelines found in sport methodology. Besides this, the recent ability (Chen, 2014; Upadhyaya, 2017) of such software to process large amounts of data means that the trainer receives the findings much faster and can make a decision regarding the next step of the training process. One other characteristic of newer AI-driven technologies is their portability. It allows the trainer or coach to always have the AI-analysis tool at-hand, even during training sessions. Thus, portable devices can mold the conducting of a training session toward the optimal form for developing sport performance.

Moreover, AI-driven applications can be used to conduct a training session through the direct control of the environment. With some limitations regarding the type of sport or training, these applications can act as an objective means of controlling—from beginning to end—the workout session. Running on a treadmill, cycling, dry-technique swimming and racing are some example of sports where an AI-driven application can govern (Dorf, 2011) the workout. These examples have one thing in common: at least one mechanical or mechatronic or electronic part is involved directly in training (i.e. actuators and sensors). The athlete performs their activity on, in or through the use of some sort of apparatus. This is the bridge that connects the AI inference core of the application to the actual movement of the human. The structure and functions of intelligent control systems allow the AI 'brain' to constantly monitor the evolution of performance-related variables and take actions toward the optimization of the workout.

Hardware-in-the-loop and human-in-the-loop intelligent systems can be used to control a training session with a different kind of impact over the student or athlete, than a purely software application. But is the 'intelligence' aspect of a control system really needed in these cases? Certainly, and that's because of the wide array of uncertainty around the understanding of human physiology, body, mind, etc. The development of classical control systems for human-in-the-loop use is limited due to the very nature of the controlled process (Constantinescu, 2017). The more complex (interconnected, nonlinear, uncertain, etc.) a system is, the more we turn to metaheuristics, linguistic computing, emulated evolution, artificial neural networks, and so on, with a healthy dose of adaptation mechanisms, the most popular of which is the famous 'machine learning' type of enhancement of computational intelligence.

A properly designed intelligent control system has everything it needs to control every aspect of training. Different kinds of sensors, control modules, mechanical actuators or interfaces can be used to cover the vital components addressed in the training the system was constructed for. Through the use of autonomous control architectures (often hierarchical), higher level objectives can be formulated and achieved. At the moment, unlike the portable software of the AI apps, intelligent control systems are mostly stationary due to their nature. This can be a drawback, but it can also be a strong point because it shows the individualization and higher specialization of such a system. Therefore, an intelligent control system can be designed to control one aspect of training and because it can do that very well (optimally, satisfying a series of well known performance specifications), it offers a reliable way of improving that parameter which comprises its focus.

The implementation array of real world intelligent control systems is currently limited, but not impossible. Right here we can pinpoint another fertile and highly promising field of research in the near future, with expected outcomes such as wearable control technologies for various physiological aspects of training.

Indifferent of what type of control technology is being used, they all need to have the bridge (appendage) between the human (process) and the decision-making core (the AI 'brain'). With the increase in complexity (higher number of these three components), the individualization of the training session can be achieved by integrating distributed and decentralized control architectures, in which each part of the training session is carefully curated, while the whole works together in an emergent(Shah, 2007) harmony toward which researcher in the field of complex control systems aspire.

So far there has been a tentative trend regarding AI-driven technologies to use fuzzy logic controllers for the control systems (Moughamir, 2001; Biagetti, 2015; Lai, 2009; Rui, 2013; Moughamir, 2002; Su, 2006). The integration of abstract knowledge from physiology into a fuzzy logic controller has been done with great success. The controller proposed in (Jacobs, 1997) consisted of 36 if-then rules that were applied on a model that had three sets of variables. Human decision-making can be modelled using fuzzy logic set theory by including abstract notions like human drives and motives, though there is a gap in the literature describing the methodology of creating expert-driven fuzzy logic models. In (Rudas, 2012) the authors proposed a 10 step method that allowed them to include variables like motivation and drives into the controller. An evaluation of strength exercises using the fuzzy logic approach was considered in (Novatchkov, 2013), along with the observation, at the time, that there is a lack of applications of fuzzy logic control systems in the fields of sport and training. With the increasing progress in fuzzy systems implementation, this technology is becoming more and more versatile, with a wide range of applicability, from modelling non-linear systems (Precup, 2015), to detection algorithms (Moallen, 2015), to controllers and decision-support systems (Panagidi, 2014).

The real world implementation and technological readiness of these technologies in sports is lacking, however, at the moment (although companies like Fitbit and Adidas do intensive research in the field), but considering the fact that fuzzy logic mimics the logical thinking of an expert—in this case a trainer—we believe that this is a good starting point for future development of such systems.

The limitations of using AI-driven technologies lies, as stated previously in this chapter, in their complexity. The dependence on special hardware to function, the high cost of components and the constant need for maintenance from trained specialists are some of the factors that may limit popularization. Smaller scale systems have been implemented with success, but their accessibility to the greater public is still on reduced (there is a long road from the shelf of the research lab to the approval of specialized normative organization for public consumption).

SOLUTIONS, RECOMMENDATIONS, AND FUTURE RESEARCH

AI and General Physical Performance

In real world implementations there are two aspects that hinder the current endeavours into machine intelligence applications: (a) the human body is a nonlinear process, thus the tools and formalisms of linear dynamical systems are inefficient in its analysis, modeling, control—and general understanding; (b) there are risks that, in the mind of users (trainers and students alike), might outshine the rewards of using AI for improving physical performance.

Therefore, the difficulties and problems of constructing an intelligent system that tries to act upon the human body need to be investigated, while the practicality of intelligent control solutions needs to be analyzed, with emphasis on reducing exploitation risks. In this section we are discussing these two aspects through two case studies.

As we mentioned before, the groundwork for this area has only recently started to be settled, in tandem with the increase in computation power and the evolution of mobile devices and other wearables. There is no recipe we can apply here, no secret formula for evaluating any new design. Therefore, the case studies presented in this section are of our making, and through their exploitation we strive to showcase not the benefits of the models we obtained and the systems we designed, but the approach in critically analysing their performance.

The human body is a multivariable MIMO nonlinear memory system (with continuous and discrete components with a base of even-distributed parameters, with stochastic functioning having manifestations both in open and closed loop), sometimes (partly) unstable and (always) riddled with uncertainty (the formal kind). From a systems engineering perspective this is the worst kind of system to model, analyze, simulate, control, etc. From all the biosystems out there, complex living organisms (like the human body) are the hardest to tackle. In one of our first studies (Pătrașcu, 2014), we researched the possibility of constructing an intelligent control system for the human heart rate, and in the end covered the design of a fuzzy controller. During this study the biggest hurdle we had to overcome was the nonlinearities of the human heart as a process, which in turn led to the investigation of the types of models that could be used for such endeavours. So far they are all lacking, because while the nonlinearities can be modeled (Cheng, 2008), there is always the risk of hidden instability (Asheghan, 2016) and other 'surprises' that control systems validated on the model could not overcome in a real-world implementation and thus register failures or cause accidents.

The second example addresses a study that aims to design and construct an AI-driven application for mobile devices that is useful in the control the intensity of the workout over a longer period of time, through the analysis of heart rate variability (HRV) (Pătraşcu, 2016). We designed, implemented, and tested a mobile device application for an Android operating system. The software uses information from the user regarding their HRV and work heart rate (WHR) over two consecutive session and returns the degree (in percentages) with which the training intensity must either be increased or decreased for the following training session.

A fuzzy logic module analyzes the input data (heart rate variability and work heart rate), in a Mamdani type structure with a MIN-MAX inference mechanism. Fuzzy inference has an advantage over others when designing support software like this one, due to its flexibility when it comes to the particularities of each individual (human bodies are all different, respond differently, behave differently). Unknowns (such as daily meals or exact lung capacity or even running style) do not hinder the output of the system. The solution combines a non-digital method of calculating and interpreting the evolution of HRV to identify the moment physical fatigue sets in, with the use of modern equipment: heart rate monitor and the MOTION-AE app.

The experiments we conducted showed that the application is able to reliably suggest a desirable workout intensity over a period of time, to prevent both over and undertraining, while also making sure that it's impossible for chronic physical fatigue to set in. The MOTION-AE mobile app enhances the performance of aerobic training through a gradual and constant control of the workout intensity. The app can be viewed as an objective instrument for coaches that can be used in aerobic training, due to its ability to keep track of previous exercise sessions and performance markers achieved by the subject. The portability and low computational costs are two characteristics of the app that open the accessibility door to the everyday user.

AI and Accessibility

One of the principles of the educational process is accessibility. This principle refers to the ability of the educational process to be easily implemented indifferent of the widely varying particularities of a specific situation. We believe that this is an important topic to cover regarding AI and the educational process in general, and even more vital regarding individualized education.

There are many hurdles that a large scale implementation of AI-assisted education may face: access to specific hardware and its use, development and fine tuning of AI systems for use in individualized education, implementation over different age intervals or social environments, and of course their social and cultural impact.

For a long period the concept of AI-based education was considered a dream due to the low feasibility of a large scale implementation. The development of intelligent machines has advanced drastically in recent years and has offered many avenues of implementation for various AI-based technologies in many industries. The accessibility of such systems in education is still limited for a large scale implementation due to high costs (both device-wise and maintenance-wise). Nevertheless, small scale pilot implementations can still be set up and are continuously launched (Lan, 2007; Wang, 2009).

- **Infrastructure:** Most schools are not design to accommodate AI-assisted education. There may not be enough room and new buildings might need to be designed and built, which will increase costs of implementation, on top of the actual cost of the components needed. These will be more expensive depending on the field the system will be applied to. Virtual 3D imaging of a basketball game for strategy analysis sounds nifty, but what about those high-res camera? If they're too expensive for traffic monitoring, they might be an impossible investment for schools. Sad, but true.
- **Design Complexity:** Depending on the purpose and method chosen to design and AI system for educational purposes, its difficulty can vary from relatively moderate to high to near impossible (perhaps quantum computing (Li, 2015) will break through the current computational ceiling and the subsequent programming languages will be less prone to human error). The maintenance of a nationwide system could be one aspect that might hinder its implementation, while an overly complicated operation of the system will result in the need to train or retrain a large number of teachers. This can be considered by many an unfounded expense. Moreover, the retraining at such a scale of existing personnel may take too long and limit deployment.
- **The Status Quo of the Educational System:** Old methods of teaching that have offered consistent results may be too deeply rooted. Depending on the different fields of knowledge it will applied to, the system might require special hardware to function properly. Beside the electronic parts that can cover anything from computer components to mobile devices, there will be a need for other appendages or mechanical parts for the optimal functioning of the system. Purely theoretical fields might need only a classical visual interface, but fields that tend to be more practical will need to have more complex interfaces for human-machine interaction.
- **Design Effort:** Will it be ready in time and will it function as intended or will it need further work? Implementation duration is paramount for the current pace of technological progress. Embarking on a project only to have it made obsolete by some technological breakthrough is unfeasible. So, the first

concern is understandable. The second question, however, is not as evident, not for non-engineers or everyday users or decision-makers. There is always, without a doubt, the possibility that any system validated in simulation to not work optimally in the real world (Ionescu, 2018) and to require further 'tinkering'. In systems engineering we call this process tuning and it can be lengthy—up to a year for a power plant where only conventional, non-intelligent systems reside, so how much difficult would it be when humans and uncertainties are involved?

There are several stages that must be reached in the developing of an AI module: 1. identifying correctly and precisely the problem we want to build the AI for; 2. conceptualizing the relations between different components of the problem; 3. designing the solutions for the type of AI chosen; 4. implementing the optimal version of the solution; all this while continuously testing and validating each choice at each step and for each performance requirement in a long list of functionalities and under the strict eye of normative organizations.

Another aspect that must be addressed regarding AI-driven systems is their tuning. Even though at their core any AI software or application aims to be self sustainable (autonomous functions, learning capabilities, etc.), the process of configuring and setting up the AI core takes time and a continuous implementation of changes or corrections. There are some AI applications used in control systems that require constant corrections of the inference engine up until the final form. All things considered, an AI system built with the aim of being used in a country-wide educational system will need both fine-tuning from of themselves (algorithms, rules, logic, etc.) and constant updating (information, databases, internal models, etc.)

- **Social Impact:** A large scale implementation of an AI-driven educational system will also face a series of factors that may become impediments in its successful functioning, the influence of factors such as age, social environment and cultural background being impossible to ignore.

An AI-driven educational system would offer many benefits through the impact of the curriculum or the flexibility of the training methods, but it also presents a peculiarity regarding its efficiency when analyzed through the age of the person it is addressed to. Children between the ages of 5 and 12 may not have a positive reaction if an AI-driven educational system will be implemented due to their age particularities. They need to have a dynamic, movement based education, where basic orientation, coordination, fitness and balance are the main focus points of the school system. Even though they do acquire a vast amount of theoretical knowledge, it is mostly linked with practical classes that aim to transfer the theory into real world events. Considering this, we believe that an AI-driven system for small children may not be appropriate (at least at the current technological readiness level), though some aspects of it can be introduced in the form of evaluation or in some sort of curiosity classes.

At the opposite end of the age timeline are adults that have finished their core education and already start working. They find themselves immersed in what is called continuous education or formation. They do have lectures they have to attend, but their education is resumed at being in contact with newer discoveries or techniques in their respective fields. Taking this into account, we think that an AI-driven education at this stage will also have a low impact due to the fact that they are already prepared for their fields of work.

Students of middle school, high school and university levels are, we believe, optimal for an AI-driven educational system because they are on track to or in the midst of preparing for the job market. The positive benefits of using AI technologies during their formation may help improve training for future work (we would be amiss, here, not to mention that 'work' is as wide a term as it should be, for society, which includes both regulatory operations and artistic endeavors, because, in the end, society is what should serve human development and individuality and not the other way around, i.e. 'work' is all about energy overcoming entropy).

- **Social Environment:** In general, social environments vary vastly between countries and also between regions of the same country. Some areas have a higher urban population, some have a higher industrialization level, some have a higher density of minorities compared to other regions; all these converge on the idea that social environments may be a hurdle in the implementation of an AI-driven educational system.

Rural and urban cultural values will have a high impact as well. A system implemented in a rural area will have to focus on other capabilities than one implemented in a densely urban one (see irrigation optimization vs. traffic control). The development of a specific industry in a region will also impact the aim of the system. The minority population in an area may have an atypical tradition that limits their fields of study and therefore the AI-driven system must be molded accordingly.

All these considered we believe that these may, in the end, be minor obstacles due to the beauty of machine intelligence: its adaptability. We believe that, if an AI-driven educational system is well designed, it can take into consideration all these aspects, accommodate them, and grow from there. The cultural limitation of a large scale AI-driven educational system can be minimized due to the fact that its implementation wouldn't be on a worldwide scale, but at country (or regional) level, where the cultural differences are minimal. Even though there are countries with significant cultural differences between their regions, the design can be adapted.

We believe that the individualization of the educational process should be the focus of any national or European educational system. Only through individualized education it is possible to obtain specialized workforce that also has the necessary flexibility to adapt to new living and societal demands. We believe that the use of AI may offer the means to achieve a shift in the educational dogma that will result in a more fluid teaching process with intrinsic individualization.

Future Research Directions

The integration of AI in an educational system is a major undertaking because the fusion of these fields is much more complex than can be observed at the surface level. The core element of an educational system is the human being, and thus the whole structure is based on a non-linear system that makes anything build around it have an intrinsic non-linear behaviour. Moreover, the multitude of subfields that makes up an educational system lead to a matrix of interconnected elements that any single AI, at the present time, may have a hard time controlling and running.

Future integrations must address the complexity of the focus system which requires that further design produce similarly complex AI structures, i.e. one must consider a decentralized, networked approach. We believe that any future studies have to identify methods for AI systems to integrate different elements of the non-linear foundation of the educational matrix. We believe that the cultural and social aspects of the educational systems are the hardest to integrate and therefore further research must make an effort to transform and adapt to techno-social, cultural, and economic trends. Future studies may allow for an increased adaptability of AI systems as new tech should be able to mold itself over cultural and social spectra and, through this, should be able to offer correct information, in a suitable manner, to any student that uses it, and in the end, should facilitate the evolution of a more efficient educational system.

CONCLUSION

In recent years, AI-driven technology has made significant advances. The nature of AI-driven software offers many advantages for its implementation in an educational system. The adaptation, interactivity, flexibility and accessibility of such applications will transfer these qualities toward the educational process. We have identified a series of factors that may limit the implementation of a nationwide AI-based educational system: age, social environment or cultural implications to name a few. Even though these are important and must be taken into account, the basic nature and scope of an intelligent machine, through its adaptability, should be malleable enough to incorporate most of these aspects.

AI systems can be useful in the training of future teachers in field of physical education. The latter can link the theoretical knowledge accumulated by future teachers with the practical situations and events they may face. The curriculum can be modified through the use of intelligent algorithms and apps to allow an individualized education molded to specialized needs and resources. Portable AI-driven modules have been found to be reliable enough to become objective means used in physical workouts and sport performance training.

We have identified several hard limitations for the implementation of an AI-driven educational system. These are mostly dependent on the novelty of the field that comes with a high price tag attached. Beside the high costs, large scale development is also currently faced with the lack of both physical space and specific hardware.

REFERENCES

Abiyev, R. H., Sadikoğlu, G., & Abiyeva, E. (2015). Fuzzy Evaluation of Job Satisfaction of Hotel Employees. *The 2015 World Congress in Computer Science, Computer Engineering, and Applied Computing*.

Adam, C., & Gaudou, B. (2016). BDI agents in social simulations: A survey. *The Knowledge Engineering Review*, *31*(3), 207–238. doi:10.1017/S0269888916000096

Aguilar, J., Valdiviezo, P., Cordero, J., & Sánchez, M. (2015, January). Conceptual Design of a Smart Classroom Based on Multiagent Systems. *Proceedings on the International Conference on Artificial Intelligence (ICAI),* 471.

Asheghan, M. M., & Míguez, J. (2016). Stability analysis and robust control of heart beat rate during treadmill exercise. *Automatica*, *63*, 311–320. doi:10.1016/j.automatica.2015.10.027

Baker, R. S., & Inventado, P. S. (2014). Educational data mining and learning analytics. In *Learning analytics* (pp. 61–75). New York, NY: Springer.

Barmaki, R., & Hughes, C. E. (2015). Providing real-time feedback for student teachers in a virtual rehearsal environment. *Proceedings of the 2015 ACM on International Conference on Multimodal Interaction,* 531-537. 10.1145/2818346.2830604

Bartlett, J. D., O'Connor, F., Pitchford, N., Torres-Ronda, L., & Robertson, S. J. (2017). Relationships between internal and external training load in team-sport athletes: Evidence for an individualized approach. *International Journal of Sports Physiology and Performance, 12*(2), 230–234. doi:10.1123/ijspp.2015-0791 PMID:27194668

Biagetti, G., Crippa, P., Falaschetti, L., Orcioni, S., & Turchetti, C. (2015). A rule based framework for smart training using sEMG signal. In *Intelligent Decision Technologies* (pp. 89–99). Cham: Springer. doi:10.1007/978-3-319-19857-6_9

Boril, J., Jirgl, M., & Jalovecky, R. (2016, September). Use of flight simulators in analyzing pilot behavior. In *IFIP International Conference on Artificial Intelligence Applications and Innovations*. Springer. 10.1007/978-3-319-44944-9_22

Brabazon, T. (2016). *The University of Google: Education in the (post) information age*. Routledge. doi:10.4324/9781315551838

Chen, M., Mao, S., & Liu, Y. (2014). Big data: A survey. *Mobile Networks and Applications, 19*(2), 171–209. doi:10.100711036-013-0489-0

Cheng, T. M., Savkin, A. V., Celler, B. G., Su, S. W., & Wang, L. (2008). Nonlinear Modelling and Control of Human Heart Rate Response During Exercise With Various Work Load Intensities. *IEEE Transactions on Biomedical Engineering, 55*(11), 2499–2508. doi:10.1109/TBME.2008.2001131

Chu, S. K. W., Reynolds, R. B., Tavares, N. J., Notari, M., & Lee, C. W. Y. (2017). *Twenty-first century skills education in Switzerland: An example of project-based learning using Wiki in science education. In 21st Century Skills Development Through Inquiry-Based Learning* (pp. 61–78). Singapore: Springer. doi:10.1007/978-981-10-2481-8_4

Constantinescu, V., & Patrascu, M. (2017). Route encoding in evolutionary control systems for emergency vehicles. In *ITS Telecommunications (ITST), 2017 15th International Conference on*. IEEE. 10.1109/ITST.2017.7972216

Dorf, R. C., & Bishop, R. H. (2011). *Modern control systems*. Pearson.

Dubois, D., Lorini, E., & Prade, H. (2017). The Strength of Desires: A Logical Approach. *Minds and Machines, 27*(1), 199–231. doi:10.100711023-017-9426-5

Ernst, J., & Monroe, M. (2004). The effects of environment-based education on students' critical thinking skills and disposition toward critical thinking. *Environmental Education Research, 10*(4), 507–522. doi:10.1080/1350462042000291038

Fister, I. Jr, Ljubič, K., Suganthan, P. N., Perc, M., & Fister, I. (2015). Computational intelligence in sports: Challenges and opportunities within a new research domain. *Applied Mathematics and Computation, 262*, 178–186. doi:10.1016/j.amc.2015.04.004

Galway, L. P., Corbett, K. K., Takaro, T. K., Tairyan, K., & Frank, E. (2014). A novel integration of online and flipped classroom instructional models in public health higher education. *BMC Medical Education, 14*(1), 181. doi:10.1186/1472-6920-14-181 PMID:25169853

Gao, Y., & Wu, X. (2015). User Acceptance of Learning Technology: The Case of Using Moodle. *International Journal of Learning: Annual Review, 21.*

Haber, M. G., Mazzotti, V. L., Mustian, A. L., Rowe, D. A., Bartholomew, A. L., Test, D. W., & Fowler, C. H. (2016). What works, when, for whom, and with whom: A meta-analytic review of predictors of postsecondary success for students with disabilities. *Review of Educational Research, 86*(1), 123–162. doi:10.3102/0034654315583135

Ionescu, T. C., & Patrascu, M. (2018). *Control systems for time delay processes.* Bucharest: Politehnica Press.

Jacobs, R. (1997). Control model of human stance using fuzzy logic. *Biological Cybernetics, 77*(1), 63–70. doi:10.1007004220050367 PMID:9309863

Jarke, M., Neumann, B., Vassiliou, Y., & Wahlster, W. (1989). KBMS requirements of knowledge-based systems. In *Foundations of knowledge base management* (pp. 381–394). Berlin: Springer. doi:10.1007/978-3-642-83397-7_17

Jony, A. I., Rahman, M. S., & Islam, Y. M. (2017). ICT in higher education: Wiki-based reflection to promote deeper thinking levels. *International Journal of Modern Education and Computer Science, 9*(4), 43–49. doi:10.5815/ijmecs.2017.04.05

Kim, J., & Fesenmaier, D. R. (2015). Measuring emotions in real time: Implications for tourism experience design. *Journal of Travel Research, 54*(4), 419–429. doi:10.1177/0047287514550100

Ku, H., Choi, J. J., Lee, S., Jang, S., & Do, W. (2018). Shelly, a Tortoise-Like Robot for One-to-Many Interaction with Children. *Companion of the 2018 ACM/IEEE International Conference on Human-Robot Interaction*, 353-354. 10.1145/3173386.3177824

Lai, D. T., Begg, R. K., & Palaniswami, M. (2009). Computational intelligence in gait research: A perspective on current applications and future challenges. *IEEE Transactions on Information Technology in Biomedicine, 13*(5), 687–702. doi:10.1109/TITB.2009.2022913 PMID:19447724

Lan, Y. J., Sung, Y. T., & Chang, K. E. (2007). *A mobile-device-supported peer-assisted learning system for collaborative early EFL reading*. Academic Press.

Lancor, R. A. (2014). Using student-generated analogies to investigate conceptions of energy: A multidisciplinary study. *International Journal of Science Education, 36*(1), 1–23. doi:10.1080/09500693.2012.714512

Lang, M. (2017). Beyond Fitbit: A critical appraisal of optical heart rate monitoring wearables and apps, their current limitations and legal implications. *Alb. LJ Sci. & Tech., 28*, 39.

Li, Y., Humphreys, P. C., Mendoza, G. J., & Benjamin, S. C. (2015). Resource costs for fault-tolerant linear optical quantum computing. *Physical Review X, 5*(4), 041007. doi:10.1103/PhysRevX.5.041007

Malone, J. J., Lovell, R., Varley, M. C., & Coutts, A. J. (2017). Unpacking the black box: Applications and considerations for using GPS devices in sport. *International Journal of Sports Physiology and Performance, 12*(s2), S2–S18. doi:10.1123/ijspp.2016-0236 PMID:27736244

Merchant, Z., Goetz, E. T., Cifuentes, L., Keeney-Kennicutt, W., & Davis, T. J. (2014). Effectiveness of virtual reality-based instruction on students' learning outcomes in K-12 and higher education: A meta-analysis. *Computers & Education, 70*, 29–40. doi:10.1016/j.compedu.2013.07.033

Metzler, M. (2017). *Instructional models in physical education*. Routledge. doi:10.4324/9781315213521

Moallem, P., Mousavi, B. S., & Naghibzadeh, S. S. (2015). Fuzzy Inference System Optimized by Genetic Algorithm for Robust Face and Pose Detection. *International Journal of Artificial Intelligence, 13*(2), 73–88.

Moughamir, S., Manamanni, N., Zaytoon, J., & Afilal, L. (2001). Control law implementation for Multi-Iso: a training machine for lower limbs. *Engineering in Medicine and Biology Society, 2001. Proceedings of the 23rd Annual International Conference of the IEEE*, 2, 1477-1480. 10.1109/IEMBS.2001.1020484

Moughamir, S., Zaytoon, J., Manamanni, N., & Afilal, L. (2002). A system approach for control development of lower-limbs training machines. *Control Engineering Practice, 10*(3), 287–299. doi:10.1016/S0967-0661(01)00155-1

Nilsson, J., & Klügl, F. (2015). Human-in-the-Loop Simulation of a Virtual Classroom. In *Multi-Agent Systems and Agreement Technologies* (pp. 379–394). Cham: Springer.

Novatchkov, H., & Baca, A. (2013). Fuzzy Logic in Sports: A Review and an Illustrative Case Study in the Field of Strength Training. *International Journal of Computers and Applications, 71*(6), 8–14. doi:10.5120/12360-8675

Panagidi, K., Kolomvatsos, K., & Hadjiefthymiades, S. (2014). An intelligent scheme for concurrent multi-issue negotiations. *International Journal of Artificial Intelligence, 12*(1), 129–149.

Pătraşcu, A., Pătraşcu, M., & Hanţiu, I. (2014). Nonlinear Fuzzy Control of Human Heart Rate During Aerobic Endurance Training with Respect to Significant Model Variations, *Proc. of the International Conference on System Theory, Control and Computing ICSTCC*, 311-316 10.1109/ICSTCC.2014.6982434

Pătraşcu, A., Ungureanu, A., Pătraşcu, M., Drăgoicea, M., & Hanţiu, I. (2016). MOTION-AE: an Intelligent Mobile Application for Aerobic Endurance Training. *International Journal of Artificial Intelligence, 14*(2), 42-59.

Precup, R. E., Bojan-Dragos, C. A., Petriu, E. M., Radac, M. B., & Stinean, A. I. (2015). Results on Optimal Tuning of Fuzzy Models of Magnetic Levitation Systems. *International Journal of Artificial Intelligence, 13*(2), 57–72.

Richards, D., & Taylor, M. (2015). A Comparison of learning gains when using a 2D simulation tool versus a 3D virtual world: An experiment to find the right representation involving the Marginal Value Theorem. *Computers & Education, 86*, 157–171. doi:10.1016/j.compedu.2015.03.009

Rudas, I. T. (2012). Risk and Uncertainties of Physiological Processes Handled by the Fuzzy Implementation. *WSEAS International Conference on System Science and Simulation in Engineering*, 37-43.

Rui, S. (2013). Identification method of sports throwing force based on fuzzy neural network. *Journal of Networks, 8*(7), 1574.

Seneviratne, S., Hu, Y., Nguyen, T., Lan, G., Khalifa, S., Thilakarathna, K., & Seneviratne, A. (2017). A survey of wearable devices and challenges. *IEEE Communications Surveys and Tutorials, 19*(4), 2573–2620. doi:10.1109/COMST.2017.2731979

Shah, N. B., Hastings, D. E., & Rhodes, D. H. (2007). Systems of systems and emergent system context. *5th Conference on Systems Engineering Research.*

Sheridan, T. B. (2016). Human–robot interaction: Status and challenges. *Human Factors, 58*(4), 525–532. doi:10.1177/0018720816644364 PMID:27098262

Su, S. W., Wang, L., Celler, B. G., & Savkin, A. V. (2006). Heart rate control during treadmill exercise. *Engineering in Medicine and Biology Society, 2005. IEEE-EMBS 2005. 27th Annual International Conference of the,* 2471-2474.

Toro, C., Barandiaran, I., & Posada, J. (2015). A perspective on Knowledge Based and Intelligent systems implementation in Industrie 4.0. *Procedia Computer Science, 60*, 362–370. doi:10.1016/j.procs.2015.08.143

Upadhyaya, J., & Ahuja, N. J. (2017). Quality of service in cloud computing in higher education: A critical survey and innovative model. *I-SMAC (IoT in Social, Mobile, Analytics and Cloud)(I-SMAC), 2017 International Conference on,* 137-140 10.1109/I-SMAC.2017.8058324

Van Gogh Museum. (2015). *App Touch Van Gogh.* Retrieved from: vangoghmuseum.nl/en/app-touch-van-gogh

Verma, A., Rathore, S., Vishwakarma, S., & Goswani, S. (2017). Multilevel Analysis of Student's Feedback Using Moodle Logs in Virtual Cloud Environment. *International Journal of Computer Science and Information Technology, 9*(5), 15–28. doi:10.5121/ijcsit.2017.9502

Wang, M., Shen, R., Novak, D., & Pan, X. (2009). The impact of mobile learning on students' learning behaviours and performance: Report from a large blended classroom. *British Journal of Educational Technology, 40*(4), 673–695. doi:10.1111/j.1467-8535.2008.00846.x

Zheng, B., Niiya, M., & Warschauer, M. (2015). Wikis and collaborative learning in higher education. *Technology, Pedagogy and Education, 24*(3), 357–374. doi:10.1080/1475939X.2014.948041

KEY TERMS AND DEFINITIONS

Artificial Intelligence: The science and engineering of building intelligent machines.

Education System: Generally refers to public schooling starting from kindergarten and through high school programs. It comprises everything that goes into educating the population.

Implementation: the process of putting a decision or plan into effect.

Intelligent Control: Is a class of control techniques that use various artificial intelligence computing approaches like neural networks, Bayesian probability, fuzzy logic, machine learning, evolutionary computation and genetic algorithms.

Model: An abstract representation of a physical entity or process.

Physical Activity: Is defined as any bodily movement produced by skeletal muscles that require energy expenditure.

Physical Education: Instruction in the development and care of the body ranging from simple calisthenic exercises to a course of study providing training in hygiene, gymnastics, and the performance and management of athletic games.

Simulation: The representation of the behaviour or characteristics of one system or process through the use of a model.

Sport: An activity involving physical exertion and skill in which an individual or team competes against another or others for entertainment.

Chapter 3
Revolution by Evolution:
How Intelligent Tutoring Systems Are Changing Education

Stefka Tzanova
York College (CUNY), USA

ABSTRACT

This chapter will discuss the development of intelligent tutoring systems (ITSs) for education in the last decade and will trace the challenges they meet. The author will examine the social and cultural impacts of several types of ITSs, from data-driven ITSs, which became the backbone of educational data mining approaches, to model-based adaptive systems. The latter utilizes artificial-intelligence-based tools that can provide dialogue to engage students in the learning process, to provide open learning models in order to promote self-awareness, to adopt meta-cognitive scaffolding, to use social simulation models, and to use cultural models. The layout of the chapter is as follows: the author will describe the technology of various ITSs with a focus on implementation of different techniques and algorithms in ITS modules (e.g., student modeling module, pedagogical module, and interface), followed by a discussion of how these ITSs begin to change the whole spectra of educational paradigms toward open everyone-is-a student models.

DOI: 10.4018/978-1-5225-7793-5.ch003

INTRODUCTION

Artificial Intelligence (AI) has a long history as a driving force behind many technologies – cars are using AI to adapt vehicle behavior to drivers' style, intelligent communications have become a common, and voice commands have already replaced keyboards in many interfaces. AI moved into the education field in the late 1970s, with the development of the pioneering intelligent tutoring systems (ITSs) SCHOLAR (Carbonell, 1970a) and BIP (Barr, Beard, & Atkinson, 1976). ITSs are a broad category encompassing any computer program that contains intelligence and can be used for the purpose of learning (Freedman, Ali, & McRoy, 2000). ITSs are an interdisciplinary field that investigates how to devise educational platforms providing instruction that fits the learning needs of each individual. In order to fulfil this mission, ITSs are designed to support various models of learning, such as one-to-one learning, collaborative learning, and learning with examples. Undoubtedly, one-to-one tutoring is the most desirable and effective form of teaching (Bloom, 1984). However, it is often out of the reach for many students, not only because of the lack of so many tutors, but also because of the financial, social, cultural, and linguistic limitations. In this sense, ITSs have huge social and cultural impact over society by providing a simulated one-to-one tutoring, which best matches the cognitive needs of the student without an actual tutor present. Collaborative learning is a valuable form of learning where the students participate in a common learning activity (e.g., online course or group project). Collaborative learning across diverse groups may be impacted by lack of social interaction skills, language or cultural differences. Many modern ITSs use AI technologies to facilitate the learner group formation and the discussions within the group. One of the most commonly used approaches in group formation is to explore student models according to some pre-defined criteria (i.e., adaptive group creation). The latter could be a group of students with the same or similar skills level or a group of students with complementary skills. Other approaches in group formation utilize internal models of collaborative patterns, which ITSs use to recognize the level of understanding of a concept across the group or use of intelligent agents to simulate a particular type of participant into a group–from the tutor to a member of a group and to a virtual test student.

The learning process has cultural and social dimensions. In this sense, ITSs may be designed as culture-neutral or culture-specific. However, transferring knowledge across multinational and multicultural groups requires consideration of culture (Chung & Miller, 2011). Simply put, the design of an effective ITS requires an understanding of the social and cultural background of the students, in order to provide individual instruction and adequate feedback to the user. The culturally aware ITSs are very specific and explore specific frameworks that guide the design of intercultural virtual humans and software (Raybourn & Waern, 2004). The U.S.

military developed three main culturally aware ITSs: Tactical Iraqi, Vector, and Elect-Bilat (Young, 2011). The latter is used to teach U.S. military personnel how to conduct business negotiations and meetings in cultural context. Tactical Iraqi teaches language in a cultural context, while Vector teaches cultural familiarity.

Tutoring with computers attracted much interest in academia in 1980s as a way to achieve more effective education. Early systems were in fact standalone computer based systems, sometimes also called computer aided learning (CAL) or Computer Assisted Instruction (CAI), which offered static interfaces and a simple feedback system. In 1970 Carbonell argued that application of AI in CAI will help to overcome the limitations seen in initial tutoring systems (Carbonell, 1970b). That led to development of Intelligent Computer Assisted Instruction (ICAI) systems. The term ICAI was later replaced by the term Intelligent Tutoring System (ITS). Twenty years later in 1990, Self (Self, 1990) defined ITS as an engineering product the effectiveness of which depends on quality of used design techniques.

Despite the great expectations, the first studies on the ITS' educational outcome revealed a modest improvement in terms of educational quality which couldn't be justified by the time and efforts invested in creating the content. For example, it has been estimated that one hour of educational content requires about 300 hours from highly qualified developers (Murray, 1999). It has been acknowledged that educational effectiveness of ITSs depends on their ability to cover ill-defined domains, their ability to adapt to students' behavior along with their ability to give feedback, and their cultural awareness, but also depends on some other aspects of the learning process. In their meta-analysis of the effectiveness of ITSs, Steenbergen-Hu and Cooper pointed out that ITS does not demonstrate significant positive effect on students' learning when ITSs are used as standalone programs and for the short term (Steenbergen-Hu & Cooper, 2014). Similarly, the research done by Ma and his colleagues revealed that applications of ITSs have positive educational outcomes only for large groups, but have no positive effect for small groups and with individualized tutoring (Ma, Adesope, Nesbit, & Liu, 2014). Both these studies were conducted on well-defined subject domains (mathematics, physics, chemistry etc.) and not on ill-defines ones. For the latter, the data-driven ITS has been seen to have the potential to overcome "ill-domain" obstacles because they can generate their content on the fly. There is no universal agreement how to evaluate the effectiveness of ITS. With lack of systematic approach to evaluate the educational effectiveness of ITS it makes sense to evaluate ITS' educational outcome as part of the educational outcome of complex Learning Management Systems and in the context of the four great challenges of AI in education: to provide a virtual tutor for every learner, to take learning outside the classroom, to do analysis of interaction data, and to address 21st century skills (Woolf, Lane, Chaudhri, & Kolodner, 2013).

This chapter is organized as follows. First, we will outline types, structure and classification of ITS. Our focus is on those defining aspects in evolution of the tutoring systems in the last decade which caused conversion of ITS from standalone learning system toward a component in a complex learning environment. Then, we will discuss those changes in ITS which go beyond simple improvements of elements of ITS structure and which require inputs from the humanities - cognitive science, pedagogy, cultural anthropology, psychology, data and information science and didactics. Lastly, we will discuss the transformation of ITS from a learning program to a core element of a complex leaning system and the social and cultural impact of that transformation.

INTELLIGENT TUTORING SYSTEMS VS. COMPUTER-BASED TUTORING SYSTEMS

Attempts to use computers in education dated back to late 1960 (Atkinson, 1968), but the academic interest in intelligent tutoring systems became significant in late 1980s. In contrast to industrial/engineering AI applications, ITSs operate in a realm of the human reasoning process, where the decisions are made based on inputs (experiences) and outputs (actions) (Sleeman & Brown, 1982). As such, ITSs are defined as computer programs which are specifically designed to perform tutoring functions by implementing a specific learning strategy, which is derived from cognitive research in human tutoring. The main goal of any ITS is effective knowledge transfer, which is achieved by providing information to students, assigning learning tasks, and providing optimal hints (feedback) according to task, all in order to provoke motivational and metacognitive changes. In this sense, ITSs differ significantly from computer-based tutoring systems (CBTSs). The latter (sometimes also called computer aided instruction systems) restrict the learning process to a simple model, in which the CBTS presents a lesson and tests the student knowledge with an objective test (quite often multiple choice). In CBTSs, the knowledge is presented as a static set of interconnected structures which are specifically designed to hold both the domain and expert knowledge. Typically, CBTSs utilize specific software engineering approaches in order to map pedagogical decisions into the framework of the educational system. Unfortunately, the successful mapping is not always possible or optimal, which causes the appearance of unwanted knowledge constructions. The main problem in CBTSs, however, is the lack of multidimensionality and thus the inability to track students' knowledge based only on a single parameter. More precisely, the ability of a student to solve a set of control tasks does not necessarily determine the desired outcome of education, because, quite often, the instructional schema guides the student only over problem-solving method(s) or techniques, but does little toward the actual reasoning process (step generating behavior).

Unlike CBTSs, ITSs, which apply AI to education and instructional design, track students' "progress" and provide adaptive instructions. Under the hood, ITSs create a multidimensional user/student model (also called knowledge tracking) which is as comprehensive as possible and use this model to provide adaptive tutoring responses. The comprehensive student model is critical for high learning outcome because it describes the student's psychological state, such as subject matter knowledge, emotions, and learning progress. Thus, at each stage of the learning process, ITSs collect student response via a specific interface in order to fit one or more of the tutoring functions. Indeed, on the one hand, ITSs aim to correct specific misconceptions and to provide very specific knowledge, but, on the other hand, the type of domain impacts the choice of the approach in building the user modelling module. Knowledge-driven approaches (i.e., cognitive tutors, constrain tutors) require the availability of a large amount of knowledge on a subject, because the latter is used to program knowledge representations and constraints of ITSs. In such knowledge-driven systems, the user model utilizes a wide spectrum of AI techniques and algorithms, such as production systems, Bayes networks, theorem proving, case-based reasoning, and constraint modelling. For example, the cognitive tutors student model is established as a set of probabilities assigned to production rules (Anderson, Corbett, Koedinger, & Pelletier, 1995; Ritter, Anderson, Koedinger, & Corbett, 2007). In constraint tutors (Mitrovic, Koedinger, & Martin, 2003; Mitrovich, Martin, & Suraweera, 2007), the student model is typically a set of constraints from three classes (i.e., relevant, fail, and satisfied). The following knowledge-driven ITSs have been reported to be quite successful and to show high learning gains for disciplines such as mathematics, programming, physics, information technology, and engineering: Cognitive tutors (Anderson et al., 1995), ALEKS (Canfield, 2001), Andes (VanLehn et al., 2005), KERMIT (Suraweera & Mitrovic, 2002), and Thermo-Tutor (Mitrovic et al., 2011).

BASIC STRUCTURE AND CLASSIFICATION OF INTELLIGENT TUTORING SYSTEMS

"Classical" ITSs consist of two nested loops in which the internal one holds the cognitive model, help/hint sub-system, student evaluation subsystem, along with individual student model. The outer loop is responsible for selecting tasks and updates on student model, according to the student performance and the hints provided. The core of the inner loop includes the cognitive model, which maps the defined knowledge components (i.e., facts, concepts, and skills) to the tasks which are used to measure the student performance, and the student model, which models the student's psychological state. The types of ITSs can be classified in general terms, that is based on the domain (e.g., mathematics, physics, and linguistics), based on the type of domain (i.e., ill-defined or well-defined), or based on the type of knowledge they provide (i.e., depth in knowledge or breadth in knowledge). In depth in knowledge tutoring, the ITS acts as a specialized tutor with the goal of covering one or few topics in great depth. In breadth in knowledge, the ITS aims to teach a diversity of subjects. Despite the domain or the type of knowledge transfer or content, all ITSs focus onto updating the student model. As such, the most suitable classification is based on the approach which is used in student modelling. In this sense, ITSs can be classified as of being a model tracing type, expectations and misconception tailoring type, constraint-based modeling type and Bayesian network modeling type (Ma, Adesope, Nesbit, & Liu, 2014).

The model tracing approach is based on Anderson's (Anderson, Matessa, & Lebiere, 1997) ACT-R theory of human learning. In this theory, the skills to be leaned are modelled as a set of production rules. As the student selects actions, the model tracing procedure maps them to sets of production rules, in order to evaluate the student's responses and also to suggest hints. Further, the results of tracing are used in some statistical inference procedure to predict-as a set of probability estimates of mastering each knowledge component-of the level of obtained knowledge by the student in a target domain. The obtained probability estimates constitute a probabilistic model of student learning which estimates the student's understanding of the knowledge components used in particular unit. The information about the level of knowledge is then transferred back to the task selection module, which generates the next task.

The expectations and misconception tailoring approach relies on natural language to provide instructions. The student provides a response to text, which represents expectations and anticipated misconceptions for the domain. Together, misconceptions and expectations form a multidimensional domain model. The student's responses are aggregated and matched to expectations and misconceptions for the domain; then, the resulting metric is used to generate hints. For example, in AutoTutor ITS (Graesser, Chipman, Haynes, & Olney, 2005), the similarity metric is generated by the implementation of the well-known LSA algorithm (Dumais, 2004; Landauer, 2006; Landauer, Foltz, & Laham, 1998).

Constraint-based modeling uses the theory of learning from performance errors. The domain knowledge is represented as a set of logical constraints, which relate all possible states that could arise in the solution of the problem. Thus, each logical constrain which combines several linear constraints (e.g., logical-and and logical-or) and conditional statements (e.g., if ... then ...) can express the complex relations between states. Further, the module which calculates the current state of student's solution vs. applicable logical constraint generates an error and advises the student about a violated principle in the student's solution (Martin, Mitrovic, Koedinger, & Mathan, 2011).

In the Bayesian network modeling approach, the multiple variables, which represent misconceptions and concepts in the domain, are organized in a network. The actual value of each variable is determined by Bayesian calculations on other variables which are connected to it. The student input on a given test generates values for test variables, which are used to calculate the probability of misconception or concept for each student for each task. It is important to note that Bayesian networks are the probabilistic tool to calculate the probability of reaching a target (in terms misconception and concept) which is not directly connected to the particular student model (i.e., implementation of different student models are possible).

ASPECTS OF THE EVOLUTION OF INTELLIGENT TUTORING SYSTEMS

Since the establishment of the basic three-model structure of the ITS, research efforts have been focused on increasing the effectiveness of the ITS both in ill- and well-defined domains. From the technological perspective, researchers implemented and evaluated a wide range of machine learning techniques (e.g. learning by examples, reinforcement learning) together with applications of multiple intelligence algorithms. The main research is focused on the improvement of the elements of canonical ITS structure, namely the development of advanced cognitive models, automatic update of cognitive models, tools and technologies for development of adequate cognitive models, further personalization of the education by automatic tweaking of a student model, development of interfaces for capturing the emotions, incorporation of interactive and multichannel interfaces, interfaces for communication of for self-assessment, use of natural language processing, advanced hint system, and some more. From the educational perspective, ITSs have evolved toward support for sophisticated educational paradigms and models, such as learning-by-teaching, space learning, collaborative learning, perspective learning, Web-based learning, peer-to-peer learning, and social network learning. In a context of increasing of educational effectiveness, modern ITSs evolve toward incorporating AI modules for evaluation and control of the effective state of the student(s) (sensor or non-sensor), module for automatic insertion of subject content, dynamic control of level of personalization, module for sentiment analysis, module for self-assessment, dynamic task generation, and many others.

Another aspect of the evolution of ITSs is a steady move from "fixed" preprogrammed systems to data-driven ITSs, especially in the areas of ill-defined domains and where the creation of the explicit cognitive model (i.e., not everything can be programmed) is not possible. These systems go beyond branching (i.e., ITSs that are able to provide feedback on students' responses) by adding the ability to formulate, generate, and solve important problems themselves. The data-driven systems pioneered automatic optimization of the cognitive model by generation alternative knowledge representations and testing these against real data. In addition, teaching agents (TA) have been implemented as a possible alternative to create/ modify cognitive model(s) in real time and by non-experts. The latter, of course, raised the question of correctness and misconception, which is addressed with the introduction of meta-tutor modules.

IMPROVEMENT OF THE COGNITIVE MODEL: LEARNING VIA TEACHING AGENTS

Building a cognitive model is a highly specialized and time-consuming process. Some data-driven systems seek to employ other knowledge transfer techniques and algorithms which explore new cognitive learning theories with the goal to allow non-AI specialists to create adequate cognitive models for many different disciplines. For instance, the learning environment called APLUS (Artificial Peer Learning Environment Using SimStudent) (Matsuda et al., 2013) employs the well-known tutor-learning effect. The latter covers the phenomena when the students learn by teaching others. In the core of APLUS is SimStudent, that is a synthetic pedagogical agent (i.e., teaching agent) that the student can interactively tutor. In the context of ITSs, the SimStudent performs inductive learning by examples, generalizing the examples given by the student. As some examples can be wrong and because students may not recognize their own misconceptions and errors, APLUS utilizes a metatutor in a similar manner as multiagent learning systems do (Vassileva, McCalla, & Greer, 2003). The metatutor module provides help to students with proper tutoring methods (metacognitive help) and domain knowledge (cognitive help) (Biswas, Jeong, Kinnebrew, Sulcer, & Roscoe, 2010). The main types of TA are three: Knowledge-sharing TA, knowledge-tracing TA, and knowledge-learning TA. The first two-knowledge-sharing and knowledge-tracing TA-implement incremental learning scaffolding strategies to expand the level of skills to the TA. In the systems which utilize knowledge-sharing TA *Betty's Brain* (Biswas et al., 2010; Emara, Tscholl, Dong, & Biswas, 2017), knowledge is shared between the student and the agent. In the knowledge tracing TA approach, a small set of skills is prescribed to the teaching agent and the student goal is to expand it by teaching the agent (Pareto, Arvemo, Dahl, Haake, & Gulz, 2011). In a process of teaching, the model tracer identifies the new skill learned from the student and adds it to the cognitive model.

The knowledge-learning TA utilizes various machine learning engines in order to learn skills dynamically and more accurately than the other two approaches. For example, SimStudent implements programming by a demonstration technique which is well-known in robotics and which allows generalizations from the user's demonstration on a concrete example of a robust solution that will work in new situations. SimStudent provides the TA with both positive and negative examples as hints and feedback from students to generate a set of production rules that can reproduce all positive examples and exclude all negative examples. SimStudent learns from rules and generates a set of hypotheses using a given set of background knowledge which is sufficient to interpret (or "explain") the examples. The effectiveness of the tutor-learning effect depends on a domain. Indeed, it has been shown that teaching-learning approach is most effective in math and sciences (Annis, 1983; Cook, Scruggs, Mastropieri, & Casto,1985; Greenwood, Delquadri & Hall, 1989). Teaching-learning is a paradoxical approach, which requires further research, but systems which explore this method may be useful to teach metacognitive skills both in a classroom or in an online environment (Matsuda, Sekar, & Wall, 2018).

OPTIMIZING THE COGNITIVE MODEL

Optimizing of the cognitive model involves dynamic generation of alternative knowledge representations and sequential comparison of these to a current model (Cen, Koedinger, & Junker, 2006). Koedinger, McLaughlin, and Stamper developed a system called DataShop which explores the abovementioned idea in a framework of modified learning factor analysis (LFA) algorithm (Koedinger, McLaughlin, & Stamper, 2012). The LFA uses a Q matrix representation (Tatsuoka & Tatsuoka, 1983), in order to map knowledge components to tasks. The elements of Q matrix represent rules simplifications of the production rules defined in the cognitive model. The learning algorithm searches over Q matrices to find the one which best predicts the student's learning status. The latter is defined as the success rate of knowledge component (i.e., skill and fact) over time. The LFA applies step regression, starting with a large set of predictor variables organized in P-matrix, which are hypothesized of the learning factors that may affect the student performance. Then, the LFA splits, merges, and adds variables, thus creating new knowledge component columns and expanding search space of Q matrices. The P matrix is computed as the union of the previously generated set of Q matrices which are associated with a data set generated by human experts. The LFA starts with the simplest possible Q matrix which represents a single skill needed to be present at all problem-solving steps and generates two new Q matrices by splitting with a negative-result (*Neg-result*) factor from the P-matrix. Thus, the new model has two knowledge components (i.e., positive and negative) which replace the old single knowledge component. The accuracy of the model is controlled by the application of a heuristic procedure that estimates the knowledge component learning rate over predictive Q matrices. The proposed approach has been tested with several datasets. Results showed that the machine-generated model matches and, in some data sets, outperforms (in terms of root-mean-square deviation between predicted vs. observed student success) the hand-generated model. However, in one data set, the best-machine model based on a discovery made entirely from the LFA outperforms the best-human model significantly, meaning that the best decision was not even anticipated by human-experts. More generally, this suggests that the LFA can be used to produce practical recommendations about tweaking hints or task selecting functions.

OPTIMIZING THE STUDENT MODEL

In most current ITSs, the evaluation of the student progress uses the same model parameters for all students (Koedinger, McLaughlin, & Stamper, 2012). Bayesian knowledge tracing (Corbett & Anderson, 1994) is a common technique for continuously tracking the process of student knowledge acquisition. It models students' skills as binary variables (i.e., mastered vs. nonmastered) and describes learning as a transition between these two states. However, the Bayesian knowledge tracing model only tracks the same type of information (i.e., longitudinal data) on the same subjects at multiple points in time. In other words, it does not allow student specific or subject specific parameters. Some recent systems, however, have pioneered the individual approach by adding student-specific variables to describe probabilities of knowing the material in a task (Pardos & Heffernan, 2010) or adding individual weights to knowledge tracing parameters (Anderson et al., 1995). The ITS ASSISTments (Lee & Brunskill, 2012; Pardos & Heffernan, 2011) incorporated knowledge tracing hidden Markov model for each student with four parameters: 1. The probability of giving correct answer; 2. the probability of giving an incorrect answer, but student mastered the skill; 3. probability to transition to master level; 4. the probability of mastery. Each knowledge tracing hidden Markov model is fit to student data using the expectation maximization procedure. As it is possible to get the probability of "guessing correctly" higher than "right answer" under the condition of mastered skill, the constraint of parameters was introduced (i.e., brute force search), which enforces the plausibility of parameters. The initial probability and learning probability are computed with the expectation maximization algorithm. In addition, the proposed approach links the parameters on an individual level by whether this resulted in changes in the instructional decision or not.

Another aspect of optimizing the student model is to define the optimal number of opportunities which are given to every student to master a skill. Computing this number is viewed as policy evaluation in Markov decision process, in which the state is the current probability of master level. Brunskill and her team (Brunskill, Garg, Tseng, Pal, & Findlater, 2010) used forward searching algorithm to evaluate the parameters of the policy on the individual level. Test simulations with resulting parameters demonstrate a significantly better fit of the observed data, compared to a generic model (likelihood ratio test, $p < 0.0001$) and also that at least 20% of the students would need more opportunities than those the generic model suggested (Ma et al., 2014). The improvement of the student model by adjusting model parameters individually has a direct impact on individual learning rates, on one hand, and on improved of the instructions, on the other.

USING THE MULTIAGENTS METHODOLOGY: ADDING NEW FEATURES

The multiagents methodology has been used for many years in designing of complex software systems. In ITSs, it is used to add modules which are aimed to provide a specific and complex model of tutoring, to add support for advanced interfaces (e.g., natural language processing, facial recognition, and emotions recognition), and, most importantly, to provide software support for advanced scaffolding metacognitive processes, such as judgments of learning, feelings of knowing, or content evaluation. For instance, Meta Tutor (Azevedo, Witherspoon, Chauncey, Burkett, & Fike, 2009) was developed as very adaptive multiagents-based ITS, specifically designed to promote Self-Regulated Learning (SRL). Meta Tutor employs a network of pedagogical agents who moderate student learning behaviors. The agents provide hints on the fly and are engaged in learning dialogues with the student(s). Meta Tutor uses scaffolding strategy (based on agents input) to help students to choose appropriate sub goals and suitable learning strategy. The interface of the system includes separate SRL dialogue, which allows students to choose (from a six-level scale) the level of understanding they think they may have. Based on that information, the pedagogical agents generate a quiz, which constitutes the feedback from the system, apart from regular dynamic hint mechanism. This approach allows students to get involved in a selection of appropriate sub goals, and to develop metacognitive judgements and skills to pick up and use a particular learning strategy. In addition, another agent is responsible for collecting information about students' SRL behavior.

For example, students may be involved in the system-initiated judgement of learning by being asked to perform a self-assessment of their understanding. The results from self-assessment are matched against actual students' performance, and feedback is provided. It is important to mention that Meta Tutor supports several SRL scenarios, such as note-taking, content evaluation, summary and prior knowledge activation.

Multiagents are used also in emotionally aware cooperative learning ITSs which are applied in distance learning. These ITSs employ collaborative virtual environments as communication technology. Cooperative learning ITSs (also called social learning systems) use a different strategy, since they do not necessarily apply the tutor-student model. Instead, such systems focus on communication between peers–both virtual and human. An early example of such systems is I-Help (Vassileva et al., 2001), which is a Web-based multiagents learning environment and which allows students to allocate peers (both human and artificial), in order to get help during the learning process.

In the more modern EMASPEL system (emotional multiagents system for peer to peer e-learning) (Neji & Ammar, 2007), the student's facial expression is captured and converted to human-computer interaction. The agent behind that process is called emotional embodied conversational agent and is capable not only to communicate information in a regular way, but also to interact with the learner on the emotional level by expressing emotions to the learner's actions and by having its own "personality" and behavior. Since the agent exhibits an emotional behavior, the student treats it like a human. This cuts the interpersonal distance between the system and the user, making the educational process more individualized and thus much more effective. The emotional agents also capture and analyze the learner's emotions. These agents detect the face, extract the permanent features of the face (e.g., eyes, eyebrows, and lips), and transmit this information to the module responsible for the interpretation of the facial expression.

INCORPORATING ANALYSIS AND CONTROL OF EMOTIONS

Emotionally aware ITSs (EITSs) are a new class of systems. They explore the results from research in neurology, which suggest that emotions are an important element of problem solving, cognition, and intelligence. EITSs seek to capture or to model the basic human emotions and use them to determine the learner's emotional state. It has been shown that the students' emotional state has a strong impact on their learning. Emotions may influence the decisions a student makes both in a negative or in a positive way in every step of the educational process. Recognizing the student's emotional state (e.g., satisfaction, confidence, surprise, confusion, or frustration) has educational value, since it allows specific pedagogical decisions to be made in order to influence these emotions. On the other hand, emotions are the direct reflection of a particular student state in a context of education, such as lack of knowledge, lack of success on task, and improper meta-knowledge. As such, the analysis of an emotional state and its classification can be used to update the student model and to initiate changes in the educational strategy in real time. Thus, an EITS seeks to influence the "users'' emotional state in a controlled way by modulating the level of help that is provided to a student (Cunha-Pérez, Arevalillo-Herráez, Marco-Giménez, & Arnau, 2018; Graesser & D'Mello, 2012). For example, in a tutoring system *Ms. Lindquist* (Heffernan & Koedinger, 2002), the number of hits is reduced in order to make "ready answers" less accessible. In addition, the system understands partially correct answers and gives hints that prompt students to improve their answer to the point where the latter is fully correct. In a similar system, MOODS (De Vicente & Pain, 2002), the students are asked to report their motivational state while interacting with the ITS. Most EITSs use cameras to capture basic human facial expressions (i.e., happiness, sadness, surprise, fear, anger, and disgust), but, in reality, these types of systems could be difficult to apply/use in schools, due to cost and reliability issues. Alternative systems which model students' emotional state indirectly, without using video capture, could be more feasible.

A major advantage of an EITS is its ability to respond to learners in a way which is similar to human tutors. As such, an EITS is far more efficient in the online education system because it presents rich pedagogical content in the most learner-friendly way. Positive interactions with the ITS and a differentiated learning strategy, together with carefully applied strategies for motivation and focusing, boost the learner's confidence and help to overcome social and personal constraints.

A major problem of an EITS is how to catch and control disengaged behaviors from the students, such as taking advantage of the feedback system (gaming of the system), off-task behavior or caress errors. In order to prevent the gaming of the system, some ITSs used the student logs, which are classified (e.g., with J48 algorithm) in order to trace the gaming behavior. For the cases of off-task behavior, the system uses log data and tracks mouse movements. For cases of careless errors, the ITS uses historical data from logs along with the probability that a student knew the skill calculated from the student model.

GENERATING OPTIMAL AND SPECIFIC HELP

The effectiveness of learning also depends on the ability of the ITS to provide context-specific hints based on previously collected data of student performance. Usually, CBTSs use a very simple algorithm for hints, which requests the learner to follow the predefined problem-solving strategy and do not promote the development of actual learning skills. In CBTSs, the hints are derived from the next step in prescribed learning strategy, but not from actual performance data. Thus, the most general hint contains minimal information about the error, while the most specific hint is actually the solution to the problem. In addition, hints based on prescribed problem-solving strategy are usually delivered after each step during problem-solving interaction, despite the action or the step was correct or incorrect (Matsuda et al., 2013). Indeed, some more advanced CBTSs use a multilayer format of the hints, which divides hints into several layers or use the learner's proficiencies to select an appropriate hint. However, despite the improvements, the main problem, namely inability to generate optimal hint(s), is typical for CBTSs.

In contrast data-driven ITSs, the actions search space is very large because students may choose from many different actions, each of which may be correct, but not necessarily optimal. In other words, the optimality of the generated hint depends on student's previous decisions in a context of a task, but is also partially random due to large searching space. Consequently, the hint mechanisms in data-driven ITSs are based on stochastic control processes, rather than on prescribed strategy. For example, the hint subsystem of the APLUS builds a graph to represent a relation between scene/state (i.e., what student sees on screen) and actions, which represents the student's previous decisions to a task. The optimal solution to the problem is the best path through the graph. In order to calculate the optimal graph traversal, the latter is transformed into Markov decision process (MDP), which has a specific reward function, such that all no solution scenes get a negative reward. The overall sum of the rewards, which can be earned by following optimal policy, is calculated and that value is compared to a value for the student. Thus, when a hint is requested, the hint subsystem searches for current scene/state in the MDP and checks if the next state/scene exists. If so, the successor with the highest value is used to generate the hint. The use of a stochastic decision-making approach in hints dramatically increases the number of optimal hints. As Stamper, Barnes, and Croy (2011) study shows, the proposed approach is capable to generate correct (optimal) hints is 80% of the cases, which increases the overall effectiveness of education.

In addition, a special attention is payed to analysis of behaviors of students from different cultures which seek help in a process of knowledge transfer. The study made by Ogan (Ogan et al., 2015) revealed significant differences between help seeking behaviors of students from different cultures. The system ICON provides students with options over their cultural preferences including problem description, feedback, and presentation of images and hints (Mohamed & Mohan, 2015).

OPTIMIZING INSTRUCTIONS AND MANAGEMENT OF LEARNING DIFFICULTIES (PEDAGOGICAL TACTICS)

Generating optimal instruction flow in ITSs can be considered as an instance of a multi-criteria optimization task. As such, early ITSs used an AI procedure of reinforcement learning and myopic view to generate instructions (Chi, VanLehn, Litman, & Jordan, 2011). Recent ITSs rely on Markov decision processes, more specifically on partially observable Markov decision processes, which allows generating sequential actions in situations where important information may be unobserved. In this case, the automated teacher agent uses the learner knowledge not as facts, but as distribution, in this way preserving the uncertainty of the student's actual knowledge. The big advantage of partially observable Markov decision processes is that any effect of a particular action is incorporated automatically without application of any heuristics about most effective teaching actions. Quite often, the students experience learning difficulties, which result in students' poor performance Learning difficulties may be caused by, for example, insufficient vocabulary, bad reading habits, lack of basic knowledge on the subject, nonlinguistic skills on low-level processing level, inability to process high-order knowledge in text representation, and inability to integrate ideas.

DATA-DRIVEN INTELLIGENT TUTORING SYSTEMS

Data-driven ITSs (DDITSs) have the potential to expand the presence and success of ITSs in nontraditional domains, where the creation of a cognitive model is too complicated. In addition, DDITSs open an avenue to explore new educational paradigms which utilize vast data from simulations, labs, homework, tutoring systems, and open online courses, expanding in this way the availability and access of educational technology out of the classroom. Machine learning approaches in DDITSs offer the opportunity to generate improved student model in ill-defined domains. Some experiments already prove the value of data-driven approaches (Forbus, Usher, Lovett, Lockwood, & Wetzel, 2008).

Data-driven approaches first appeared in early 1990 (Self, 1998), but have had a significant push in development more recently as possible avenues to explore the educational potential of a vast amount of data accumulated via simulations, experiments, open courses, and home works. In addition to these options, it is recognized that data-driven approaches provide opportunities to rapidly develop ITSs in domains for which it is too difficult to create an explicit cognitive model. DDITSs rely on machine learning techniques and algorithms to define and support their own evaluation capabilities. For example, in a detector approach, the detector (classifier) is trained with experts' provided labels on desired student actions (Sao Pedro, Baker, Montalvo, Nakama, & Gobert, 2010). Each label represents how appropriate (or inappropriate) the students' inquiry strategy is in a particular segment (i.e., in designing experiment and testing hypothesis). Each detector is trained individually by each student, meaning that each student should pass the simulation process a few times. The output of the detectors is the input to the pedagogical unit which evaluates students' actions, identifies best and worst strategies, and provides students with feedback and hints. Sao Pedro reported that the resulting models not only better capture the complex relationships (compared to humans), but also define the boundary conditions more precisely (Sao Pedro et al., 2010).

In DDITSs, rules are not prescribed, but discovered and cross-validated by machine learning techniques from given data, human labels, P-matrices, and feature sets. Further, the intrinsic learning abilities have been used to optimize the cognitive model of the ITS. In their work, Koedinger and his team proposed a procedure for cognitive model optimization, based on the evaluation of alternative knowledge representations (Koedinger, McLaughlin, & Stamper, 2012). In their approach, the skills, called knowledge components, are related to tasks via Q matrices (Tatsuoka & Tatsuoka, 1983). The LFA algorithm (Cen, Koedinger, & Junker, 2006) searches across Q matrices to find the one that best predicts the student learning status which is represented as a success rate over knowledge components. In the model discovery process, the LFA operates with two objects: A set of predictor variables called P-matrix, which represents learning factors that may impact the student learning rate, and a set of Q matrices. In the beginning, the LFA is seeded with the simplest possible Q matrix which represents the single skill that is needed for all problems and then the matrix is "split" with P matrix to generate new Q matrices. It has been reported that discovered models are very close to existing ones, but the results of discovery process may be used to improve the teacher behavior.

Data-driven approaches allow the introduction of examples in the educational process. In the ITS Deep Thought (Mostafavi, Zhou, Lynch, Chi, & Barnes, 2015), the knowledge about tutor-student performance is extracted from historical data, and used to evaluate the student performance and select structured problem sets. Similar approach is used in a system DeepTutor, an ITS developed for education in classical physics (Rus, Niraula, & Banjade, 2015). The system Deep Thought hypothesizes that students who have completed Deep Thought in the past have acquired a coherent skill set for proof problem solving and rule application. Then, by splitting the problem set to new sets with the same level of difficulty, the new students are evaluated. Based on performance, the new working examples are generated and added to the existing problem set.

In ill-defined domains, the data-driven approach has been applied to define a cognitive model of the ITS. The human expertise is introduced by a set of human labels of desired/undesired students' actions and then a formal classifier is trained over this data. In a tutor for scientific inquiry developed by Sao Pedro and his team (Sao Pedro et al., 2010), the human experts label by hand the students' logs which they obtain through interaction with the ITS. The labels mark if an appropriate or inappropriate learning strategy was used for each particular task. Further, the labels are used to train the agents responsible to recognize the students' skills, which are called detectors. Obviously, detectors need enough data to be trained successfully, but it has been reported that the student must run only three or four times the simulations, before the detectors can make accurate enough inferences about a specific student's inquiry skill. The detector itself is a part of the pedagogical agent, which evaluates students' actions and progress, identifies improper strategies, and provides hints. In order to decrease the domain experts' time which is needed to generate and code the tasks the ITS offers, some DDITSs use automatic problem generation techniques and algorithms to provide suggested tasks. For example, Singh, Gulwani, and Rajamani (2012) presented an algorithm which generates a set of new, similar, but nontrivially different problems from a given example. This helps the ITS to operate with more examples which are specifically designed and tuned to address the student's error or misconception

In DDITSs, the tutoring system represents and uses the whole knowledge on a particular/given subject to make pedagogical decisions. These decisions may not be the same or may not be even anticipated by the human experts and thus, under the DDITS, a different teaching style may take place. In addition, the process of knowledge communication in DDITSs is different and involves the use of a limited set of communication channels and communication operations. Historically, in the development of ITSs, the focus has been on gaining the computational understanding of the processes of knowledge transfer via modelling of the student, modelling of the communication process (tutor), and modelling of a domain. This three-model architecture (i.e., student, domain, and tutor) has been challenged recently by adding the fourth component, user interface, which reflects the impact of the communication channels onto knowledge transfer. Adding the user interface opens an avenue to implement some different learning paradigms, such as learning perspective (Hwang, 2014). Even more, involving the user interface as forth DDITS component causes the evolution of the core DDITS model from student, domain, and tutor toward situation, interaction, and affordance.

SOCIAL IMPACT AND FUTURE OF INTELLIGENT TUTORING SYSTEMS

The core idea of ITSs was to replace the teacher in a classroom. However, the technological advances, developments in machine learning, along with advances in teaching methodologies, cognitive science, neurology, and pedagogy have made the modern ITSs capable to achieve a much broader scope and consequently to have a much higher impact over society. The synergy between ITSs and communication technologies have raised up the e-Learning concept that allows millions of people to gain knowledge without getting into the classroom. In addition, e-Learning has omitted the time restrictions of class schedules and has decreased the credit prices making this way the education accessible to almost everyone. The synergy between ITSs and adaptive hypermedia raised up the class of adaptive hypermedia ITSs. The latter adds adaptive presentation and adaptive navigation support for hypermedia in their expert model, along with ITS features (Pipatsarun & Vicheanpanya, 2010). The development of the technologies for automatic content insertion, along with automatic task generation, have helped to alleviate the problem of bad students/teacher ratio in remote or underdeveloped areas. In addition, modern ITSs have become cultural and emotionally aware, and this is the critical factor to make knowledge transfer universal and free of cultural prejudice.

The primary goal of education is to teach skills in the most effective way. ITSs seek to achieve this goal by incorporating various new types of cognitive learning theories, such as peer-to-peer knowledge transfer, collective learning, self-regulated learning, and tutor-learning. All of these, when combined with methods for control of students' emotions and motivation, have allowed modern ITSs to be able to teach skills for the 21st century. The effectiveness of education is rooted in the personalization of the education. ITSs address effectiveness problem with models and techniques for "just-in-time" specialized feedback and hints, dynamic tweaking of student model, and rich interfaces with natural language capabilities.

However, modern education goes beyond simple skills, toward the development of metacognitive abilities, critical thinking, and problem-solving abilities. In a modern educational environment, ITSs get incorporated into learning management systems (LMSs). The latter provides content creation, delivery solutions, visualization, forums, and streaming services and, most importantly, the media and infrastructure to support distance and online learning. In the realm of LMSs, the focus has been moved toward instructional expertize which can use learners' interaction data and domain knowledge, along with pedagogy knowledge, to provide an as individualized as possible learning experience. As such, the role of ITSs is to furnish effective education on a subject in a framework of LMSs where the global intelligence is shared between software, instructional and domain experts, and network. The instructional experts collect the data with pedagogical goals and interact with the computational elements of the system. As such, the particular type of ITSs may be assigned as part of the educational process.

Indeed, the network support provided by LMSs allows ITSs to reach global scale, but, most importantly, ITSs become an element of the data-assisted approach to education which is aimed to overcome cross-cultural differences and specific learning habits. On the global scene, the sophisticated ITS interfaces can capture the learners' emotional state and adjust the learning strategy, despite the students' social or cultural status. In addition, the learners' experience may be augmented even further by using other knowledge sharing channels out of the capabilities of particular ITSs, such as chats, messengers or discussion boards. Being in a framework of LMSs, the learners' data are collected, classified and further used by instructional experts. The same data, however, may be transferred back to ITSs and used to adjust the student model.

DDITSs address specificity of education and are especially suitable for ill-defined areas. In a context of LMSs, DDITSs provide a specific educational model which matches overall an educational strategy which is designed by instructional experts. In this sense, the rich data capturing capabilities and vast network capabilities of LMSs compliment DDITSs.

CONCLUSION

In the current technology-driven society, the need for high-quality computer-supported education is a critical component to human tutoring in many fields and settings, from mathematical computation to subject matters with the huge verbal reasoning in the humanities. The applications of ITSs encompass AI with cognitive science and education, in order to deliver to students an autonomous educational experience that is tailored to their specific needs. Providing technically sophisticated, culturally adequate and emotionally savvy ITSs poses unique challenges, because they have to satisfy not only the model domain, but the whole spectra of student behavior as well. Perhaps, the ideal ITSs are the ones that emulate equally well both human tutors and complex computations, achieving the perfect equilibrium of conditions on content, time on task, and other variables which are relevant to pedagogy.

Armed with technological advantages in communications, advances in learning theories, computational methods, and cognitive science, and being the core element of LMSs, the modern ITSs are well posed to answer the challenges of AI in education. As time progresses, more empirical studies affirming the advantages of ITSs over human tutors will possibly be conducted, since well-designed ITSs capture the wisdom of thousands of human tutors.

REFERENCES

Anderson, J. R., Corbett, A. T., Koedinger, K. R., & Pelletier, R. (1995). Cognitive tutors: Lessons learned. *Journal of the Learning Sciences*, *4*(2), 167–207. doi:10.120715327809jls0402_2

Anderson, J. R., Matessa, M., & Lebiere, C. (1997). ACT-R: A theory of higher level cognition and its relation to visual attention. *Human-Computer Interaction*, *12*(4), 439–462. doi:10.120715327051hci1204_5

Annis, L. F. (1983). The processes and effects of peer tutoring. *Human Learning: Journal of Practical Research & Applications*, *2*(1), 39–47.

Atkinson, R. C. (1968). Computerized instruction and the learning process. *The American Psychologist*, *23*(4), 225–239. doi:10.1037/h0020791 PMID:5647875

Azevedo, R., Witherspoon, A. M., Chauncey, A., Burkett, C., & Fike, A. (2009). MetaTutor: A metacognitive tool for enhancing self-regulated learning. In *Proceedings of the AAAI Fall Symposium on Cognitive and Metacognitive Educational Systems* (pp.14-19). Menlo Park, CA: Association for the Advancement of Artificial Intelligence (AAAI) Press.

Barr, A., Beard, M., & Atkinson, R. C. (1976). The computer as a tutorial laboratory: The Stanford BIP project. *International Journal of Man-Machine Studies*, *8*(5), 567–596. doi:10.1016/S0020-7373(76)80021-1

Biswas, G., Jeong, H., Kinnebrew, J. S., Sulcer, B., & Roscoe, R. (2010). Measuring self-regulated learning skills through social interactions in a teachable agent environment. *Research and Practice in Technology Enhanced Learning*, *5*(2), 123–152. doi:10.1142/S1793206810000839

Bloom, B. S. (1984). The 2 sigma problem: The search for methods of group instruction as effective as one-to-one tutoring. *Educational Researcher*, *13*(6), 4–16. doi:10.3102/0013189X013006004

Brunskill, E., Garg, S., Tseng, C., Pal, J., & Findlater, L. (2010). Evaluating an adaptive multi-user educational tool for low-resource environments. In *Proceedings of the IEEE/ACM International Conference on Information and Communication Technologies and Development* (pp. 13-16). New York, NY: ACM.

Canfield, W. (2001). ALEKS: A Web-based intelligent tutoring system. *Mathematics and Computer Education*, *35*(2), 152.

Carbonell, J. R. (1970a). *Mixed-initiative man-computer instructional dialogues (No. BBN-1971)*. Cambridge, MA: Bolt, Beranek, and Newman.

Carbonell, J. R. (1970b). AI in CAI: An artificial-intelligence approach to computer-assisted instruction. *IEEE Transactions on Man-Machine Systems, 11*(4), 190–202. doi:10.1109/TMMS.1970.299942

Cen, H., Koedinger, K., & Junker, B. (2006). Learning factors analysis–a general method for cognitive model evaluation and improvement. In *Proceedings of the International Conference on Intelligent Tutoring Systems* (pp. 164-175). Berlin: Springer. 10.1007/11774303_17

Chi, M., VanLehn, K., Litman, D., & Jordan, P. (2011). An evaluation of pedagogical tutorial tactics for a natural language tutoring system: A reinforcement learning approach. *International Journal of Artificial Intelligence in Education, 21*(1-2), 83–113.

Chung, M. H., & Miller, J. (2011). Do we live in a box of crayons? Looking at multicultural metaphors written by teachers. *Multicultural Education, 18*(4), 39.

Cook, S. B., Scruggs, T. E., Mastropieri, M. A., & Casto, G. C. (1985). Handicapped students as tutors. *The Journal of Special Education, 19*(4), 483–492. doi:10.1177/002246698501900410

Corbett, A. T., & Anderson, J. R. (1994). Knowledge tracing: Modeling the acquisition of procedural knowledge. *User Modeling and User-Adapted Interaction, 4*(4), 253–278. doi:10.1007/BF01099821

Cunha-Pérez, C., Arevalillo-Herráez, M., Marco-Giménez, L., & Arnau, D. (2018). On incorporating affective support to an intelligent tutoring system: An empirical study. *IEEE Revista Iberoamericana de Tecnologias del Aprendizaje, 13*(2), 63–69. doi:10.1109/RITA.2018.2831760

De Vicente, A., & Pain, H. (2002, June). Informing the detection of the students' motivational state: an empirical study. In *International Conference on Intelligent Tutoring Systems* (pp. 933-943). Berlin: Springer. 10.1007/3-540-47987-2_93

Dumais, S. T. (2004). Latent semantic analysis. *Annual Review of Information Science & Technology, 38*(1), 188–230. doi:10.1002/aris.1440380105

Emara, M., Tscholl, M., Dong, Y., & Biswas, G. (2017). Analyzing students' collaborative regulation behaviors in a classroom-integrated open ended learning environment. In B. K. Smith, M. Borge, E. Mercier, & K. Y. Lim (Eds.), *Making a difference: Prioritizing equity and access in CSCL, 12th International Conference on Computer Supported Collaborative Learning (CSCL)* (*vol. 1*, pp. 319-326). Philadelphia, PA: International Society of the Learning Sciences.

Forbus, K. D., Usher, J. M., Lovett, A. M., Lockwood, K., & Wetzel, J. (2008). CogSketch: Open-domain sketch understanding for cognitive science research and for education. *SBM*, *8*, 159–166.

Freedman, R., Ali, S. S., & McRoy, S. (2000). Links: What is an intelligent tutoring system? *Intelligence*, *11*(3), 15–16. doi:10.1145/350752.350756

Graesser, A. C., Chipman, P., Haynes, B. C., & Olney, A. (2005). AutoTutor: An intelligent tutoring system with mixed-initiative dialogue. *IEEE Transactions on Education*, *48*(4), 612–618. doi:10.1109/TE.2005.856149

Graesser, A. C., & D'Mello, S. (2012). Emotions during the learning of difficult material. In B. Ross (Ed.), *Psychology of learning and motivation* (Vol. 57, pp. 183–225). Cambridge, MA: Academic Press. doi:10.1016/B978-0-12-394293-7.00005-4

Greenwood, C. R., Delquadri, J. C., & Hall, R. V. (1989). Longitudinal effects of class wide peer tutoring. *Journal of Educational Psychology*, *81*(3), 371–383. doi:10.1037/0022-0663.81.3.371

Heffernan, N. T., & Koedinger, K. R. (2002). An intelligent tutoring system incorporating a model of an experienced human tutor. In *Proceedings of the International Conference on Intelligent Tutoring Systems* (pp. 596-608). Berlin: Springer. 10.1007/3-540-47987-2_61

Hwang, G. J. (2014). Definition, framework and research issues of smart learning environments-a context-aware ubiquitous learning perspective. *Smart Learning Environments, 1*(4).

Koedinger, K. R., McLaughlin, E. A., & Stamper, J. C. (2012). Automated student model improvement. In *Proceedings of the 5th International Conference of Educational Data Mining* (pp. 17-24). Worcester, MA: International Data Mining Society.

Landauer, T. K. (2006). Latent semantic analysis. In *Encyclopedia of Cognitive Science*. London: Wiley. doi:10.1002/0470018860.s00561

Landauer, T. K., Foltz, P. W., & Laham, D. (1998). An introduction to latent semantic analysis. *Discourse Processes*, *25*(2-3), 259–284. doi:10.1080/01638539809545028

Lee, J. I., & Brunskill, E. (2012). The impact on individualizing student models on necessary practice opportunities. In *Proceedings of the 5th International Conference of Educational Data Mining* (pp. 118-125). Worcester, MA: International Data Mining Society.

Ma, W., Adesope, O. O., Nesbit, J. C., & Liu, Q. (2014). Intelligent tutoring systems and learning outcomes: A meta-analysis. *Journal of Educational Psychology*, *106*(4), 901–918. doi:10.1037/a0037123

Martin, B., Mitrovic, A., Koedinger, K. R., & Mathan, S. (2011). Evaluating and improving adaptive educational systems with learning curves. *User Modeling and User-Adapted Interaction*, *21*(3), 249–283. doi:10.100711257-010-9084-2

Matsuda, N., Sekar, V. P. C., & Wall, N. (2018, June). Metacognitive Scaffolding Amplifies the Effect of Learning by Teaching a Teachable Agent. In *Proceedings of the International Conference on Artificial Intelligence in Education* (pp. 311-323). Cham: Springer. 10.1007/978-3-319-93843-1_23

Matsuda, N., Yarzebinski, E., Keiser, V., Raizada, R., Cohen, W. W., Stylianides, G. J., & Koedinger, K. R. (2013). Cognitive anatomy of tutor learning: Lessons learned with SimStudent. *Journal of Educational Psychology*, *105*(4), 1152–1163. doi:10.1037/a0031955

Mitrovic, A., Koedinger, K. R., & Martin, B. (2003). A comparative analysis of cognitive tutoring and constraint-based modeling. In *Proceedings of the International Conference on User Modeling* (pp. 313-322). Berlin: Springer. 10.1007/3-540-44963-9_42

Mitrovic, A., Martin, B., & Suraweera, P. (2007). Intelligent tutors for all: Constraint-based modeling methodology, systems and authoring. *IEEE Intelligent Systems*, *22*(4), 38–45. doi:10.1109/MIS.2007.74

Mitrovic, A., Williamson, C., Bebbington, A., Mathews, M., Suraweera, P., Martin, B., . . . Holland, J. (2011). Thermo-Tutor: An intelligent tutoring system for thermodynamics. In *Proceedings of the IEEE Global Engineering Education Conference (EDUCON)* (pp. 378-385). Piscataway, NJ: IEEE.

Mohammed, P., & Mohan, P. (2015). Dynamic cultural contextualisation of educational content in intelligent learning environments using ICON. *International Journal of Artificial Intelligence in Education*, *25*(2), 249–270. doi:10.100740593-014-0033-9

Mostafavi, B., Zhou, G., Lynch, C., Chi, M., & Barnes, T. (2015). Data-driven worked examples improve retention and completion in a logic tutor. In *Proceedings of the International Conference on Artificial Intelligence in Education* (pp. 726-729). Cham: Springer. 10.1007/978-3-319-19773-9_102

Murray, T. (1999). Authoring intelligent tutoring systems: An analysis of the state of the art. *International Journal of Artificial Intelligence in Education*, *10*, 98–129.

Neji, M., & Ben Ammar, M. (2007). Agent-based Collaborative Affective e-Learning Framework. *Electronic Journal of e-Learning, 5*(2), 123-134.

Ogan, A., Walker, E., Baker, R., Rodrigo, M. M. T., Soriano, J. C., & Castro, M. J. (2015). Towards understanding how to assess help-seeking behavior across cultures. *International Journal of Artificial Intelligence in Education, 25*(2), 229–248. doi:10.100740593-014-0034-8

Pardos, Z. A., & Heffernan, N. T. (2010). Modeling individualization in a Bayesian networks implementation of knowledge tracing. In *Proceedings of the International Conference on User Modeling, Adaptation, and Personalization* (pp. 255-266). Berlin: Springer. 10.1007/978-3-642-13470-8_24

Pardos, Z. A., & Heffernan, N. T. (2011). KT-IDEM: Introducing item difficulty to the knowledge tracing model. In *Proceedings of the International Conference on User Modeling, Adaptation, and Personalization* (pp. 243-254). Berlin: Springer. 10.1007/978-3-642-22362-4_21

Pareto, L., Arvemo, T., Dahl, Y., Haake, M., & Gulz, A. (2011). A teachable-agent arithmetic game's effects on mathematics understanding, attitude and self-efficacy. In *Proceedings of the International Conference on Artificial Intelligence in Education* (pp. 247-255). Berlin: Springer. 10.1007/978-3-642-21869-9_33

Pipatsarun, P., & Vicheanpanya, J. (2010). Adaptive intelligent tutoring systems for e-learning systems. *Computer and Information Science, 2*(2), 4064–4069.

Raybourn, E. M., & Waern, A. (2004). Social learning through gaming. In *CHI'04 Extended Abstracts on Human Factors in Computing Systems* (pp. 1733–1734). New York: ACM.

Ritter, S., Anderson, J. R., Koedinger, K. R., & Corbett, A. (2007). Cognitive tutor: Applied research in mathematics education. *Psychonomic Bulletin & Review, 14*(2), 249–255. doi:10.3758/BF03194060 PMID:17694909

Rus, V., Niraula, N., & Banjade, R. (2015, March). DeepTutor: an effective, online intelligent tutoring system that promotes deep learning. *Twenty-Ninth AAAI Conference on Artificial Intelligence.*

Sao Pedro, M., Baker, R. S., Montalvo, O., Nakama, A., & Gobert, J. D. (2010). Using text replay tagging to produce detectors of systematic experimentation behavior patterns. In *Proceedings of the International Conference on Educational Data Mining 2010* (pp. 191-200). Worcester, MA: International Data Mining Society.

Self, J. (1990). Theoretical foundations for intelligent tutoring systems. *Journal of Artificial Intelligence in Education*, *1*(4), 3–14.

Self, J. (1998). The defining characteristics of intelligent tutoring systems research: ITSs care, precisely. *International Journal of Artificial Intelligence in Education*, *10*, 350–364.

Singh, R., Gulwani, S., & Rajamani, S. K. (2012). Automatically generating algebra problems. In *Proceedings of the Twenty-Sixth AAAI Conference on Artificial Intelligence*. (pp.1620-1627). Menlo Park, CA: AAAI Press.

Sleeman, D., & Brown, J. S. (1982). *Intelligent tutoring systems*. London: Academic Press.

Stamper, J., Barnes, T., & Croy, M. (2011). Enhancing the automatic generation of hints with expert seeding. *International Journal of Artificial Intelligence in Education*, *21*(1-2), 153–167.

Steenbergen-Hu, S., & Cooper, H. (2014). A meta-analysis of the effectiveness of intelligent tutoring systems on college students' academic learning. *Journal of Educational Psychology*, *106*(2), 331–347. doi:10.1037/a0034752

Suraweera, P., & Mitrovic, A. (2002). KERMIT: A constraint-based tutor for database modeling. In *Proceedings of the International Conference on Intelligent Tutoring Systems* (pp. 377-387). Berlin: Springer. 10.1007/3-540-47987-2_41

Tatsuoka, K. K., & Tatsuoka, M. M. (1983). Spotting erroneous rules of operation by the individual consistency index. *Journal of Educational Measurement*, *20*(3), 221–230. doi:10.1111/j.1745-3984.1983.tb00201.x

VanLehn, K., Lynch, C., Schulze, K., Shapiro, J. A., Shelby, R., Taylor, L., ... Wintersgill, M. (2005). The Andes physics tutoring system: Lessons learned. *International Journal of Artificial Intelligence in Education*, *15*(3), 147–204.

Vassileva, J., McCalla, G., & Greer, J. (2003). Multi-agent multi-user modeling in I-Help. *User Modeling and User-Adapted Interaction*, *13*(1-2), 179–210. doi:10.1023/A:1024072706526

Woolf, B. P., Lane, H. C., Chaudhri, V. K., & Kolodner, J. L. (2013). AI grand challenges for education. *AI Magazine*, *34*(4), 66–84. doi:10.1609/aimag.v34i4.2490

Young, P. A. (2011). The significance of the Culture Based Model in designing culturally aware tutoring systems. *AI & Society*, *26*(1), 35–47. doi:10.100700146-010-0282-6

Chapter 4
Concerning the Integration of Machine Learning Content in Mechatronics Curricula

Jörg Frochte
Bochum University of Applied Science, Germany

Markus Lemmen
Bochum University of Applied Science, Germany

Marco Schmidt
Bochum University of Applied Science, Germany

ABSTRACT

Machine learning is becoming more and more important for mechatronic systems and will become an ordinary part of today's student life. Thus, it is obvious that machine learning should be part of today's student's curriculum. Unfortunately, machine learning seldomly is implemented into the curriculum in a substantial or linking manner, but rather offered as an elective course. This chapter provides an analysis of how machine learning can be integrated as a mandatory part of the curriculum of mechatronic degree courses. It is considered what the required minimal changes in fundamental courses should be and how traditional subjects like robotics, automation, and automotive engineering can profit most of this approach. As a case study, this chapter utilizes an existing German mechatronic degree course specialized on information technology, which covers most of the discussed aspects.

DOI: 10.4018/978-1-5225-7793-5.ch004

INTRODUCTION

Mechatronics is a multidisciplinary field that includes mechanical engineering, electronics, and computer engineering. Typical application areas are industrial automation, robotics, and automotive engineering. Especially for the latter two, control theory has become an important topic.

Within mechatronic systems, software and intelligent systems play a crucial role as they are the key drivers for innovation and added value of modern mechatronic systems. Nowadays, also machine learning is a new major factor in this field, and very often it interacts closely with control theory. Some techniques will be or are already integrated into modern mechatronic systems as standard components, like e.g. image and speech recognition. Usually, these components are simply licensed and integrated from suppliers. Nevertheless, in many cases the integration of machine learning requires a deep understanding of the technical behavior of a mechatronic system. Therefore, engineers should have a basic understanding of common machine learning approaches. This is especially true for the field of robotics, flexible manufacturing, vehicles and logistics.

This demand in mechatronic engineering practice has a strong impact on mechatronics and computer science engineering curricula at universities: While machine learning is increasingly important for the mechatronic systems, the mechatronic degree courses at universities often lack integration of this subject, and usually the different curricula are not ready to integrate this subject into fundamental courses of a degree curriculum. We will show, that with minor changes in the curriculum, seamless integration of machine learning contents is achievable. In that way, a university can enhance the attractiveness of a degree course without additional expenses.

In the following sections of this paper, we analyze the requirements for integrating machine learning into mechatronic degree courses based on an existing (example) degree course. In order to be able to choose a proper approach to integrate machine learning, it is essential to understand, which part of machine learning offers the strongest connections to the courses under discussion and therefore candidates are to be integrated into the courses. Next, the interaction to control theory and simulation will be highlighted; both topics have already (classically) a big influence on mechatronic degree courses. The subsequent section will show, which new requirements for degree courses have to be considered, and which already established approaches and topics can be utilized for this purpose by slight re-arrangements, e.g. in control theory.

AN OVERVIEW ON MACHINE LEARNING

Which aspects of machine learning are now the most important ones for mechatronics? One taxonomy for machine learning approach divides them into

- Supervised,
- Unsupervised
- And reinforcement methods.

Supervised methods can be broadly divided into two groups of tasks: regression and classification. Regression is about estimating or predicting a continuous quantity, like e.g. the probability of failure. Classification deals with assigning a given set of features into discrete categories, like e.g. categorizing objects into animal or furniture. Both techniques are important when it comes to mechatronics with a wide field of applications like Predictive Maintenance, see e.g. (Ahmad et al 2012), automated/autonomous driving (Vallon et al 2017) and Convolutional Neural Networks and Deep Learning are more and more used in medical systems see e.g. (Lee et al 2017) and healthcare, see e.g. (Esteva et al 2019). Beyond the technical application areas, it becomes more important in production planning, logistics and cost estimation (Börzel et al 2019) closely linked to curricula's and professional opportunities of engineers. One aspect is which methods one should teach to mechatronic engineers from the rich family of possible algorithms and techniques. To answer this question, it is important to mention the nature of the data. We have two major types of data: structured and unstructured data. Structured data is organized in a data frame, e.g. in rows (data records) and columns (features). In unstructured data, the information is in the data record, but there is no clear relation of the information and the individual data bits. Take for example the picture of a dog as a bitmap. It is clear that the picture shows a dog but the contribution of every pixel to this class is unclear. Both kinds of data suggest different tools. For unstructured data, the family of neuronal networks is most important. For classification of classes from pictures etc. convolutional neural networks are important and should be taught. For structured data, it is important for students to know approaches like CART because a learned tree addresses the problem of transparency in technical applications and leads easily to ensemble methods like random forest. A tool-kit could be set-up with the following methods:

- K-nearest neighbors (lazy learner, to illustrate the principle and often quite efficient)
- CART (Classification and Regression Trees)
- Random Forest

- Dense Neural Networks
- Convolutional Neural Networks (CNN)

Beyond this there is a class of tools like YOLO, see e.g. (Redmon, J. et al, 2016) widely used in robotics for real-time segmentation and classification. It is in general not possible in a mechatronic machine learning course to cover the detailed theory of this approaches, but they are related to CNN, therefore a less theoretical use in e.g. a practical session might still be possible.

Furthermore, there exists a different class of algorithms referred to as unsupervised learning. While supervised learning is based on datasets of labeled answers to learn from - e.g. sensor data, which is annotated either as a failure or as working correctly - unsupervised learning tasks identify patterns without labels. The main task here is clustering. Clustering refers to grouping things together in such a way, that members of a group are similar to each other. The last category is reinforcement learning. In order to be able to conduct reinforcement learning, it is essential to provide a signal suitable for rewarding and quantifying the amount of reward. Consequently, one does not in general know in advance, what the (final) solution will be. Thus, in general, the result is usually of less quality than in the supervised learning case. Reinforcement learning is very useful in cases, where the algorithm can be thought of as an agent interacting with its environment. In mechatronics that can be a robot, a vehicle or even a whole factory.

As one can see, every category of machine learning approaches can be used in mechatronic products like robots, vehicles, and factories. If one has to make a ranking, one might end up with reinforcement learning and supervised learning as most important categories, especially because modern approaches of reinforcement learning like Q-Learning require regression learning techniques like neural networks to represent the Q-Function (Wiering & Otterlo, 2012). Therefore, we will focus on the demands of reinforcement learning to illustrate connections and requirements, as an example.

MACHINE LEARNING AND MECHATRONICAL SYSTEMS

Machine learning enables predictions to be made based on data to elaborate knowledge and relationships out of experiences / data sets. For this purpose, it makes use of some mathematical fields, mainly regression, optimization, and statistics.

Application Areas

One area of application is Industry 4.0, also referred to as smart factory. In smart factory, production processes are connected and a lot of data can be collected in order to optimize the manufacturing process. In this context, machine learning supports e.g. process optimization by changing and adapting manufacturing settings or automatically improving quality assessment. In the application area of vehicle technology, machine learning can mainly be found as a tool to support autonomous driving and comfort functions or features. Furthermore, a lot of companies can make use of machine learning in maintenance and support services. By means of sensors the energy consumption of individual machines can be monitored, maintenance needs can be predicted, and maintenance cycles can be optimized. If a smart system is designed to continuously learn, it is very likely that it will improve performance based on more accurate and actual predictions.

Links to Robotics and Control Engineering

Machine learning approaches for robotic applications have grown quite popular in the last decade. Recent success in the fields of robotics vision and AI robotics showed the benefits in many applications.

Prior to the increased popularity of machine learning in robotics, mainly control engineering approaches were used to ensure safe and autonomous operation of robotic systems.

Nowadays, robotic platforms are getting more and more complex, including a variety of different sensors, increasing computational power, and network capabilities.

Figure 1. Frequency range of control cycles, translated from (Hertzberg, J. et al. p. 262, 2012)

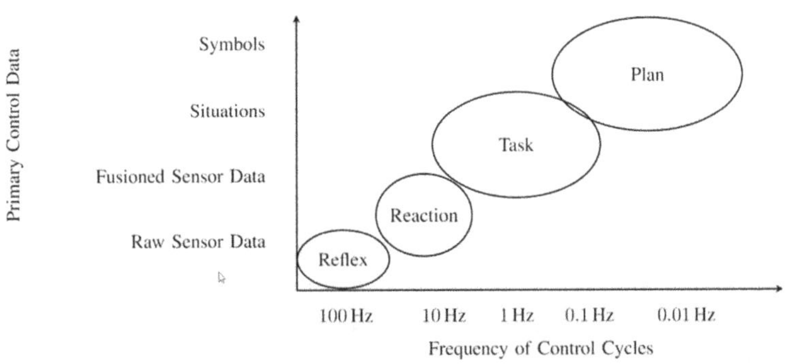

The challenge to achieve intelligent behavior of the robot in an unknown and dynamic working environment leads to challenges combining recent machine learning approaches with traditional control engineering aspects in a neat manner.

At first glance, this seems quite difficult, as on the one hand control loops require real-time behavior of the system and on the other hand machine learning approaches are often computationally expensive. A common model for the design of a robot control system in a layered structure is given in (Hertzberg, Lingemann, & Nüchter, 2012) and is illustrated in figure 1.

The layers of the control structure in figure 1 can be seen as complexity levels to be handled from the robot, ranging from obstacle avoidance to path planning:

- **Reflex:** Describes the lowest level of control and uses raw sensor data to immediately react to changes in the environment. This layer is often directly implemented in hardware.
- **Reaction:** Implements reactions that rely on filtered or fused data. Software modules process the sensor data and build the basic behavior for robotics.
- **Task:** Controls the achievement of small tasks given to the robot. The task is only a small step to achieve a final goal.
- **Plan:** Creates a global plan to be executed from the robot. The global plan is divided into several tasks, which are executed from the layer below.

The execution frequency of the control cycles decreases with growing complexity. The lowest layer (reflex) directly uses the sensor data to react as fast as possible to changes in the environment, typically with a frequency of about 100 Hz. If an obstacle or hazardous area is detected, the system should stop its motion without any delays. It is highly required for security reasons that a real-time response of the system is possible, thus a direct implementation in hardware can be found in many systems. The frequency of the control layer above is already an order of magnitude larger. Reactions rely on fused sensor data, i.e. several sensors are used to derive more knowledge about the environment and to initiate behaviour of the robot. For example, the robot could avoid an obstacle by detecting an alternative path with a variety of navigation sensors. The two lower layers, reflex and reaction, are closely related to the hardware of the robot. In contrary, the upper layers are independent of the robot hardware, they are responsible for the planning process. In this context, planning is related to reaching a final goal or solving a given problem. The planning process on a global scale is performed from the highest layer (plan), which is only executed at minute intervals. The result of the global planning process is divided into several tasks, which are given to the task layer for execution. These upper layers are well suited to apply machine learning algorithms, as they are not time critical.

The task and plan layers are commonly used for path planning and scheduling. This layered structure demonstrates, how the connection of control engineering and machine learning can be integrated into a modern robotic system.

Today, at first quite often simulated environments are being used. The reason is that for modern reinforcement approaches (e.g. (Otterlo, 2012)) using deep neuronal networks a lot of data is necessary for training purpose. This amount of data is typically hard to acquire just from real life tests.

Thus, pre-training based on simulation is quite commonly found.

A similar challenging application area is automotive engineering / vehicles. As established state-of-the-art vehicle technology, many control tasks have to be performed on a millisecond calculation time basis performing on cost-optimized ECUs, while the environment sensing, classification and path planning performs on a different scale, still.

In particular, in the context of fully automated driving, there are still many challenging aspects to provide suitable control structures and vehicle control architectures to cope with this challenge, though many OEMs and suppliers are working on these topics with very high effort and promising results.

Placing of Machine Learning Contents in a Generic Curriculum Framework

The analysis of the requirements necessitates mathematical fundamentals as well as programming skills to be taught prior to any machine learning module. As discussed, it makes sense to focus on reinforcement learning in mechatronics, since it is helpful to be able to rely on basics in physics, simulation, and control theory before the machine learning module pops up in the study curriculum. Control theory is not really mandatory but very useful, since many standard problems, like e.g. the inverted pendulum, are being used as examples in control theory courses.

These application examples from control theory courses can then be adopted in machine learning as well in order to illustrate to the students, how reinforcement learning approaches may achieve similar or equal results based on completely different approaches. A machine learning module can be sped up significantly if the students have already participated in such control engineering experiments and have prior knowledge in application examples.

Nevertheless, machine learning is by no means a separated degree course in mechatronics, and it makes the most sense if it is integrated into advanced courses of application areas like robotics, intelligent or automated driving or automation. Consequently, there should be still sufficient time following the machine learning course to integrate this approach into those fields of application.

Implications to Mechatronics Curricula and Deduction of a Generic Framework

In this section we will discuss the implication of successful integration of machine learning to the curricula of a mechatronic degree course plan; to the complete study plan as well as to individual existing modules. Even though today's European degree courses are based on the idea of modules, usually almost no module is separated from all other modules. Most courses base on fundamental courses and thus, rely on skills set up before.

Prerequisites and Requirements for Machine Learning Contents

Nowadays the availability of many easy-to-use machine and deep learning packages, such as scikit-learn (Pedregosa et al., 2011) (Python), Weka (Hall et al., 2009) (Java), Tensorflow (Abadi et al., 2015) (Python) etc. makes it easier for engineers to use state-of-the-art machine learning algorithms in and for their products. Especially the Keras-API was a big step forward for the usage by different professions than mathematicians and computer scientists (Chollet, 2015).

Nevertheless, machine learning is a field, that intersects statistics, optimization, computer science, and algorithmic aspects. Despite the immense possibilities of existing tools, at least a rough mathematical understanding of many of these techniques is necessary in order to obtain satisfactory or good results. Examples of this requirement are

- Selecting appropriate algorithms regarding aspects like e.g. the required accuracy, suitable training time, adequate model complexity, number of parameters and number of features.
- Choosing parameter settings and validation strategies.
- Identifying under- and over-fitting by understanding statistics, regression and function approximation.

Therefore, one can conclude, that the fundamentals for understanding machine learning are mainly programming skills and knowledge about algorithms and mathematics. Fortunately, a lot of the necessary concepts are already part of the mathematical education of e.g. mechanical engineers.

Let's have a look at the list of the main mathematical aspects needed for machine learning:

1. Ordinary one-dimensional basic calculus
2. Basic Linear Algebra, especially vector spaces, Projections, Eigenvalues & Eigenvectors, norms and metrics
3. Some parts of higher dimensional calculus, especially how to determine or estimate gradients and derivatives
4. Basics in optimization approaches like Gradient descent, Newton's Methods and similar methods
5. Curve fitting and basic regression like least squares methods
6. (Basic) Mathematical statistics

While the first five aspects are usually part of the mathematical education of engineers -- maybe optimization sometimes needs slightly more attention -- the last point is only rarely taught in engineering mathematics. Consequently, the question has to be answered, how deep and how much of these new aspects are needed?

The answer to this question cannot uniquely be given and depends on the choice, how machine learning is presented. If one chooses a more algorithmic approach in teaching of machine learning like in (Marsland, 2014) in contrast to a quite probabilistic perspective as in (Kevin, 2012), the topic of machine learning fits quite well to common fundamental engineering mathematics courses. The basics for an engineer can be handled in between three and five weeks during a semester. Therefore, 2 European Credit points (ECTS) are somehow a lower boundary for the additional statistics needed. Of course, more ECTS would allow for a broader basis, such as also up to 4 European credit points could be reasonable.

From fundamental computer science courses some other subjects including the following are required:

1. Procedural and Object-Oriented Programming
2. Practical skills in Python and/or Java
3. Basics in Algorithm analysis
4. From Physics, some newton mechanics and advanced topics like friction models are useful in order to understand some important effects within the simulated environments.
5. For a Simulation and Modelling course the concept of models in simulation is important as well as some basic practical skills in this topic.

The first two items are mainly covered in typical mechatronic degree courses as part of programming courses. The third topic, basics in algorithms, is not necessarily covered in a mechatronics curriculum. Nevertheless, it can be easily integrated into any computer science related lecture. From our perspective, reinforcement learning is one of the most relevant machine learning disciplines for mechatronics students,

Figure 2. Generic Curricula Framework for 6 semester degree courses with application areas

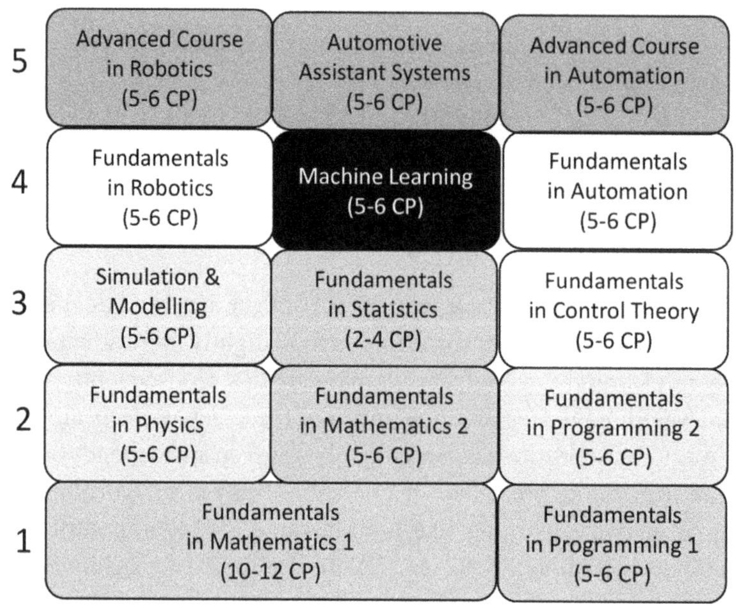

therefore items number four and five become mandatory. To understand the physics behind a system is especially important when reinforcement learning is applied to a real-world system.

Achieving this is more demanding within a six semester degree course, though these are quite common in traditional universities as bachelor degree curricula. Of course, it is much easier to realize it in a seven semester curriculum, which is often being chosen by most universities of applied sciences.

Figure 2 sketches some possible solutions to set up a curriculum for a six semester version of a bachelor study program. Dark grey filled elements highlight mandatory prerequisites for the machine learning module depicted in black. Light grey filled courses are highly desirable, while white filled courses are needed for the advanced machine learning courses filled in red.

Of course, the fundamentals of statistics need to be integrated into the general mathematics fundamentals. They are displayed separately because this is, in general, the only really new aspect next to machine learning itself required in the degree courses. On the one hand, it is very encouraging that this new topic fits in so well. Still, on the other hand, there are at least seven or eight credit points that need to be re-assigned in the existing bachelor courses. Beyond this, it only fits in easily, if the existing degree course comes up with sufficiently integrated credit points for mathematical fundamentals and focus on principals and ideas rather than training to solve more complicated integrals by hand or handle conic sections. Therefore, the integration of machine learning shifts the focus in mathematics from human computation to more general principals and more linear algebra and statistics.

In the whole degree course plan, it shifts the course plan more into the direction of computer science, because the total amount of credit points is limited and transferred from mechanics and/or electronics.

PERSPECTIVES AND BENEFITS OF LINKING MACHINE LEARNING, AUTOMOTIVE, ROBOTICS, AND AUTOMATION

In this section, we discuss, why in our option it is worth to integrate machine learning to keep mechatronic degree courses up-to-date and to satisfy the demands of the typical mechatronics application areas. Of course, the benefit strongly depends on the seamless integration of machine learning contents on module level and the cooperation of different lectures across module borders.

Table 1. Study Plan Bachelor Mechatronic & Information Technology (2019) from the Bochum University of Applied Sciences

Semester	Course / Module	Provides Prerequisites
1	• Analysis 1 • Linear Algebra • Fund. Programming 1	• One-dimensional basic calculus • Basic Linear Algebra • Curve fitting and basic regression • Procedural Programming • Basics in Algorithm analysis
2	• Analysis 2 • Physics 1 • Fund. Programming 1	• Higher dimensional calculus, Basics in optimization approaches • Basic Knowledge for e.g. simulated environments • Object-Oriented Programming
3	*No machine learning related contents in this semester*	
4	• System Analysis & Simulation • Fund. Control Theory	• Basics in Simulation and Modelling • Basics in Control Theory
5	• Machine Learning • Fund. Robotics • Fund. Automation	• (Basic) Mathematical statistics • Application areas
6	• Advanced Robotics • Advanced Automation	• Application areas

Examples of Machine Learning in Robotic Applications

Especially in the field of robotics, machine learning plays an important role. Thus, the students of mechatronic courses strongly benefit from integrated machine learning contents in their curriculum when working on robotics-related projects. It will be shown in the three following examples; how machine learning is used in robotics context to realize an application.

- Machine learning had a big influence on many computer vision approaches. Camera systems are standard equipment in any mobile robot platform, they are available as low-cost commercial of the shelf components. These camera systems in combination with machine learning are often used for the identification of objects in the robot environment or for obstacle detection in navigation tasks. Especially in the field of object detection are a number of libraries available, which can be easily adapted to detect objects in the robot's environment. It is important to have a basic understanding of the used key technologies to utilize the libraries appropriately in a robotic context. A well-known library to realize object detection in a robotic scenario is YOLO (Redmon et al., 2016). To use YOLO on a mobile robot, one has to take into account that many mobile platforms have only very limited computing resources. It is important to understand how neural networks work and what makes them computationally expensive when applied to a robotic application. An example picture from our Turtlebot is shown in figure 3 where YOLO is used on a Turtlebot platform for object detection. If students acquire skills in machine learning and neural networks, they are able to realize their own implementations in a timely manner.
- Another important application field of machine learning is the mobility of robots. The control of challenging robot kinematics, such as humanoid robots or mobile platforms with legged locomotion, is quite demanding. Control software development for unknown terrain or noisy environments is very sophisticated. Control engineering is in many mechatronic engineering courses already an integral part and is a necessary requirement for stabilizing the movement of a robot. But if the kinematics of a robot is very sophisticated and the environment is unknown and additionally very dynamic, reinforcement learning is an important tool to realize a stable and adaptive behavior of the robot. The idea of reinforcement learning is, to define a reward for the desired behavior (in this case a movement in the desired direction). While many movements of the legs to not lead to any movement of the robot, a combination of movements might lead to the goal of moving into the correct direction. A good example is the crawling robot (Tokic & Ammar, 2012),

which is able to adapt its locomotion strategy according to the characteristics of the underground surface. Even further challenging is when the scenario involves multiple agents acting and learning (Weiss, 2013).

- A third example shows the importance of machine learning in the field of industrial manipulators. For many decades, industrial manipulators were mainly used for repetitive tasks with high accuracy requirements. In a pick and place scenario, where the manipulator moves a workpiece from a start location to an end location, the workpieces need to be placed with high accuracy in the work environment. Meanwhile, it is quite common to use vision systems to be able to dynamically grasp well-defined workpieces (see figure 4). Recent developments based on machine learning approaches do not even require the workpieces to be well defined or separated on a feeding system. The dex net project (Mahler et al., 2017) enables grasping of arbitrary objects with the help of a neural network approach.

Examples of Machine Learning in the Field of Automotive Engineering

Similar developments to the ones just discussed within the fields of robotics can be observed in automotive engineering, too. Machine learning techniques have played crucial roles, in particular in the area of systems trying to investigate the environment of vehicles. Examples are camera systems for speed sign recognition, radar, lidar or ultrasonic sensors in addition to mono and stereo cameras. They are used to detect possible paths to follow for the car or to identify obstacles within or near to the planned paths as part of advanced driver assistance systems of manual-driven cars. Beyond this, they can be used as part of vehicle controllers for trajectory tracking of (partly) automated driving vehicles; see e.g. (Ersoy & Gies, 2017) as an introduction to these topics. The impact of machine learning techniques even become more important due to the very manifold development challenges, validation tasks for components, systems and full vehicles and also for the driving tasks of the individual vehicle to be engineered and during lifetime of each vehicle making use of modern driver assist systems or future (partly) automated driving.

Thus, summarized, machine learning will get increasingly important as the enabler for functions or features for vehicles to be engineered as part of components or systems, and machine learning is being investigated to support the tuning and validation processes of these functions or features, as well.

In order to give an example of how a university automotive application courses for machine learning could look like, will be discussed here. Already in classical (machine-learning-free) mechatronics engineering curricula we gained experience with some elective courses for problem-based-oriented model-based software development.

Figure 3. Object detection with YOLO on a Turtlebot

Figure 4. Grasping an object based on a visual system

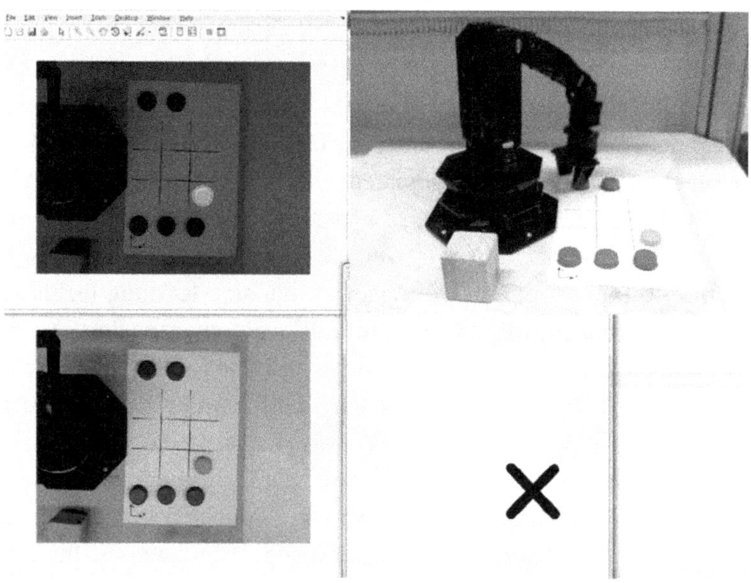

The task for the students of the course is to build up (step by step with the increasing complexity of tasks) some LEGO-EV3-based vehicle which should perform certain tasks.

During the course, the tasks get more and more complicated. At first, the students have to implement vehicle speed control and lateral control (following path marks) for arbitrary vehicle speed set points.

Then the next complex task is to implement an adaptive speed/distance control in order to prevent the own vehicle from crashing into a slower preceding vehicle. Next comes vehicle location and online map generation of the driven tracks. Then the task is to stop the vehicle at some pre-defined location of the map. The final task then is to re-use the sensors for adaptive speed/distance control for sideways detection of potential parking lots and implement automated reverse parallel parking to the left and then to the right including each time a return on the path markings (lane/street). These tasks have to be performed completely stand-alone on the EVO3-LEGO-Brick, which only has rather limited computation power and memory space. Last but not least the student's final task has been to re-do all these development steps for a new vehicle designed by the students themselves. The only restriction is, that it needs a driven rear axle (preferable with rear differential) and a steered front axle. Up to this point, the course does not need artificial intelligence or machine learning. This changes now, since the already developed tasks are extended by two very basic changes:

First, the reference vehicle set point (given from outside by the student) shall be overruled by traffic signs like "STOP" or speed limits. Second, the lateral vehicle controller based on the idea of controlling the desired measured reflected light intensity of a lane mark by the reference orientation calculated by a lane detection algorithm. Both additional tasks depend on cameras and additional computation power which the LEGO-Brick cannot perform by itself. For this purpose, a mobile phone has been fixed on the LEGO-vehicle, the camera-data is transferred to a computer in the lab performing the camera-based traffic sign recognition and the lane / track identification.

Figure 5 depicts the signal flow structure of the set-up. This setup and separation of tasks can be done since Matlab-EV3-Release 2018. Since then, a rather reliable UDP signal transmission is available for information fed from outside to the (comparable slow) real-time calculation being done on the LEGO-Brick EV3. Both tasks are being performed with AI tools, in particular, neuronal networks. The calculated information results in vehicle speed setpoint correction values for the vehicle speed controller and into steering angle set or yaw rate points for the lateral controller of the student's vehicle running on the LEGO-Brick.

Figure 6 illustrates the tracking task, while figure 7 shows the situation for identifying a STOP-sign.

Figure 5. Set-up for extending a LEGO-brick vehicle by AI camera-based traffic sign recognition and lane tracking (Simic & Heller, 2019)

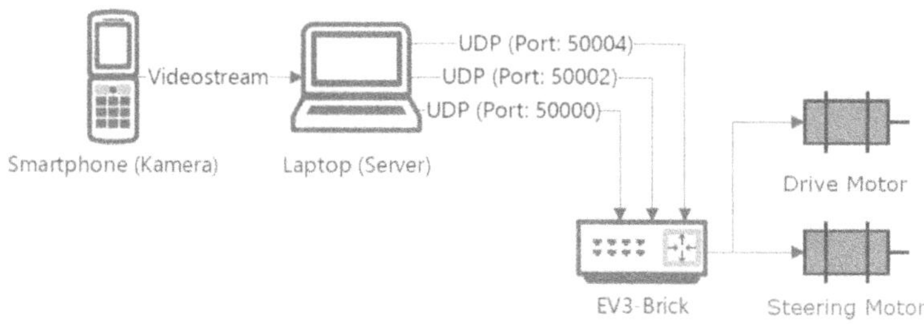

Figure 6. Tracking of the LEGO brick by identification of the lane markings (Simic & Heller, 2019)

Figure 7. Identification of a STOP-sign (Simic & Heller, 2019)

For a bachelor course, the amount of content can be scaled by the amount of reduction of degrees in freedom for the student and increased predefined structures in terms of software running on the Brick and type and structure of networks and training methods and also for the used signals.

Case Study on the Bachelor Degree Course Mechatronic and Information Technology

The considerations mentioned above provide a theoretical approach to cover relevant machine learning contents into a curriculum. Now, it will be shown in a case study, how this has been achieved in an existing mechatronics degree program. The main issue with new content is, that existing study plans are quite often fully packed and there is no further degree of freedom to place new contents. In general, there are two approaches to this: On the one hand, the establishment of a suitable specialization subject or on

the other hand, the development of a specialized degree program. The framework described in the section "placing of machine learning contents in a generic curriculum framework" places the machine learning lecture in the fourth semester of a six-semester course. In this way, a specialization subject in machine learning can be implemented. In the presented case study, we look at a seven-semester bachelor's degree program in mechatronics and information technology, which belongs to the genre of specialized degree programs. Table 1 shows an excerpt of the study plan, which only shows the contents related to the framework of the section "placing of machine learning contents in a generic curriculum framework".

The third semester contains lectures such as electrical engineering and mechanics. These are not contents of our framework; thus it is kept blank in Table 1. This is possible because it is a seven- and not six-semester degree course. The module System Analysis & Simulation mainly covers the required skills in modeling and simulation. The machine learning module will be followed by two specialization subjects. First of all, this shows that integration is possible in the sense of the framework. At the same time, however, there are also challenges that make a seamless integration difficult, which will be similarly found in other degree programs. The first challenge lies in teaching the subject of machine learning with regard to the available mathematical basics. Mathematics in the degree program is sufficiently represented with 18 ECTS credits and further expansion is not possible without going at the expense of other subjects. However, the mathematical courses are already filled with traditional engineering subjects and are under increasing pressure to deal with the heterogeneous admission requirements of the students. Therefore, statistical basics are only discussed in terms of the equilibrium calculation as they are necessary for the fitting of measurements. Corresponding contents are therefore first and foremost imparted in machine learning and partly in System Analysis & Simulation. This is accompanied by a reduction in the amount of the core substance, which has been minimized by an algorithmic orientation of machine learning.

The second challenge concerns the application areas. As it is often the case in modular degree programs, these are also used as compulsory or optional subjects in other degree programs. Therefore, the lecturers cannot assume that all participants have dealt with machine learning beforehand. This prevents integration as an integral part of the course, although the majority of participants are familiar with it. The chosen solution for this is the integration of modern teaching concepts which are especially suitable for advanced students. These events are partly enhanced by aspects of problem and project-based learning. This differentiation allows the integration of machine learning in selected projects and problems as well as a stronger practical activation of the advanced students. In general, problem-based learning has shown itself to be an excellent integration option, which offers interested students opportunities and at the same time takes the individual interests of the students into account. Focusing on the students as initiating partners leads to more active learning, better understanding and stronger anchoring of what has been learned. In addition, this learning approach promotes the acquisition of interdisciplinary skills -- important for mechatronics -- and soft skills, see e.g. (Wood, 2003) discussing this for medicine. The most common difficulties in implementation, which (Wood, 2003) also mentioned, are the need for more personnel and, in certain areas of expertise, for more equipment per student. Therefore, it is in general, a good approach to use this technique in higher semesters. Nevertheless, the open design of problem-oriented learning scenarios as well as in social aspects such as group dynamics are still aspects of research (Antonietti, 2001; Henry et al., 2012; Neville, 2009). The practical experience in the *Bachelor Mechatronic & Information Technology* of the Bochum University of Applied Sciences is that project and problem-based learning in the advanced courses can, as illustrated in the section before, in the context of machine learning in automotive, robotics and automation has the potential to provide experiences for students with this mathematical subject in an applied context. This includes problem solving in the application domain as well as applying methods learned in machine learning courses.

In our work, we focused mainly on machine learning contents to be integrated into the curriculum. It should be mentioned, that there is a strong demand to include in modern engineering curricula additional contents like personal and professional skills, like proposed in the CDIO approach (Crawley et al., 2011). These additional qualifications were not covered in this work, but a number of different courses (e.g. English classes, scientific writing courses) are available and are mandatory for all bachelor students in our engineering department. The feedback from the students regarding the new lecture contents was very positive. It was very motivating for them to apply latest approaches from the field of machine learning to different applications. In the lectures they were able to include their new skills in robotic projects and show impressively the application of machine learning in a mechatronic system. As many students study at our university in the scope of dual study program, they were even able to transfer their knowledge successfully in their companies, for example in a case study for CAD based cost estimations (Börzel 2019).

CONCLUSION

This work introduced a framework to integrate machine learning contents in a modern mechatronics curriculum. The relevance of machine learning disciplines for mechatronics applications has been discussed, and a framework with required course contents has been derived. The framework has been formulated in a modular way to enable seamless integration in any engineering degree program. The successful integration has been demonstrated with a case study at the University of Applied Sciences Bochum. Benefits and drawbacks of this solution have been presented and discussed. Beyond this and (Frochte, J. et. al) some examples for possible application areas and project-based learning in the context of robotics and autonomous driving where given and discussed.

REFERENCES

Abadi, M., Agarwal, A., Barham, P., Brevdo, E., Chen, Z., Citro, C., . . . Ghemawat, S. (2015). *TensorFlow: Large-scale machine learning on heterogeneous systems*. Software available from tensorflow. org: http://tensorflow. org

Ahmad, R., & Kamaruddin, S. (2012). An overview of time-based and condition-based maintenance in industrial application. *Computers & Industrial Engineering*, *63*(1), 135–149. doi:10.1016/j.cie.2012.02.002

Antonietti, A. (2001). Problem based learning--A research perspective on learning interactions. *The British Journal of Educational Psychology*, *71*, 344.

Börzel S., & Frochte, J. (2019). Case Study On Model-based Application of Machine Learning Using Small CAD Databases for Cost Estimation. *Proceedings of KDIR 2019*.

Castle, R. (in press). Shadowing a police officer: How to be unobtrusive while solving cases in spectacular fashion. *Professional Writers' Journal.*

Crawley, E. F., Malmqvist, J., Lucas, W. A., & Brodeur, D. R. (2011). *The CDIO Syllabus v2. 0: An Updated Statement of Goals for Engineering Education. In Proceedings of the 7 th Intl. CDIO conference.* Copenhagen: University of Demark.

Ersoy, M., & Gies, S. (Eds.). (2017). *Fahrwerkhandbuch: Grundlagen–Fahrdynamik–Fahrverhalten–Komponenten–Elektronische Systeme–Fahrerassistenz–Autonomes Fahren–Perspektiven.* Springer-Verlag. doi:10.1007/978-3-658-15468-4

Esteva, A., Robicquet, A., Ramsundar, B., Kuleshov, V., DePristo, M., Chou, K., ... Dean, J. (2019). A guide to deep learning in healthcare. *Nature Medicine, 25*(1), 24–29. doi:10.103841591-018-0316-z PMID:30617335

Frochte, J., Lemmen, M., & Schmidt, M. (2018). Seamless Integration of Machine Learning Contents in Mechatronics Curricula. In *2018 19th International Conference on Research and Education in Mechatronics (REM)* (pp. 75-80). IEEE. 10.1109/REM.2018.8421794

Hall, M., Frank, E., Holmes, G., Pfahringer, B., Reutemann, P., & Witten, I. H. (2009). The WEKA data mining software: an update. *ACM SIGKDD Explorations Newsletter, 11*(1), 10-18.

Henry, H. R., Tawfik, A. A., Jonassen, D. H., Winholtz, R. A., & Khanna, S. (2012). "I know this is supposed to be more like the real world, but...": Student perceptions of a PBL implementation in an undergraduate materials science course. *Interdisciplinary Journal of Problem-based Learning, 6*(1), 5. doi:10.7771/1541-5015.1312

Hertzberg, J., Lingemann, K., & Nüchter, A. (2012). *Mobile Roboter: Eine Einführung aus Sicht der Informatik.* Springer-Verlag. doi:10.1007/978-3-642-01726-1

Kevin, P. M. (2012). *Machine learning: a probabilistic perspective.* Academic Press.

Lee, J. G., Jun, S., Cho, Y. W., Lee, H., Kim, G. B., Seo, J. B., & Kim, N. (2017). Deep learning in medical imaging: General overview. *Korean Journal of Radiology, 18*(4), 570–584. doi:10.3348/kjr.2017.18.4.570 PMID:28670152

Mahler, J., Liang, J., Niyaz, S., Laskey, M., Doan, R., Liu, X., . . . Goldberg, K. (2017). *Dex-net 2.0: Deep learning to plan robust grasps with synthetic point clouds and analytic grasp metrics.* arXiv preprint arXiv:1703.09312

Marsland, S. (2014). *Machine learning: an algorithmic perspective*. Taylor & Francis Inc. doi:10.1201/b17476

Neville, A. J. (2009). Problem-based learning and medical education forty years on. *Medical Principles and Practice*, *18*(1), 1–9. doi:10.1159/000163038 PMID:19060483

Pedregosa, F., Varoquaux, G., Gramfort, A., Michel, V., Thirion, B., Grisel, O., ... Vanderplas, J. (2011). Scikit-learn: Machine learning in Python. *Journal of Machine Learning Research*, *12*(Oct), 2825–2830.

Redmon, J., Divvala, S., Girshick, R., & Farhadi, A. (2016). You only look once: Unified, real-time object detection. In *Proceedings of the IEEE conference on computer vision and pattern recognition* (pp. 779-788). IEEE. 10.1109/CVPR.2016.91

Simic, B., & Heller, A. (2019). *Autonomes Fahren: Spur- und Schilderkennung mit einem LEGO-Fahrzeug unter Matlab und Simulink. Bochum University of Applied Sciences, Höseler Platz 2, D-42579 Heiligenhaus*. Project Documentation.

Tokic, M., & Ammar, H. B. (2012). Teaching reinforcement learning using a physical robot. *Proceedings of the ICML Workshop on Teaching Machine Learning*.

Vallon, C., Ercan, Z., Carvalho, A., & Borrelli, F. (2017, June). A machine learning approach for personalized autonomous lane change initiation and control. In *2017 IEEE Intelligent Vehicles Symposium (IV)* (pp. 1590-1595). IEEE. 10.1109/IVS.2017.7995936

van Otterlo, M. (2012). *Reinforcement learning: State-of-the-Art*. Springer Berlin Heidelberg.

Weiss, G. (2013). *Multiagent Systems, ser.* EBSCO ebook academic collection.

Wiering, M., & Van Otterlo, M. (2012). *Reinforcement learning. Adaptation, learning, and optimization*. Academic Press.

Wood, D. F. (2003). Problem based learning. *BMJ (Clinical Research Ed.)*, *326*(7384), 328–330. doi:10.1136/bmj.326.7384.328 PMID:12574050

KEY TERMS AND DEFINITIONS

Machine Learning: A branch of artificial intelligence. Summarizes different approaches to "learn" from data.

Mechatronic Degree Courses: A complete mechatronics course at the university with a total length of 6 to 8 semesters. The student completes the course with a bachelor thesis.

Reinforcement Learning: Machine learning approaches often used in robotics. A reward is used to teach a system a desired behavior.

Supervised Learning: Machine learning approaches often used for regression and classification.

Unsupervised Learning: Machine learning approach used for clustering. Learns from unlabeled data (i.e., there is no supervision from a human who specifies the labels for the data).

Chapter 5
Robotics E-Learning Supported by Collaborative and Distributed Intelligent Environments

Maki K. Habib
https://orcid.org/0000-0001-8088-8043
The American University in Cairo, Egypt

ABSTRACT

Robotics e-learning environment that facilitates tailored learning for individual students studying robotics is developed. The developed collaborative and distributed intelligent environment (CoDIE) enables multi-users to access simultaneously remote and integrated mixed reality facilities through the web. The developed system constitutes a robotic center to help in transferring theoretical knowledge enhanced by simulation and practical experience. It enables realistic interaction by immersing users in a shared 3D CoDIE. The system enables users to do programming, simulations, experiments, manipulating data and objects, diagnostics and analyses, control and monitor actions. Also, users can receive feedback from the system or instructors. The developed system has been implemented and tested using two real manipulators and virtual robots supporting real-time tracking and simulation. Three modes of operations have been implemented, individual robot training mode through virtual robot models, multi-user mode working together, and individual or group-based training by instructor.

DOI: 10.4018/978-1-5225-7793-5.ch005

INTRODUCTION

There is no agreed universal definition of artificial intelligence (AI). However, in a general sense, it is the synergy of multiple technologies that together can create systems that can perform tasks (by applying algorithms and models to find patterns in large amounts of data) usually require human expertize. With the convergence of disruptive technologies (Robotics, nanotechnologies, genetics, 3D printing, etc.), the emergence of every new technologies are accelerating the growth and the capabilities of AI to address new opportunities and challenges (D2L 2018; Luckin et al, 2017). However, the new technologies disrupting the job market will always demand new skills. Hence, new evolution is taking place impacted by AI to lead the development transforming education, teaching and learning into a new era with aim to meet the need by enriching education techniques and methods. The use of AI in education and learning provides classrooms, teachers, schools and universities with innovative ways to understand how to support students' learning process and assess their learning and skills as well as allowing better ways to enhance course content, individualized tutoring and facilitate tailored and adaptive learning experience. The principles of AI in higher education underlie a range of innovative systems that may include for example: analytics, robots, virtual experiences, advising, grading and intelligent tutoring (Wolf, 2009). AI will significantly influence what we teach and learn, as well as how better it can be done. Furthermore, the usage of machine learning, deep learning, and neural networks in AI systems beside the increased computational power represents effective AI-driven tools that facilitate and expand the opportunities to support and improve the education and learning process. New generation of students are living the new ear of education as they are growing up with the latest and smart technologies integrated through Internet and other networks.

Since the beginning of E-learning in 1997 it was associated with interactive learner-centered distance learning with aim to enhance knowledge and performance and it is expanded with the evolution of the information and communication technologies that support the growth of the Internet based technologies which evolved to support wide range of web-based applications using resources of various digital technologies (Mori, 1997; Rosenberg, 2001; Rossett, 2001; Cross, 2004; Khan, 2005). Robotics integrated with AI supporting automation along with service robots are influencing current and future industry, economies and society (Wolf, 2009).

This chapter aims to establish effective synergy between robotics, education with AI techniques by synergizing it with the integration of information and communication technologies with the necessary expertize beyond space and time constrains. Information, equipment, devices and expertize along with other resources are scattered across our planet and these resources may not be available where they are needed at the necessary time. The quality of communication technology and infrastructures of networking are forcing for definite move towards a rethinking of the physical structures and spaces needed for living, learning and working. As physical presence is no longer a prerequisite for physical influence there is a need to look for alternative forms of physical movement of people, knowledge, equipment, records and information, etc. This approach is evolving to address the issues of universal sense of connectivity and global access to information; easy control and use of globally linked physical devices, databases and processes, facilitating real time interaction and awareness along with supporting mobility and portability of people and enhance access to experts and other dispersed and valuable resources (Habib, 2008). Efforts to develop frameworks aiming to understand and design intelligent tutoring that facilitate robots tutoring with AI techniques. This is facilitated by the use the perception-planning-action to establish effective teaching-learning relationship between the education-learning domain and the robotics content domain (Truong, 2016).

In order to facilitate remote access by multiusers to the resources, information and expertize beyond space and time constrains, Telecooperation is an outstanding example for the power of enabling technologies that stands for the fusion of computer science, telecommunication and multimedia facilities to carry out a cooperative process among organizations, individuals, systems or combination of them by having better access to resources and share timely information over geographically distributed locations that lead to make well informed decisions (Habib 2001, Habib 2006; Habib 2008). The most suitable development environment that realizes telecooperation among dispersed people and other resources is the Internet. The Internet represents effective open network infrastructure technologies that facilitate virtual presence via electronic communications between entities, human populations and machines. The Internet provides low cost and widely available media rich interface that can make resources accessible to a broad range of users regardless of geographic location and the type of operation system they are using. Internet based systems with tools supporting human communication and interaction with real world, will inevitably lead to many useful applications in various sectors of the society, professionally and socially. Internet is a rich, interactive and engaging environment and it is a challenging way of providing training and education to assist learner in developing knowledge and skills through a well-planned, well designed educational/ training environments (Habib 2008).

Within the global and rapid development of educational needs “virtuality” indicates to the aspect of introducing a telematic network into the process and interaction of teaching and learning while realizing the requirements of telepresence concept supported by AI techniques. The characteristic of virtuality incorporates a vision that no physical campus or training center as a separate organization will be needed but that learning place with its facilities and the supporting organization may be created as a virtual network of elements and contributions of different organizations (Galkin et al, 1998; Wagner, 1998; Kruse & Dai, 2001). The virtual campus refers to the environment that supports its research/educational and administrative activities that leap over the boundaries of time and space.

COLLABORATIVE AND DISTRIBUTED INTELLIGENT ENVRIONMENT (CoDIE)

In Merging virtuality and reality in unique and innovative ways takes new meanings and its implication is extensive. Users of the system are immersing themselves into 3D based mixed realities environments, which create illusion of physical presence at the physical place where robots with their models and other equipment, devices and information are available and supported by sensory devices that can create better understanding and appreciation of both realities (virtual and real). The developed a multiuser 3D virtual, interactive and collaborative environment is easy to be re-configurable and its space is divided into segments called zones. The functional capabilities of each zone are adaptable and it is not necessary to have the same attributes and capabilities in all zones. Users of the system can move between the zones of the virtual, interactive and collaborative environment seamlessly. The appearance and capabilities of graphically represented task environment as space, equipment and people are displayed in 3D and tracked when they are logged in to the system.

The developed system architecture uses four-tier architecture as shown in Figures 1 and 2 respectively with new concept of portable process servers to support dynamic and fast reconfiguration for equipment, devices, resources and other facilities.

The four-tire levels are,

1. Device level,
2. Process servers / File server,
3. The system server/Web Server, and
4. Integrated Client/Server level.

The communication structure is based on a client/server architecture written mainly in the Java and VRML programming languages and their supporting utilities.

Figure 1. The distributed architecture of the system

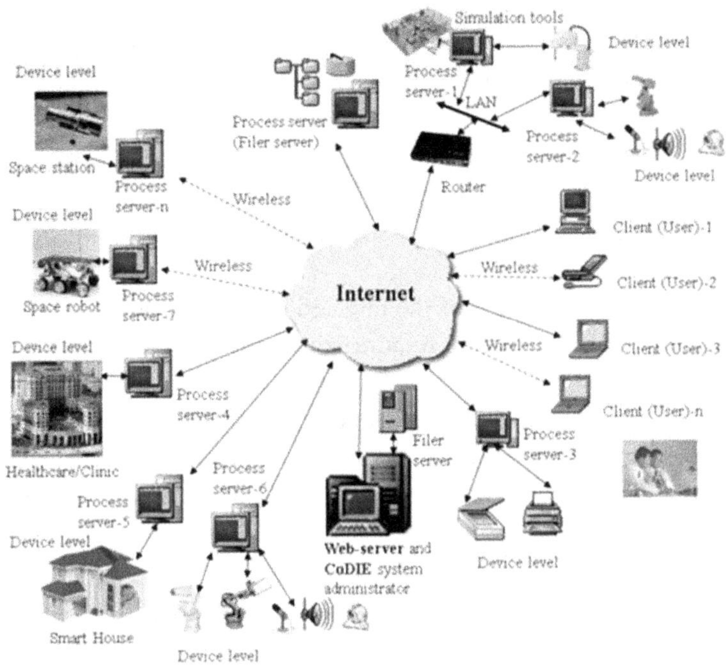

Figure 2. The four-tires outline of developed architecture

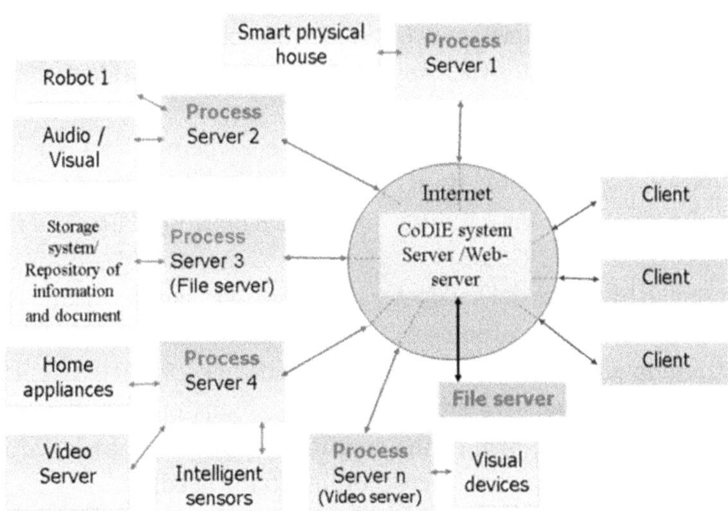

1. Device Level

This layer represents the lowest layer in the developed architecture. It includes all distributed devices, equipment, databases and other hardware & information that are needed for the purpose to,

a. Fulfill the goals associated with an application domain. Such devices and equipment may include robots and their models, experimental systems, manufacturing processes, etc.
b. Simulate and model some of the targeted equipment/process, or design and analyze new ones. Such needs require to have software tools/packages relevant to equipment/process, and
c. Facilitate interactive individual and team based training work among collaborating members. This is done, by integrating wide range of devices, such as cameras, printers, faxes, scanners, cellphones, computers and memory devices, media based technology, etc.

The mentioned categories of devices, equipment, other hardware and software packages/tools,

i. Do not require to be physically located at the physical spaces or environments modeled as a part of the shared spaces,
ii. Can be distributed as long as there is a mean to be reached through the open network, and some of them may be collocated within the same physical space without the necessity for such space to be represented inside the application environment,
iii. Should be interfaced to one or more computers where at least one of them at each physical space should be assigned as a server with IP address to assure portability and also connectivity with the open network. This server is called, a process server,
iv. Represented by 3D model and integrated inside the shared space. It is the duty of the collaborative environment administrator to place the model(s) of any device, equipment, and other hardware of the device level at the right location/ Zone within collaborative environment in association with the application domain and the work plan of the authorized teams. The assigned location/ zone can be changed at any time according to the needs,
v. Each device, equipment and other hardware at this layer has an interactive applet. The applet pops up once an authorized user is getting within a certain distance from the device or equipment while moving inside the interaction and collaborative environment. In the case of a simulation tool, it can be lunched

either interactively through the popped applet representing the tool or directly by the user without the need to be within the tool area. All these applets are bound together using the Hypertext Transfer Protocol (HTML), which can easily support adding new features, new applets or delete applets,

vi. Command control protocol has been developed to define general and device specific command structures to enable the process server receive data and sensory information through its interface with the connected devices/equipment, and send control signals and requests to the relevant device or equipment as necessary.

2. Process Servers–File Server–Video Server

Process server is a software server dedicated to handle communication between the system server/Web-server from one side and the device level from the other side. Each process server has the following features,

a. A process server can be hosted by an independent computer or a single card computer embedded with any of the globally distributed hardware and software tools at the device level. The computing and interfacing power of a process server is based on the requirements of the application domain and the complexity of the facilities available at the device level,
b. Each process server has a unique IP address. Hence, it requires having networking card. Such capability helps to plug-in any computer hosting a process server to the open network from any place that can facilitate such connection,
c. The process servers are connected to an open network such as the Internet or LAN. The network could be wired or wireless and it may utilize a variety of communication protocols as necessary.
d. All IP addresses of the assigned process servers on the open network should be defined at the system server/Web-server. This allows secure connection as only the system server has the right to connect authorized users to any of the process servers with the defined list of IPs. Process servers will not allow any connection from coming from IPs other than that of the system server. In addition, the unique IP for each process server supports the portability and re-configurability,
e. Once a process server is connected to the open network, the system server/ Web-server can recognize it by the availability of its active IP. Accordingly, the interactive applets of devices and /or equipment at the device level and connected to that process server are automatically activated within the collaborative and interactive environment. In contrary to this, when a process server is unplugged from the open network (Internet), the system server can

detect that and accordingly, the system server deactivates the interactive display of all device level model(s) associated with the unplugged process server while displaying a message describing the case,

f. The concept of the process server helps to modularize the system in terms of
   - Programming as it separate the device level codes from the administrator type codes,
   - Allowing flexible future extensions in adding new distributed process servers with their associated devices/equipment/tools, and
   - Supporting efficiently the integration of distribute resources.

g. Command control protocol has been developed to enable each process server executes commands received from the system server/Web-server, and reports back any change within its remote environment and the associated device level.

h. The process server may host video or media server, a file server, etc. The file server may act as repository of information and document related activities at the local environment associated with the process server, or the local environment may have a separate file server that interacts directly with both, the process server and the main server. This depends on the size of document, required update and sharing activities at the local level.

i. Each process server has a set of safe guard functions to assure protection and safe operation, monitoring and control for all hardware connected to it. Such functionality can deal with abnormal actions through command control coming from the main server, and the unavailability of the network connection during the operation.

3. The System Server/Web Server

The system server

a. Acts as administrator and provider for all interaction functionalities of client users,
b. It host the communication middleware that facilitates the interaction and communication between client users and all available process servers,
c. Integrates into the shared space all 3D elements of the considered environments (physical and virtual)
d. Allows the administrator to reconfigure any part of the collaborative and interactive environment,
e. It host a file server that acts as document related activities, or the system may has a separate file server interacting directly with the main server.

f. A process server may be collocated within the physical location of system server to facilitate interaction with people administering the system and authorized client users of the system,
g. Analyzes logging messages,
h. Assure secure access-right to collaborative and interactive environment (this includes the 3D shared space and all facilities immersed inside it). In addition, the server logs all IPs of the users and their actions/activities with their date and time,
i. Apply access control policy to access zones, facilities and other resources within the application environment. In addition, it is responsible to schedule the time and the use of the facilities under demand through access management system. The interaction with access management system is done at the web browser side,
j. Etc.

Access controls is a feature integrated to the server. Each command sent by the client is checked against his/her assigned permission and accordingly allow or deny access as defined by the permissions list assigned by administrator according to the adopted access control strategy. When a user aims to access the system and controls a physical device or equipment, the server serves as the source of communication with the process servers. Users will have to connect first to the system server/Web server and the server will connect them to the relevant process server as required.

4. The Integrated Client/Server Level

The client-server model adopts an integrated design, where core classes exist at each side. These classes are the Client-Applet class for the client, and the Admin-Server class for the server as well as the core listening and sending classes whose sole purpose are to handle the network data transfer and packet forwarding between classes. The core classes aim to provide share functionalities and to handle inter-component communication functionalities, i.e., all subclasses are connected to the relevant core class at each side. This design introduces a sense of modularity while minimizing inter-component dependencies as much as possible. Such approach helps to facilitate some level of plug-in interface, which is good to separate between each component package for both, the server and the client sides. All function associated with this design model have been implemented.

The server is implemented as a java application that communicates with all authorized client users and provides them with update on their views (first person or second person views) within the 3D model of the application environment according to their current locations, and provides them with responses on their requests.

Industry standard Virtual Reality Modeling Language (VRML) was used to create a full 3D model representing any of the discussed types of system spaces. The type and complexity of the model depends on the application domain and the associated requirements. The client user applet controls the local VRML(viewer) plug-in browser through the External Authoring Interface (EAI) periodically to update his/her own scene during the user's own movement and/or due to changes in location of other users. This requires sending user's new location to the server continuously. In order to support the interoperability, portability and enables maximum adaptation to the user's computing environment, the web-interface of the client side is implemented as a VRML coupled with Java technology through EAI.

Notice that the functions and software associated with GUI can be transferred from the system server/Web-server, and some functions may come from a relevant process server on demand, and no specific software is required to be installed at the client site a priori. In addition, the client computer should support media streaming as necessary.

ROBOTICS E-LEARNING AND TELECOOPERATION

The developed concept of collaborative, distributed and interactive intelligent environment was used to develop an educational and training robot center integrated with distributed physical and virtual facilities. The center aims to help in transferring theoretical knowledge into practice and enables geographically dispersed people to interact individually and in teams by immersing them within the customized shared space of the application domain of type (e). The center is dedicated to provide users access to remote virtual and physical real industrial robots through the application environment while interacting with their colleagues and instructors as needed.

The 3D model of the shared space and its application domain consists of following,

1. The shared space of the application environment. The considered space under the selected application domain constitutes the following (See Fig.3),
    a. Virtual entrance space,
    b. A 3D virtual lobby for the training center,
    c. A virtual space supporting virtual training. This space consists of a group of 3D virtual training cells arranged as independent rooms with a separate entrance and ID assigned to each of them. Each cell includes 3D robot model (See Fig.4), and
    d. A virtual space represents 3D models a virtual robot laboratory linked with physical counterpart (equipment and space).
2. Equipment, devices, sensors and software tools

Figure 3. The shared space of the application domain

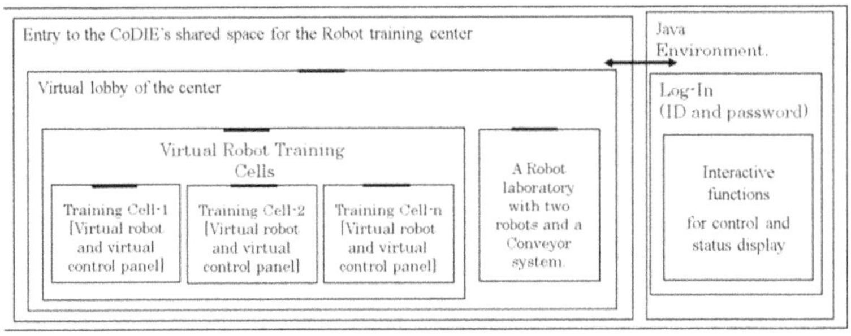

a. The virtual robot laboratory includes the models of two real physical robots (KUKA KR-6) and two conveyor systems (one with each robot) and other mechanical elements that are located at the physical counterpart (See Fig.5). In addition, audio, and visual sensors with text messaging capability are integrated within the real physical environment for control, monitoring, awareness, etc. about the physical robot environment and the relevant task. The robots, conveyor systems and sensors are integrated with two process servers (Process server 1 and 2 were) to facilitate the mentioned purpose. In addition, a simulator integrated with a rigid 3D model of KUKA KR-6 supported by all kinematics functions, analysis, monitoring, and control capabilities has been developed and integrated to the robots at the relevant process server. Two process servers were used and linked to the internet with their unique IDs to illustrate the capability of global distribution and independent access by multi-user without space and time constraints for equipment, devices and other facilities.

Figure 4. The virtual training cells at the robot training center

Figure 5. The developed robot training center architecture

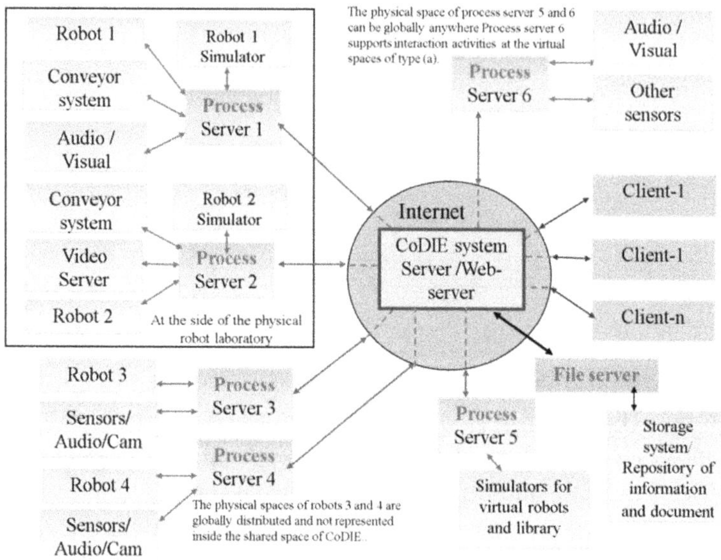

b. Each of the virtual training cells includes 3D interactive model of a real industrial robot along with the virtual model of its control panel (See Fig.6). A robot model can be selected from a robot model library according to the training need. In addition, a robot simulator for the selected robot is integrated with each cell. The instructors has the authority to link any of the selected virtual robot model in any of the training cells to an identical physical robot that is globally distributed while its physical environment is not represented in the shared space of the application environment. For this purpose, the physical robot KUKA has been selected along with its developed virtual model and simulator. Two globally physical robots with no representation of their physical space inside collaborative and interactive environment have been connected to the process servers 3 and 4. While, the virtual models of the robots, the simulators and the robot library are all connected to one process server 5 that be anywhere too.
c. Virtual lobby with integrated webcam, audio for announcement, and variety of sensors. Also, variety of functions and capabilities has been integrated to facilitate conferencing, public message board, instant private and public messaging, etc.
d. Users (trainees and instructors) can use visual and audio sensors to interact by activating a chat session supported by text, voice and vision. Each zone has its assigned capabilities that can support different activities.

Figure 6. A virtual robot (KUKA) and its virtual control panel at a robot training cell

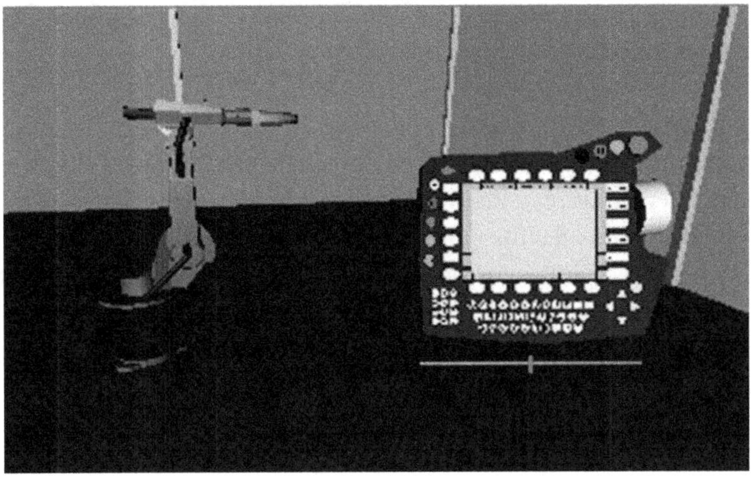

E-LEARNING TRAINING MODES

Three E-learning modes for training have been designed and integrated with the developed system. In each educational mode, the user has different functional capabilities assigned by the system. The implemented training modes are,

1. Individual education mode. In the Individual training mode, the user is given the right to learn how to control the virtual robot within a virtual training cell where a virtual control panel and a virtual robot are available. Upon entering this mode, the user will be able to navigate inside the environment of the virtual cell and move around the robot while the panel control will be always in the view of the user. In this mode, each trainee has the opportunity to control the virtual robot that he/she initiates. Currently there are 10 virtual training cells and users can access and use them simultaneously. Each virtual cell is dedicated to one user.
2. Multi-users education mode. The multi-user mode has been implemented to enable group of users (more than one) to communicate, coordinate and cooperate with each other inside the shared virtual cell. The users can recognize each other through avatars with a name attached to it representing each user. All communication, messaging, conferencing, tracking and other functionalities integrated with the virtual environment are available for the users to use.
3. Instructor guided educational mode. The purpose of this mode is to provide a real time guide through an expert for the trainees to enable them to refer or to discuss with when they are face problems during their training. Also,

the instructor may have a class with multiple users to demonstrating either a virtual robot programming or an implementation and execution of programs on the physical robot integrated with the system.

In addition, the system provides components for user authentication during log-in process, access to training material and facilities, resource management, sharing, etc.

The client users (trainees and instructors) are the authorized users that can access the environment and its facilities through the open network by logging-in using a web browser. The administrator of the application environment assigns the role and states the access right for each user while managing the whole environment in terms of, add and delete physical and virtual devices/equipment and software tools, add and delete client users, reconfigure the environment, implement access control policy, security, etc.

Once a client user enters the URL of the system, the HTML browser displays the interactive graphical user interface (GUI) associated with relevant application domain. In this case the application domain is the robot training center. The browser loads the client software as Java applets from the server and starts them. The Java applet provides inputs for Login ID and password. Other possible authentication techniques can be used as necessary. Each authorized client user is identified by 3D avatar that identifies him/her when entering CoDIE environment. When a client user is logged-in successfully into the application environment, he/she would appear at the entrance of the robot training center within the shared space. The user appears in the environment with its avatar with a default first person view while a second person view can be selected as required. The users accessing the application environment can mutually see each other avatars from their locations if they are sharing the same space without barriers between them. When a user within the application environment enters the robot laboratory and comes closer to any of the robots, the user interface applet of that robot will be popped-up.

All functions of the collaborative and interactive application environment and other application related have been implemented and tested successfully. Access control and user tracking features have been implemented. Two tracking methods were developed based on the graphical map and the hierarchical tree structure. Figure 7 shows a snapshot from the Internet browser.

CONCLUSION

Robotics E-Learning based interactive 3D environment that facilitates tailored learning experience for individual and multi students learning Robotics was developed. The developed environment enables multi users to access simultaneously remote mixed

Figure 7. The user interface applet with the 3D model of the physical robot laboratory

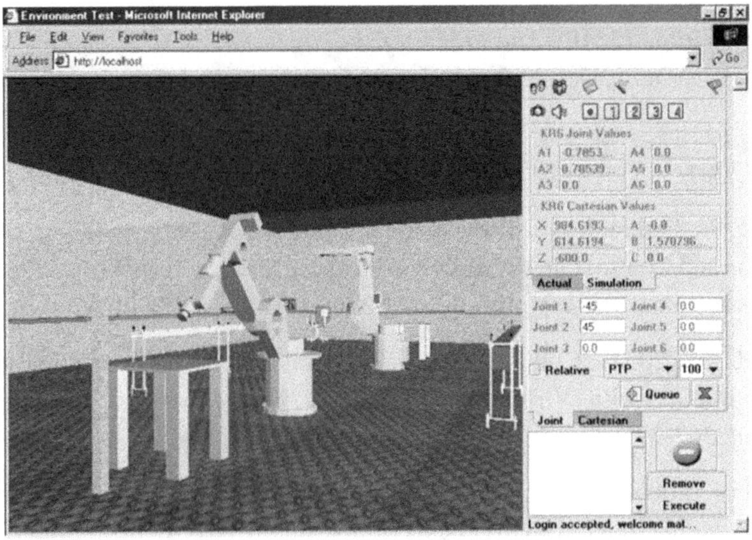

realities facilities through a Web-based collaborative and distributed intelligent environment (CoDIE). A prototype was built and demonstrated, The main purpose of the developed mixed realities robot system) is the education/training of robotics as well as web-technology and virtual reality. Current work is focusing on enhancing robot functionalities, having seamless interaction capabilities, awareness capabilities among users and environment, and adding more features to the implemented training modes. The developed CoDIE based interactive E-Learning system for robotics can connect resources from any universities-classrooms, industries, research centers and laboratories across the globe regardless of their physical locations. More analysis are currently investigated

AI and automation usage raises ethical, moral, privacy and security concerns. Among the negative effect automation and AI will eliminate jobs and open the way to demand people with new skills.The alignment of education and the need of the future labor market in the 21st century with jobs demand skills that are not considered with the current job market. Hence, it is the responsibilities of Education, policymakers, educators, academics, companies and individuals to conduct such transformation that facilitate the creation of new jobs. The developed system in this chapter can contribute to such needs.

REFERENCES

D2L Cooperation. (2018). *The Future of Work and Learning in the Age of the 4th Industrial Revolution.* Developed in Partnership with Colleges and Institutes Canada (CICAN).

Cross, J. (2004). An Informal History of E-Learning. *On the Horizon, 12*(3), 103-110.

Galkin, D. W., Parkin, R. M., Safaric, R., & Czarnecki, C. A. (1998). Visualisation, Simulation and Control of a Robotic System using Internet Technology. *Proc. of the 5th International Workshop on Advanced Motion Control*, 399-404.

Habib, M. K. (2001). Collaborative Telecontrol and Integrative User Interface Merging Reality with Virtuality. *IEEE-RAS 2nd International Conference on Humanoid*, 367-376.

Habib, M. K. (2006). Telecooperation Through Shared & Integrated Distributed and Collaborative Intelligent Environments Supporting Mixed Realities. *International SICE-ICCAS Conference*, 2639-2643.

Habib, M. K. (2008). Distributed Teleoperation and Collaborative Environment for Robotics E-Learning and Cooperation. *IEEE International Conference on Industrial Informatics (INDIN 2008)*, 1358-1363. 10.1109/INDIN.2008.4618315

Khan, B. H. (2005). *Managing E-Learning Strategies – Design, Delivery, Implementation and Evaluation*. Bangladesh: Information Science Publisher. doi:10.4018/978-1-59140-634-1

Kruse, E., & Dai, F. (2001). Virtual Training Using Web and Interactive Visualisation. *Proc. of the IFAC International Conference: Telematics Applications in Automation and Robotics*, 517-522. 10.1016/S1474-6670(17)41704-6

Luckin, R., Holmes, W., Griffiths, M., & Forcier, L. B. (2017). *Intelligence unleashed: An argument for AI in Education.* Pearson.

Morri, A. (1997). *Bright Future for Distance Learning: One Touch/Hughes Alliance Promotes Interactive 'E-learning' Service*. Telephony Online - Chicago, Telephony Penton Media.

Rosenberg, M. J. (2001). *E-Learning: Strategies for Delivering Knowledge in the Digital Age*. New York: McGraw-Hill.

Rossett, A. (2001). *Beyond The Podium: Delivering Training and Performance to a Digital World.* San Francisco: Jossey-Bass/Pfeiffer.

Truong, H. M. (2016). Computers in Human Behavior Integrating Learning Styles and Adaptive E-Learning System: Current Developments, Problems and Opportunities. *Computers in Human Behavior, 55*, 1185–1193. doi:10.1016/j.chb.2015.02.014

Wagner, E. (1998). Creating a Virtual University in a Traditional Environment. *Proceedings of the 7th European Distance Education Network.*

Wolf, B. P. (2009). *Building Intelligent Interactive Tutors: Student-Centered Strategies for Revolutionizing E-Learning*. Morgan Kaufmann Publishers.

KEY TERMS AND DEFINITIONS

Artificial Intelligence: Artificial intelligence (AI) is intelligence demonstrated by machines by adopting self-learning algorithms.

Artificial Neural Network (ANN): ANNs are computational networks composed of multiple nodes named neurons interacting with each other. The nodes can take input data and perform simple operations on the data.

Augmented Reality: Is an interactive experience of a real-world environment where the objects that reside in the real-world are enhanced by computer-generated perceptual information.

Data Mining: Is the process of discovering patterns in large data sets involving methods at the intersection of machine learning, statistics, and database systems.

E-Learning: It is interactive learner-centered interactive distance learning with aim to enhance knowledge and performance and it is expanded with the evolution of the information and communication technologies.

Industry 4.0: Is a name given to the current trend of automation and data exchange in manufacturing technologies.

Chapter 6
Virtual Laboratory to Face New Challenges in the Industry:
Virtual Laboratory as Part of the New Education Age

Arturo Soriano
https://orcid.org/0000-0003-3299-9851
Tecnologico de Estudios Superiores de Ixtapaluca, Mexico

Pedro Ponce
Tecnologico de Monterrey, Mexico

Arturo Molina
Tecnologico de Monterrey, Mexico

ABSTRACT

The fast-growing field of technology allows for the development, design, and implementation of smart solutions to several industries such as smart grid, manufacturing, automotive, and robotics. Trends in smart solutions are based on providing a certain degree of intelligence to the process and products through intelligent artificial and machine learning algorithms. It also involves further use of devices based on power electronics elements, fast microcontrollers, intelligent algorithms, and processing of information via local or cloud. Hence, a new workforce that possesses multidisciplinary skills (i.e., dealing with different fields of knowledge in order to find solutions to complex problems) is required. Recently, virtual laboratories have emerged so as to aid in the improvement of forming engineers. In this chapter, a virtual co-simulation laboratory is proposed to deal with the lack of engineers with multidisciplinary skills in mind; additionally, a new framework based in co-simulation, co-modeling, and co-design is proposed in order to maximize the use of the laboratory proposed.

DOI: 10.4018/978-1-5225-7793-5.ch006

INTRODUCTION

The recent inclusion and adoption of power electronics devices into several areas of the industries has enabled a fast production with high quality and low cost (van Wyk & Lee, 2013). The incorporation of these devices increases the functionality, security, reliability, efficiency, and interoperability of various process. Nowadays, the industries such as the smart-grid, manufacturing, automotive, and robotics have implemented and developed smart environments and smart devices in order to increase their functionalities and benefits (Quinn & Dalal, 2017). Smart-grid industry includes a high implementation of power electronics devices, and it promotes the interoperability between all stakeholders in the electrical grid. The modernization of power grids represents a reduction of global warming and greenhouse emissions. In order to achieve this renovation, the electrical industries require a workforce with multiple abilities and knowledge in several fields such as power electronics, automatic control, communication technologies, information technologies, public policy, algorithms to mention some (Shahidehpour, 2011; Steinbrink et al., 2017).

In the same direction, industrial advances combine production system planning, operation, and engineering with communication and information technologies (Colombo, Karnouskos, Shi, Yin, & Kaynak, 2016). The automatization in different industrial fields frequently is supported by industrial robots, which integrates the mechanized technology, electronic technology, material technology, and control technology in order to increase productivity in the industry (Yasuda, 2017). New production demands are related to manufacturing equipment, production line, and data acquisition. According to (Chen et al., 2018), the production objectives require a workforce with knowledge associated with the configurable controllers, self-configurable robots, data acquisition, communication protocols, and information algorithms. Similarly, the automotive industry has been dealing with different technical issues such as real-time data analysis, software, and hardware complexity, moreover non-technical issues like consumer preferences, and ethical concerns (Zhang, Zhang, Zhang, & Edmonds, 2016; Hussain & Zeadally, 2019).

Industrial problems and their solutions are moving towards the smart era which includes several fields of knowledge and requires a specialized workforce that posses multidisciplinary skills (Shahidehpour, 2011; Kurth, Schleyer, & Feuser, 2016; Potkonjak et al., 2016). The World Economic Forum presents the 10 skills which are recommended for the new workforce. Creativity, cognitive negotiation, coordination with others, and emotional intelligence are abilities which are added to the traditional abilities such as complex problems, critical thinking, people management, judgment and decision making, service orientation, and negotiation (World Economic Forum, 2018). In recent years, remote and virtual laboratories have been implemented in order to provide a real scenario to learn, practice, and understand real-world applications (Budai & Kuczmann, 2018). The remote and virtual laboratories help to improve the learning outcome such as practical skills, inquiry skills, analytical skills, perception, knowledge and understanding (Brinson, 2015). The remote laboratory enables a remote connection to a real laboratory, which is commonly used to manipulate, operate, and made experiments of a specific area of knowledge. In like manner, the virtual laboratory is a local server network that enables a virtual space to simulate, analyze, and control specific systems (Kumar et al., 2018; Potkonjak et al., 2016).

This chapter is divided into six sections, the first section a brief description of recent advances of the smart-grid industry, manufacturing industry, automotive industry, and the robotics industry is presented. The second section shows the architecture, advantages, and disadvantages of virtual laboratories. The third section introduces C^3 framework which is based on co-simulation, co-design, and co-modeling. C^3 is presented as a tool in order to maximize the virtual laboratory benefits. Section four presents and describe a virtual co-simulation laboratory proposed. Section five shows a case study about the design of power electronic drive using the laboratory and C^3 framework proposed. Finally, section six describes future research directions.

RECENT ADVANCES

The inclusion of a certain degree of intelligence into devices represents a difficult problem being that the development of solutions and applications requires specialized engineers that are able to deal with this kind of challenges. The problems in the industries have been transformed due to the high incorporation of technologies. Therefore, the aforementioned problems require solutions that involve various domains of knowledge. In this section, the transformation of the smart-grid, manufacturing, automotive, and robotic industries, as well as their necessity of engineers with multidisciplinary skills is presented.

Smart-Grid

The modernization of electrical grids represents a big challenge for governments, industries, engineers, researchers, and current users since the current electrical infrastructure will eventually transform into a smart-grid. This transformation affects all stages of the electrical grid such as generation, transmission, distribution and consumption. The advanced infrastructure installation along the electrical grid is necessary for improve the security, quality and cost of electrical grids, as well as provide resilience to the electrical grid.

The intelligent devices will be installed and integrated into this infrastructure in order to increase their functionality and provide bidirectional communication throughout the electrical grid. An intelligent device includes sensors, communication protocols, data storage and controllers. Frequently, the aforementioned devices are integrated by power electronics elements, controllers installed within of the microcontrollers, and includes communication protocols and storage functions. Electrical grid modernization takes into account several areas of knowledge such as power electronics, an automatic control, and mechanical, electrical, communication and information technologies.

Manufacturing Industry

The increase of product demand requires competitive companies that have the potential to achieve production demand with high quality in the less possible time. The recent technological advances are facilitators used to reach the major benefits in production. The common features of modern manufacturing are cost, dependability, flexibility, quality, and speed. The cost is related to machine operation and general labor, dependability focuses on delivering the demand of production on time, flexibility enables changing attributes of the production systems, and the quality is emphasized into the ability to increase the functionality of the machines material in order to deliver a product with high quality, and finally the speed is very important to respond to customer demand. Modern manufacturing considers all these features in order to gain a higher value in their process. Hence, a manufacturing system also involves activities, mechanisms, monitoring, control, communication technologies, information technologies, and the transformation of raw materials into a product.

Automotive Industry

In recent years, the applications of power electronics in the automotive industry have been growing due to development the electric vehicles (Richardson, 2013). The Modern vehicles are integrated by complex systems which increase the use of software applications since these applications are designed to improve safety, comfort, and efficiency. The modern applications in the automotive industry can be grouped as control systems, telematics systems, and advanced driver assistance systems.

The trend of vehicles is using and installing even more complex systems, which will enable new ways to use vehicles and change the way of interacting with them. The main technological advances allow the implementation and development of new platforms as well as interconnecting it with other intelligent applications in order to monitor all systems involve in the vehicles. New platforms include software applications which are focused on guarantee the passengers' security, at the same time that recollects data to share with other devices and applications, and as a result, all collected data are used to increase the capability and functionality of vehicles.

Robotic Industry

The increase of robotic adoption in several industries and applications has been growing. The robot's implementation and smart device incorporation can result in the design of a smart factory, which allows rapid manufacturing of products and optimization of the supply chain. The robots are the link between the process and the users which means that the user can access the data to improve the process. The information access that before was inaccessible can also achieve by cloud-based systems or client-server.

The incorporation of information and communication technologies enables for the acquisition and processing of data. The recent trends and problems are not only structure, control, and management, but also includes the organization and analysis of all of the collected information. The growth of virtual design as a solution of a proof concept has been gaining attention because it reduces the time and decision as well as offering several work scenarios.

Virtual Laboratory

In the past decade, virtual laboratories were developed for several reasons, for example, to improve learning quality, to allow remote access and to train a large number of people. A virtual laboratory is frequently integrated by specialized software which enables the emulation of scenarios that in real life are risky and complex (Potkonjak et al., 2016; Hircca, Necati, 2017), some examples are the design of high voltage controllers for the electrical grid, a new power drive to electric motors, the study of semiconductors lifetime.

The virtual laboratories allow the simulation of a real process through computational tools, which offer speed and security in the design solutions to complex problems (Kumar et al., 2018). These laboratories present some benefits during experimental activities since they provide a quick and safe way to make measurements, in comparison with the conventional laboratories where the same process is very slow and/or complex, and involves health risks. The advantages and disadvantages of a traditional virtual laboratory according to (Budai & Kuczmann, 2018; Potkonjak et al., 2016) can be described as shown in Table 1.

Table 1. Advantages and disadvantages of virtual laboratories

Advantages	Disadvantages
• Accessible anytime, from anywhere. • Create experiments in a self-taught way. • The experiments can be a good approximation to reality. •Mathematical models can be an approximation to reality. •Lower operational cost and it is cheaper to generate new experiments.	• Lack of hands-on contact with devices and equipment. • Low level discipline and caution. • Can be considered as a video game by students. • All details of real system transform the mathematical model in complex model. •Experiments have purpose of education and demonstration.

Architecture

The architecture of a conventional virtual laboratory can be integrated by an internet connection or a local network, a virtual server and simulation servers as shown in Figure 1. The virtual server provides and delivers applications to users through web pages. It also establishes communication between the client and simulation applications. The simulation server has applications that model, process and solve dynamic systems for a specific field. Sometimes, the simulation presents some limitations that are commonly related to the accuracy of the mathematical model. The mathematical model is an approximation of a real system that is described by differential equations. The models can consider some phenomenon or assume them and this reflects their reliability.

C^3 Framework

The recent advances in several industries such as the robotic, electrical grid, automotive, manufacturing and the use increase of device of electronic technology such as DC-DC converters, DC-AC inverts, and AC-DC rectifiers require new engineers with a multidisciplinary formation to face the new challenges head-on. The new workforce needs experience in proposing solutions which involve various fields of knowledge, for example, if it is necessary to develop a new power electronic device that includes a communication protocol for the automotive or smart-grid industry. The new engineers should be capable of proposing a solution that considers the controller design, electronic design, communication technologies to use, and their operation as a whole system. This is combined with the main objective to reduce cost, materials, and production time, as well as to increase production quality and efficiency. The multidisciplinary formation of engineers required to provide instruments and experience to new engineers in order to find solutions. The co-

Figure 1. Virtual laboratory architecture

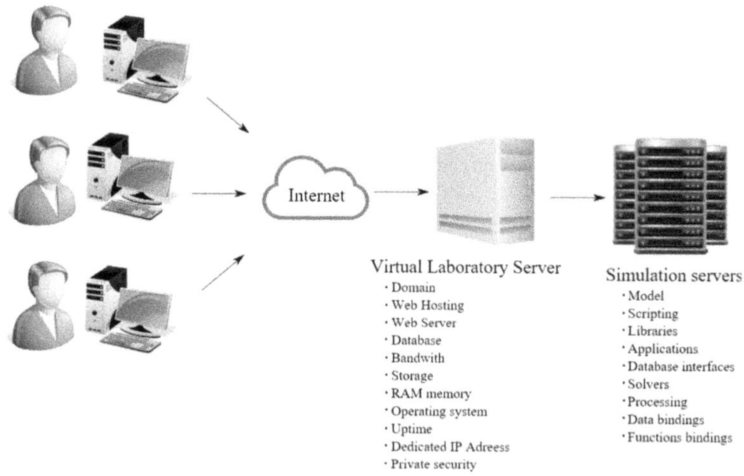

simulation, co-modeling, and co-design are instruments that help in the process of the formulation and design of solutions for complex applications. In this work, a C^3 framework is proposed in order to provide to the engineers with an instrument that facilitates the design and finding of solutions, this framework is shown in Figure 2.

Co-Simulation

Co-simulation is a solution that combines multiple domains to allow a global simulation of a coupled system through the composition of specialized simulators (Palensky, Meer, Lopez, Joseph, & Pan, 2017; Steinbrink et al., 2017). The traditional simulation design is focused on a single domain, which can be power electronics, automatic control, or communication technology. Thus, the simulation of these systems needs a dynamic model for each domain. The solution of mathematical models depends on the solvers that have each simulator. In this context, the time of implementation is affected by the difference with reality. The simulators present good results according to the parameters and solvers where are designed but a real system works as a whole. Hence, the implementation requires time for the tuning of some parameters. A co-simulation enables the reduction of time in the design process and the solution implementation as well as the tuning of parameters, and integrate several simulators in order to analyze the system as a whole.

Figure 2. Co-simulation, co-modelling and co-design framework

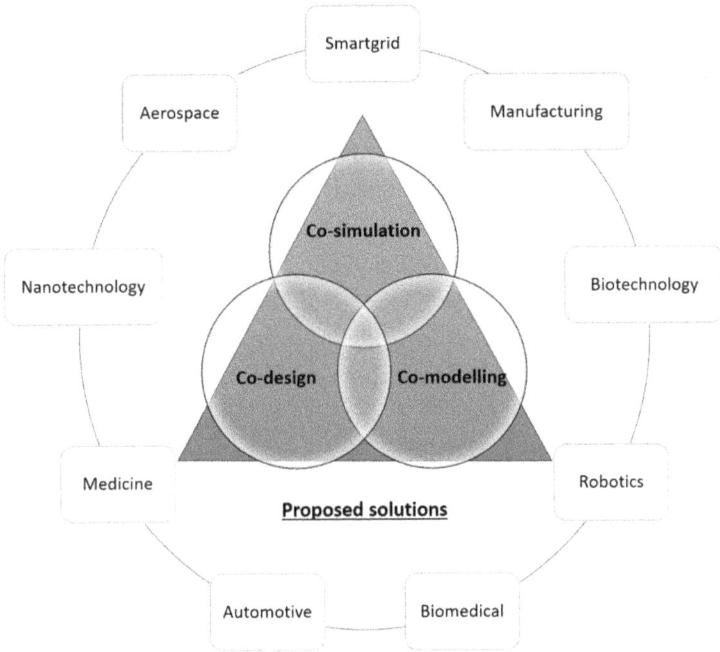

Co-Modelling

The description of reality can be performed through models, which can be classified as continuous-time and discrete-event models. Continuous-time commonly describes reality or the system dynamics through differential equations, and discrete-events is used to describe system logic. The current applications are integrated by using microprocessors and computers that increase the functionality of dynamic systems or processes (Gomes, Thule, Broman, Larsen, & Vangheluwe, 2017). The use of embedded systems has been increased in several complex applications for the industry since they provide a certain degree of intelligence for the devices. As a result, some processes are able to increase their potential. This makes the devices have a dependency on embedded systems being that they provide a computational tool.

Co-Design

The current challenges require integrating elements and tools that allow and help to design a solution for complex problems. The inclusion of consumers and users of services and products in the solution design increased the creativity, innovation, and improvements to the end proposal (Lumsakul, Sheldrick, & Rahimifard, 2018). This is called co-design which involves the experience of the end-user or service in the phase creation, design process and end products. Co-design changes the traditional way of design and enables the creative formulation, contribution and solution of complex problems. The features that describe co-design are the principles of the generation of better ideas through the feedback of stakeholders since they provide their experiences, knowledge and expert skills in the field. The principle of respect is related to all ideas and inputs are also valued, as well as iterative design because of the solutions that are continuously tested and evaluated, and finally the principle outcomes-focused is focus on the potential of the solution is rapidly tested and measured. As a result, the main idea of the co-design is to provide a structure and tools to design a solution to solve a complex problem.

Co-Simulation Virtual Laboratory

A virtual co-simulation laboratory is proposed to be an integrative, traditional class where students can improve their knowledge and gain experience regarding complex applications. Hence, the experiments and practices in a virtual co-simulation laboratory are suggested as being complementary. The laboratory can be implemented along the engineer's formation. Naturally the laboratory participant needs to possess previous knowledge being that complex applications are commonly integrated by various domains of knowledge. In this work, a novel design of virtual laboratory that considers a co-simulation as an engine that supports exchanges of different dynamic models is proposed. The co-simulation virtual laboratory enables design solution through C^3 framework and its design integrate the conventional virtual laboratory and the co-simulation features. Figure 3 shows the design of a co-simulation virtual laboratory, where FMU is the Functional Mock-up Interface which is an industrial standard (Fitzgerald, Larsen, & Verhoef, 2014). FMU is an instrument that enables the information exchange between model and co-simulation of dynamic models. The combination of c-code and XML-code files are used to support the aforementioned exchange in the FMU. This standard is designed to support the simulation of complex systems by coupling several models and their own solver in a heterogeneous environment. The advantages that the virtual laboratory presents and the C^3 uses to increase the creativity, active participation of end-users, customers, patients, and stakeholders in order to face the big issues and challenges.

Integration in Education

According to the World Economic Forum, emerging technologies are transforming the workforce (World Economic Forum, 2018). The top 10 skills are:

Figure 3. Co-simulation virtual laboratory

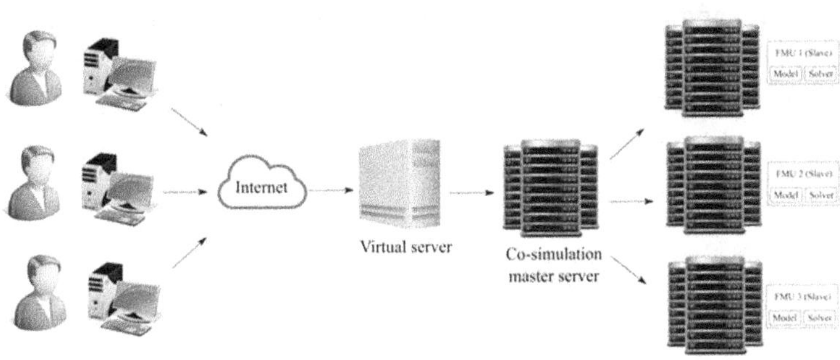

1. Complex problem solving.
2. Critical thinking.
3. Creativity.
4. People management.
5. Coordinating with others.
6. Emotional intelligence.
7. Judgment and decision making.
8. Service orientation.
9. Negotiation.
10. Cognitive flexibility.

A virtual co-simulation laboratory is proposed to be an integrative, traditional class where students can improve their knowledge and gain experience regarding complex applications. Hence, the experiments and practices in a virtual co-simulation laboratory are suggested as being complementary. The virtual laboratory can be implemented along the engineer's formation. Naturally the laboratory participant needs to possess previous knowledge being that complex applications are commonly integrated by several different domains of knowledge. Additionally, C^3 framework helps the development of multidisciplinary skills like creativity, analysis of complex problems, proposal solutions, teamwork, and gain experience in the real process to propose a solution to a complex problem. Hence, the instructors can modify their evaluations in order to consider the development of multidisciplinary skills and the acquisition of new knowledge.

There are several evaluation methodologies such as Problems Based on Research (PBR), Problems Based on Learning (PBL), and Problems Based on Challenges (PBC). Hence, the evaluation should take into account the development of new experimental, process, logic, and critical thinking skills. According to the Project Based Learning (PBL) methodology, the students can develop critical thinking, communication, and creativity skills as well as deep content knowledge when they are solving and doing a real problem. This proposal allows students to reflect and establish the link between theory and practice in addition to the skills developed by the students which are focused on developing experimental context, formulate hypotheses, experiment analysis, and critical reasoning skills.

SOLUTIONS AND RECOMMENDATIONS

Case Study

Nowadays, the design of power electronics solutions is considered a complex task since it not only involves a field of knowledge but also other fields such as the control, digital, computational systems. The case study presents the control design to improve the lifetime of an electric drive in a virtual laboratory. An electric drive is an electrical circuit or device that uses a command signal to control another circuit or device. Their main applications are in electronic circuits and electric machines which are considered to be complex applications. In these applications, the lifetime of the semiconductors is affected because they are operating at high frequencies, voltages, currents, and temperatures. These applications involve several domains of knowledge such as power electronics, an automatic control, and computing. Hence, the power electronics theory is essential in order to recognize the features and behavior of each power electronics element, thus simulation enables us to learn power electronics elements functions. In the same way, the control systems theory is necessary in order to propose solutions for complex systems. Undergraduate students should take the control systems course before enrolling in this kind of course with a virtual laboratory since the knowledge of complex applications requires students to have a previous theory about control systems. The power electronics design can be simulated in Multisim™ and the control design can be simulated in Labview™. National Instruments also provides a co-simulation tool in order to simulate a complex system as shown in Figure 4.

The fact that the sensing of the temperature of power elements during their operation is difficult, hence the co-simulation offers instruments to find and propose a solution. For example, the simulation of electronic circuit in Multisim™ and a design of controller that consider the temperature changes in the Labview™, can result in a solution that improve the lifetime of semiconductors in electric drives. Finally, the co-simulation virtual laboratory can improve student's knowledge about complex applications since they can build and analyze several scenarios and solutions, being that these kinds of problems also demand powerful and flexible as well as cost-effective solutions. Thus, a virtual co-simulation laboratory can be a solution

Figure 4. Electric drive design in the co-simulation virtual laboratory

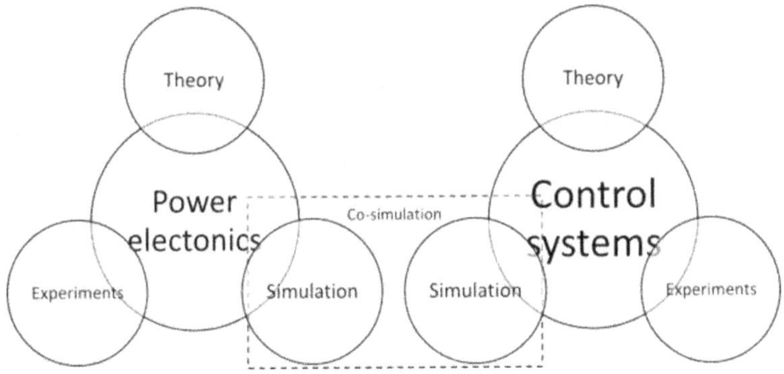

in order to reach these objectives. In addition, students can acquire perception and expertise related to designing a solution in a real-life situation through gaining experience solving complex and real applications.

FUTURE RESEARCH DIRECTIONS

Virtual and remote laboratories enable a tool in order to carry out experiments which are commonly costly and dangerous. In recent years, the development of virtual and remotes laboratories has been increased since they can benefit to many people via remote and offer a virtual space to simulate hard experiments. The new challenges in several industries demand a workforce with multidisciplinary skills, for that reason is important to develop laboratories that include several fields of knowledge. Develop new education and evaluation methodologies in order to integrate the laboratories into the traditional formation of engineers. The implementation of specialized laboratories such as smart-grid, robotic, and manufactory represent a high cost of acquisition, operation, and maintenance to several educational institutions. However, there are few advances in this direction, but they are necessary in order to face the new challenges of industries. Finally, the availability of laboratory is a distinguishing feature to take into consideration since it is required to carry out a self-management and remote access to the platform during the 24 hours and 365 days of the year.

CONCLUSION

The design of a co-simulation virtual laboratory enables the access to a specialized technology that can be integrated into an engineer's formation. This proposal increases the benefits of the conventional design of a virtual laboratory since specialized software packages can be integrated. This laboratory allows for the proposed design and solutions testing related to several different domains of knowledge. The training of a workforce that possesses multidisciplinary skills can be done through this laboratory and use of a C^3 scheme. The framework C^3 is proposed to facilitate the creative process since it involves several specialized technologies and all stakeholders, as well as offer a virtual platform to propose costly and danger solutions.

ACKNOWLEDGMENT

This research is a product of the Project 266632 "Laboratorio Binacional para la Gestión Inteligente de la Sustentabilidad Energética y la Formación Tecnológica" ["Bi-National Laboratory on Smart Sustainable Energy Management and Technology Training"], funded by the CONACYT SENER Fund for Energy Sustainability (Agreement: S0019201401).

REFERENCES

Brinson, J. R. (2015). Learning outcome achievement in non-traditional (virtual and remote) versus traditional (hands-on) laboratories: A review of the empirical research. *Computers & Education*, *87*, 218–237. doi:10.1016/j.compedu.2015.07.003

Budai, T., & Kuczmann, M. (2018). Towards a Modern, Integrated Virtual Laboratory System. *Acta Polytechnica Hungarica*, *15*(3), 14.

Chen, B., Wan, J., Shu, L., Li, P., Mukherjee, M., & Yin, B. (2018). Smart Factory of Industry 4.0: Key Technologies, Application Case, and Challenges. *IEEE Access: Practical Innovations, Open Solutions*, *6*, 6505–6519. doi:10.1109/ACCESS.2017.2783682

Colombo, A. W., Karnouskos, S., Shi, Y., Yin, S., & Kaynak, O. (2016). Industrial Cyber–Physical Systems. *Proceedings of the IEEE*, *104*(5), 899–903. doi:10.1109/JPROC.2016.2548318

Fitzgerald, J., Larsen, P. G., & Verhoef, M. (Eds.). (2014). Collaborative Design for Embedded Systems. Academic Press. doi:10.1007/978-3-642-54118-6

Gomes, C., Thule, C., Broman, D., Larsen, P. G., & Vangheluwe, H. (2017). *Co-simulation: State of the art.* Retrieved from http://arxiv.org/abs/1702.00686

Hircca, N. (2017). The Influence of Hands on Physics Experiments on Scientific Process Skills According to Prospective Teachers' Experiences. *European Journal of Physics Education, 4*(2), 6–14.

Hussain, R., & Zeadally, S. (2019). Autonomous Cars: Research Results, Issues, and Future Challenges. *IEEE Communications Surveys and Tutorials, 21*(2), 1275–1313. doi:10.1109/COMST.2018.2869360

Kumar, D., Radhamani, R., Nizar, N., Achuthan, K., Nair, B., & Diwakar, S. (2018). *Virtual and remote laboratories augment self learning and interactions: Development, deployment and assessments with direct and online feedback.* Academic Press. doi:10.7287/peerj.preprints.26715v1

Kurth, M., Schleyer, C., & Feuser, D. (2016). Smart factory and education: An integrated automation concept. 2016 IEEE 11th Conference on Industrial Electronics and Applications (ICIEA), 1057–1061. 10.1109/ICIEA.2016.7603738

Lumsakul, P., Sheldrick, L., & Rahimifard, S. (2018). The Sustainable Co-Design of Products and Production Systems. *Procedia Manufacturing, 21*, 854–861. doi:10.1016/j.promfg.2018.02.193

Palensky, P., Meer, A. A. V. D., Lopez, C. D., Joseph, A., & Pan, K. (2017). Cosimulation of Intelligent Power Systems: Fundamentals, Software Architecture, Numerics, and Coupling. *IEEE Industrial Electronics Magazine, 11*(1), 34–50. doi:10.1109/MIE.2016.2639825

Potkonjak, V., Gardner, M., Callaghan, V., Mattila, P., Guetl, C., Petrović, V. M., & Jovanović, K. (2016). Virtual laboratories for education in science, technology, and engineering: A review. *Computers & Education, 95*, 309–327. doi:10.1016/j.compedu.2016.02.002

Quinn, C. A., & Dalal, D. B. (2017). Empowering the electronics industry: A power technology roadmap. *CPSS Transactions on Power Electronics and Applications, 2*(4), 306–319. doi:10.24295/CPSSTPEA.2017.00028

Richardson, D. B. (2013). Electric vehicles and the electric grid: A review of modeling approaches, Impacts, and renewable energy integration. *Renewable & Sustainable Energy Reviews*, *19*, 247–254. doi:10.1016/j.rser.2012.11.042

Shahidehpour, M. (2011, November). *Smart Grid Education and Workforce Training Center*. doi:10.1109/ISGT-Asia.2011.6167128

Steinbrink, C., Lehnhoff, S., Rohjans, S., Strasser, T. I., Widl, E., Moyo, C., … Degefa, M. Z. (2017). *Simulation-based Validation of Smart Grids - Status Quo and Future Research Trends*. doi:10.1007/978-3-319-64635-0_13

Van Wyk, J. D., & Lee, F. C. (2013). On a Future for Power Electronics. *IEEE Journal of Emerging and Selected Topics in Power Electronics*, *1*(2), 59–72. doi:10.1109/JESTPE.2013.2271499

World Economic Forum. (2018). *The 10 skills you need to thrive in the Fourth Industrial Revolution*. Retrieved December 14, 2018, from World Economic Forum website: https://www.weforum.org/agenda/2016/01/the-10-skills-you-need-to-thrive-in-the-fourth-industrial-revolution/

Yasuda, K. (2017). The future vision of industrial robot. 2017 29th International Symposium on Power Semiconductor Devices and IC's (ISPSD), 7–12. 10.23919/ISPSD.2017.7988979

Zhang, F., Zhang, X., Zhang, M., & Edmonds, A. S. E. (2016). Literature review of electric vehicle technology and its applications. 2016 5th International Conference on Computer Science and Network Technology (ICCSNT), 832–837. 10.1109/ICCSNT.2016.8070276

KEY TERMS AND DEFINITIONS

Co-Design: The belief that the participation user in the design process of a project increases the creativity and promote their preferences, necessities, and ideology in order to find a better solution.

Co-Modeling: A belief that validation of complex systems can be via software continuous or discrete models of hardware models through a transaction-based interface, which is commonly made by FPGA devices.

Co-Simulation: The belief that exchange between specialized packages of software facilitates the analysis and design of solutions to complex systems.

Framework: A conceptual structure that facilitates the resolution of complex problems or complex process.

Multidisciplinary Skills: Abilities that can facilitate the process to find solutions to complex problems from several perspectives.

Remote Laboratory: A physical laboratory that can be accessed via remote. Secure and low-risk access is enabled by a web system in order to teleoperate specialized equipment.

Virtual Laboratory: A server of applications that offers specialized packages of software to emulate different fields of knowledge.

Chapter 7
Impact of Social and Cultural Challenges in Education Using AI

Kapil Sethi
Shoolini University, India

Ajay Sharma
Shoolini University, India

Shweta Chauhan
Shoolini University, India

Varun Jaiswal
https://orcid.org/0000-0001-8068-0672
Shoolini University, India

ABSTRACT

Learning is the main feature that is connected to education. Education increases the power of visualization and to differentiate between the right and wrong. Education in these days has become expensive for the poor guardians. Education indeed helps to know the real values in relation to social and cultural behavior so that one can become a decent person in nature in society. The role of technology in modern education helps to lookout the current trends and to solve the problems using artificial intelligence in education. AI tools play a vital role in research and help to access the literature worldwide. AI can also provide the solution to social challenges like diversity in nature, security, and privacy of the person. Apart from education, AI has made an impact in other fields like social media, communication, and technology.

DOI: 10.4018/978-1-5225-7793-5.ch007

INTRODUCTION

Education is a necessary tool for the development of the nation. The vast majority of the population in the world would believe that success and to earn money is a critical factor, however, it isn't right in light of the fact that without education, no one can get success for which learning the social and cultural values (Owens, 1995). Learning is the main feature as well as a tool which is connected to education to learn and know different things which invariably helps to educate more and more students/persons in the area around. Almost all the time one question always arises in the mind of students that "Why education is so important?" and the answer is because it is a more important part of our life (Morreale & Pearson, 2008). Education is such a great amount of imperative for accomplishment throughout our everyday life. Without the education, one cannot explore the new thoughts which indicate that they are not ready to build up the world in the light of the fact that without thoughts there is no creativity and without creativity, there is no development. Over the world, some nations may be more developed and some are certainly not (Wals & Jickling, 2002). The nation which is developing, the more educated individual's ratio compares to the nation which is not as much of developed. Education is the mechanism which gives the individuals the required learning, information, skill, technique, and allows them to know their rights and duties toward their family, society, and the country (Gartner & Lipsky, 1987). Education increases the power of visualization, so one can outlook to see the world easily. Education builds up the capacities and the capabilities to fight the unfairness, violence, exploitation and other elements (Dewey, 2007). Similarly, as the face is the reflection of the heart, the level of education builds the status of the state or the country. In many different nations, the structure resembles that rich students get gradually more education and poor won't (Delpit, 2006). Education in these days has become expensive and the poor guardians of the utmost capable students can't consider getting their wards admitted into such institutes (Sallis, 2014). We require a framework that will give an equal amount of chances to both rich and poor students who in turn can contribute to the improvement and development of the nation. By providing education, we eliminate the destitution and each individual in the nation will become popular and contributes their involvement in developing their nation (Hofstede, 1986).

According to Nelson Mandela, the most famous person tells about education "Education is the most influential weapon which you can use to transform the world" (Mandela, 2014). Education turns out to be great guardians, students, business people, specialists, relatives and honest people (B. U. Levinson, 2001). Being in contact with an educated individual and having a smart discussion with him extends learning and presents a specific inventiveness and satisfaction in the mind (Cole & Shastry, 2009). Education makes the national improvement process quick (Fägerlind & Saha,

2016). The way of life of its people can be reliant up to a great extent, the Nationals can secure. The importance of education and its essentialness can be comprehended from the way that when we are conceived, our societies begin educating us around a fundamental thing throughout in everyday life (Fägerlind & Saha, 2016). A baby starts adapting new words and builds up a vocabulary based on what his folks teach him. They teach him who is his dad, mother, sister, brother etc. and how to carry on with every individual giving them due regard (Von Glasersfeld, 1998). They also convey him precious knowledge about morals and ethics appropriate from the earliest starting point when he has a delicate nature so these characteristics remain within him for as long as he can reminisce as conditioning (Noddings, 2013).

How we act with our blood relation and how much respect we have for our seniors is an immediate result of our essential education in our childhood times (Lickona, 1996). So it is right to state that a person's underlying education starts at his home. Guardians manage their youngster not that simply into the initial steps when he begins figuring out how to walk; they also guide them on the steps to be taken with behaviour, ethical quality and regard (Eisner, 2017). They teach him about the law and values of humanity and why they should be monitored to become a decent person. As the child develops more established, his aspirations and wants to become greater and guardians attempt their best to give him the finest educational situation to make his dreams come true (Zipes, 2013). Today, the current educational structure has been reduced to an exchange of directions and information and nothing more. While in prior cases the thought process of education was to fill great qualities and ethics in a person's awareness (Best & Kahn, 2016). Today we have floated away from this ideology due to the quick commercialization in the training part.

In the present time, it is critical to think about the essentialness of a decent education. A decent education does not just comprise of going to school or college to get a degree. It goes past that. In the event that somebody can read or compose, has attended the classes and achieved a degree, it doesn't mean he is fully educated (Bourdieu & Nice, 1977). This is only a section of the education that makes one attentive of what is significant on the planet and since the vast majority of the world needs a degree. In this procedure, he gets the ability to recognize what is essential for him, what is right or wrong. In figure 1, it shows their education based problems and its solution with AI.

Some of the important factors who shows "why education is so important in our life".

1. Moral education makes an individual grow socially as well as monetarily. Education makes us loyal and encourages to perform our daily life exercises in most ideal ways (Doran, 1981), obtain new abilities, acquire new skills and

Figure 1. Common problems and their solution

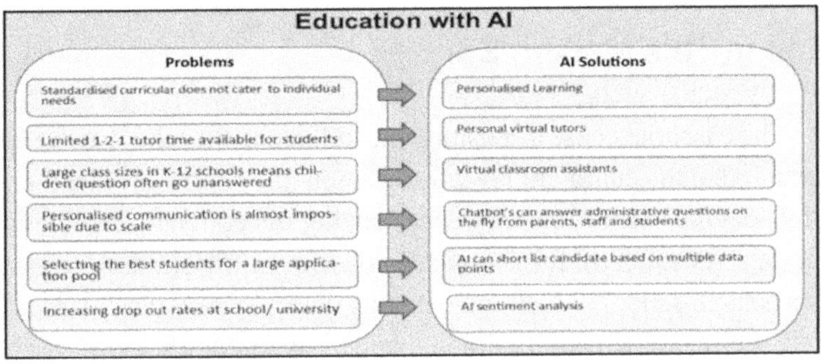

awareness that improves life throughout every day (Seligman, Ernst, Gillham, Reivich, & Linkins, 2009).

2. Education gives an individual all the essential tools and awareness about how he can earn his daily meals (Eisenberg, 2010). He always gets knowledge about how he can raise the status of life while satisfying his family's everyday necessities.
3. Education makes an individual aware of his rights and duties. He/she realizes his responsibility to practice his capacity to vote and choose a decent representative among elections (Apple, 2013).
4. A noble education enlightens the craft of living to an individual without bounds. It edifies him to best utilize the country's assets for development.
5. An individual becomes a better judge to recognize the true from false and good from bad (Stocker, 1979).
6. Education gives individual learning about great qualities, moral and good duties throughout life.
7. Being educated, a man can fight with the different social shades and feels enabled to eliminate such issues (Sharp, Green, & Lewis, 2017).
8. An educated politician knows how to behave publically and how to converse with the media appropriately. He also recognizes the requirements and aspirations of the general public and gives it his best shot to fulfill them.
9. An educated professional treats people with empathy, modesty and truly considers their welfare through every single accessible approach.
10. A talented educator teaches his students efficiently and knows how to use optimum knowledge and education for the general improvement of society (Glaser, 1984).
11. An educated society can assist everybody with individual growth and development in their separate fields.

BACKGROUND

Education in This Modern Era

1. Today the essential cause of pushing the kid into a pre-school at the tender age of three is that the guardians are worried about the possibility that their kid will be "left-behind" who are really experiencing the equivalent careless practice every day (Asis, 2006). It is a typical sight to see little children carrying really heavy bags to school, which really stunts their physical development.
2. Today, the major sensibility among student is to contest extreme challenges for a specific degree to get a specific position. Along these lines, education has turned out to be remarkably commercialised and relatively like a business today, with institutes charging high expenses for degrees which promise good placements since they have "tie-ups" with the organizations (Marginson, 2006). Yet at the same time, they are leaving their occupations following 3-4 months or the greater part of them is not fulfilled.
3. Currently, a majority of students are going into such foundations which have great marketing and promoting policy and which make grand guarantees to invite individuals amid confirmation times (Smith & Piele, 2006). So individuals are not influenced by the teachers and the excellence of teaching but the notices and special movements being controlled by the foundation.
4. It is noticed that each educated individual knows how to converse nicely with people from everywhere in this world, but they have failed to recall how to talk respectfully to elders in their own families such as parents and others. Today the only goal of getting training has been lessened to acquiring money and nothing more.
5. A person's improvement and the manner in which education is spread among individuals are affected by society's commitment to a vast degree (Lasswell, 1948; Trow, 2007). Our general public should endeavour to make a domain that is useful for all area of society in getting a decent education.

It is the education which makes us good human being and distinguishes us from further alive creatures on earth. It is our education that provides us with the learning and abilities to utilize our imaginative gifts to their greatest potential (Scott, Mcguire, & Shaw, 2003). To have a good life and to get the thoughtful and physical satisfaction that goes on for quite a while, it is significant to get taught. No one but education can assist our general public with progressing further and education is the main component that is similarly noteworthy for all organizations, ethnicity and social gatherings since it has the ability to inspire everybody (Seidman, 2013).

Education is a way of updating our aptitudes and accomplishing more learning and standout amongst other means believable (Tuckman & Harper, 2012). Education begins at home so we should find a way to guarantee that the earth in our homes is useful for our kids to learn however much as could reasonably be expected (Delpit, 1988). Other than our homes, we ought to likewise endeavor to contribute from our side as much as we can for the advancement of our society and our country.

MAIN FOCUS OF THE CHAPTER

1. The Role of Technology in the Education of the Future

As we set out on the Fourth Industrial Revolution, plainly innovation will assume a focal job in almost all parts of our lives (Cortese, 2003). Research by the World Economic Forum evaluates that 65% of kids entering elementary school will wind up in occupations that today don't exist (Elder, 2018). By 2020 its evaluated there will be 1.5 million new digitized employments over the globe. In the meantime, 90% of associations right now have IT aptitudes deficiency, while 75% of instructors and studies reflect a hole in their capacity to meet the needs of the IT workforce. To set up the ability required for the advanced economy, instructions must be adjusted as quick as the interest for IT aptitudes is growing with time (Csorny, 2013). Experiences from the impact of psychological, social and ecological factors are rising up out of "the new art of learning" (Becker & Luthar, 2002). This way to manage understanding and guidance clashes in our complex and rapidly propelling present reality, educational models in light of interdisciplinary research which are essential to make great teaching and learning conditions.

2. Collaborative Deep Learning

Today the science's extended perspective is revealing new ways to deal with education. A main logical expert on creativeness and learning, emphasises the intensity of innovation to influence and improve the academic community by giving encounters that prompt deep learning (Blumenfeld, Kempler, & Krajcik, 2006). These enable the students to learn cooperatively, test out, reshape models and grasp knowledge both visually and verbally. Imagine a classroom containing remote technology, remotely available switches, routers and a synchronized tool to create "intelligent" environment for the innovation of true Internet of Things (IoT) items, management and encounters by students (Sivakumar, Robertson, Artimy, & Aslam, 2005; Watson, McKeown, & Casado, 2006). Creation happens in various scenes for instance, in the classroom amid task-based learning or nearby energetic innovation peers by means

Figure 2. AI connect with society and culture

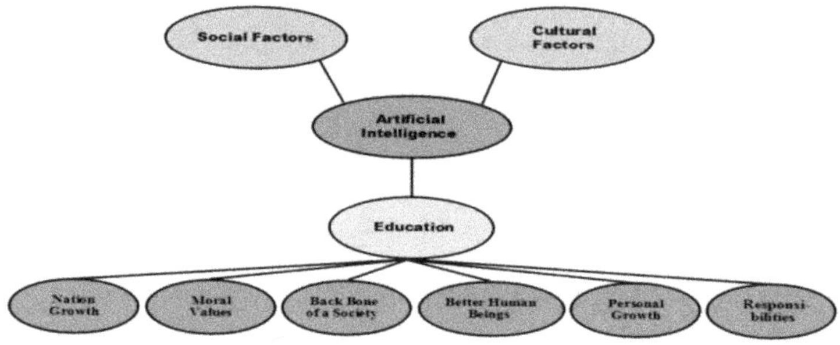

of hackathons (Nandi & Mandernach, 2016). Students display the systems they make in a test system and model with cloud-based innovation at home. Instructors are empowered with a customisable learning organization while cooperating with friend teachers over the world. Learning science's interdisciplinary bits of knowledge are innovating new ways to deal with education. By applying learning science bits of information to IT instruction [56], we can make a dynamic, mechanized and hands-on learning foundation that is specially crafted, versatile, related and developing the capacity anticipated that would control the propelled economy.

3. Understanding Learning Science's Impact on Education

Through its Education dominance model, the U.S. Naval force built up computerized reasoning based coaching framework to imitate the practices of extraordinary guides (Burton & Brown, 1979). Innovation and hands-on labs drive this framework with understudy results identical to or outperforming those utilizing the human mentor. The stage is likewise adaptable in a way not managed by face to face guides. Including advanced devices extends the alternatives and reach of customized education framework. For instance, supplementing the intensity of face to face and online instructors, learning and evaluation improved with organized advanced devices can be exceptionally powerful.

4. Society and Culture

a. Supporting The Growth of the Nation

Exceptionally educated individuals benefit the countries to grow (Faure, 1972). Strategy creators and officers continuously attempt to make a superior condition in society. A country won't be considered as a prevailing country in the event if it doesn't have great quality human resources. Educated business are producing service and paying assignment to manufacture better foundation in the nation (Jongbloed, Enders, & Salerno, 2008). Researchers are working continuously to make a superior world. There are distinct social advantages of education and the countries are its observer.

b. Moral Values

An educated individual will probably grow better for good and moral qualities contrasted with an uneducated individual. The absence of education makes problems like superstition, aggressive behaviour at home, weakness and poor expectations for everyday comforts (Hunter, 2008). An educated individual knows the significance of neatness and cleanliness. Education will rise to open the door for both man and women and educated individuals will have the capacity to make a sound society.

c. Back Bone of a Society

Educated individuals are the foundation of society. The absence of education brings forth various social issues like weakness, innermost conflict, poor expectations for everyday comforts and many more. Just educated individuals can understand the estimation of the association, framework and social insurance (Russell & Norvig, 2016). Just instructed individuals will have the capacity to frame a spotless and sound society. The right education will assist the typical individuals with finding an appropriate solution for their issues.

d. Education Can Create Better Human Beings

It isn't possible for an uneducated individual to take the correct decision. An uneducated individual will probably grow bad habits, bring low confidence and dissatisfaction. Just through the right education, a person can develop great quality, good qualities and moral qualities (Roco & Bainbridge, 2003). Only well education individual will know the estimation of instruction and they will probably have a more extensive vision. What's more, without great quality education, a sound society can't be shaped (Ary, Jacobs, Irvine, & Walker, 2018).

e. Personal Growth

we must get a decent quality of instruction with a specific end goal to get the maximum capacity (Friese, Pittman, & Hendee, 1995). In the event that we are planning for the future, a person should finish the formal education from the perceived colleges in India and self-improvement (Umashankar & Dutta, 2007). Great quality colleges know the correct method to set up a decent native. All the large associations are searching for individuals, who are profoundly prepared and have unique aptitudes. Without appropriate instruction, the person won't have the capacity to serve an association or achieve maximum capacity.

f. Understanding The Responsibilities

It is not possible for an uneducated person to be completely aware of his duties. Only an informed individual knows about his own and social duties. An uneducated individual will probably turn into a major weight or a risk to the general public, who don't have anything to offer back to the general public (Lantos, 2001). Proper education trains a person to think historically their own advantage and furthermore gives him the capacity to give something back to society. As a social being, it is an obligation to give something back to society and improve something for the next generation.

5. Challenges in Education

- Social Media
- Culture (Traditional)
- Artificial Intelligence

The culture of an educational organization is the result of the convictions, observations, connections, demeanours, composed and unwritten principles that shape and impact each part of school capacities (Bruner, 1996). School culture likewise incorporates more solid problem, for instance, the physical and enthusiastic security of understudies, the association of classrooms and open spaces, or how much a school handles and celebrates ethnic, etymological, or social assorted variety. Impacts that change or modify any part of this blend will probably affect the general culture of a school or organization (Skrtic, 1991).

6. Social Challenges in Education

a. **Diversity:** One of the challenges in education is recognizing the increased diversity of learners in our classrooms and the pedagogies that cater to diverse learners and groups of learners. Students belonging to different regions, places, religions need to be educated equally (Brown, 2000).

b. **Digital Fluency:** Education is driven by personal responsibility, aptitude to effectively and ethically elucidate information, online identity, digital literacies, citizenship, cyber security, access and equity of opportunity to each and every student (Wang, Wiesemes, & Gibbons, 2012).
c. **Digital Citizenship:** Understanding to live respectfully and dependably in the reality world with the digital advances are changing the manners where we connect, communicate, impart and identify with each other (Ohler, 2011).
d. **Identity and Privacy:** In the computerized world, understanding our identity and to shield the things we need to keep the individual's identity private and similar with the others too (B. A. Levinson, 1996).
e. **Cyber Bullying:** Understanding the impact of this kind of conduct with respect to schools and society, the long haul and enduring effect of such practices (Meredith, 2010).
f. **Global Connectedness:** Understanding the effect and Implications of living in the universally associated world including understanding and regard for the languages, culture and personality of others (Lehtomäki, Moate, & Posti-Ahokas, 2016).
g. **De-Privatized Practice:** Understanding the emergence of practice, in school's institutions where teachers and students are working together in more open environments, where the sharing of strength and learning is esteemed and empowered (Kruse & Louis, 1993). This includes the change in regarding instructors as the sole authority within their own classroom, seeing them work as a part of a team where their work with learners is always 'in view' of their colleagues.

Artificial intelligence tools used worldwide in the education are:

1. Thinkster Math
2. Brainly
3. Content Technology
4. Mika
5. Netex Learning

Considering artificial intelligence, it's reasonable that scenes from a science fiction thriller come in the mind. Robots are fighting with humans, men are falling in love with a computer who is learning to feel and understand the emotions. iPhones outflanking their client. However, shouldn't something be said about a classroom?

What About a Classroom?

For an extensive time, teachers have attempted to encourage every single understudy (school student) with their individualized instructive necessities. That gets inconceivably extreme in a classroom of twenty, thirty, forty, or fifty students all required to breeze through the equivalent government sanctioned test, paying little mind to self-awareness. The utilization of man-made reasoning can possibly upset the conventional and conceivably harming one-estimate fits all model of present-day instructions (Bergmann & Sams, 2012). Machine Learning algorithm has just started helping educators fill the empty gaps while showing which subjects' students are suffering from the most (Kotsiantis, 2012; Michalski, Carbonell, & Mitchell, 2013). AI and chalkboard go hand -in -hand will change the way of education, here are some of the Artificial Intelligence tools used worldwide in education (Martin, 2012; Ann I Morey, 2004).

1. **Thinkster Math:** A web interface "the math app that offers an unusual human touch," by The New York Times, Thinkster Math is a mentoring application that mixes genuine math educational modules with a customized teaching style (Wadhwa). The application assigned every student a background guide who watches their psychological procedure unfold well-ordered on a screen. To start with, Thinkster Math gives the client diverse issues fitting to their range of abilities, skillsets. As understudies work out how they've achieved an answer, the application breaks down their composed work to figure out where they've turned out badly or misconstrued a vital critical thinking step. Thinkster Math enhances every understudy's rationale procedure by giving video help to stuck students and immediate, personalized feedback.
2. **Brainly:** Brainly (https://brainly.in/) is the social media learning website for classroom questions. Brainly uses Machine Learning algorithm for filtering the spams. It allows the student to ask schoolwork exercise from the different subject and receive automatic, verified answers from fellow students across different location worldwide (Choi et al., 2015; Choi et al., 2016). Brainly helps students to come up with their own correct answer. On the off chance that you have an understudy who directions the classroom, he or she can give replies on answers and work towards turning into a Brainly people group arbitrator. Brainly has specialists on an assortment of school subjects and attempts to make a classroom-like network for that customized blackboard contact.
3. **Content Technologies:** Worldwide schoolbooks are useful for cardboard cut-out forms of understudies who look, think, issue unravel and process data the equivalent. Content Technologies, Inc. CTI is an AI organization utilizing deep Learning to make tweaked reading material that fit the necessities of

particular courses and students (Chen, Mashhadi, Ang, & Harkrider, 1999). Instructors import syllabus into a CTI engine. CTI hardware at that point aces the input text data and use artificial intelligence algorithm which executes computations to make customized reading material and coursework dependent on centre ideas (Brusilovsky & Peylo, 2003). At the point when was the last time, your classroom read a course reading spread to cover, used each page of training questions or really observed relationships between in-class work and appointed perusing? CTI plans to fill that hole and help distributors make powerful course books appropriate for every individual student

4. **Mika:** Mika offers AI-based training tools for learners after the school hours, Mika provide personalized attention to each student. What's more, in the event that you think balanced consideration is only for elementary school students struggling with mathematical problems like long division, multiplication. Mika has some expertise in higher education coaching to fill the gaps in university classrooms infamous for lecture-based classrooms (Mahon, Bryant, Brown, & Kim, 2010). The application is guided by each student via one of a kind learning process, keeping users mindful of their day by day advance and adjusting exercises to every student particular struggle.
5. **Netex Learning:** Netex Learning provide the teachers to design a program across a variety of digital platforms and devices for the students. The most technically unskilled students consolidate incorporate interactive components like sound, video and self-evaluations to their advanced exercise designs, all inside customized learning with a cloud-based platform (Ercan, 2010; Wadhwa). With Netex, teachers can make customized student materials to be distributed on any computerized digital platform while providing tools for video conferencing, discussion on the topic, personalized assignments and analytics learning that show a visual representation of each and every individual student and their personal growth. It will enhance awareness among the students across worldwide on the importance of education.

Risks and Limitations

There are few constraints with the execution of AI innovation:

1. **Poor Teacher Adoption:** A few instructors are impervious to this and should be overseen through the change likewise.
2. **"Fear Factor":** As with several businesses, educators may feel that AI knowledge could finally replace them and will, therefore, be reticent to push forward initiatives consuming the innovation (Winston & Prendergast, 1984).

3. **Adoption at Scale:** AI joining requires encouraging from different associates like – guardians, students, instructors, directors and policymakers. This can be hard to accomplish rapidly.
4. **Subject Limitations:** AI won't be pertinent to all subjects. For instance, customized learning and computerized reviewing are probably not going to work in reasonable subjects with a solid emotional component to evaluation, for example, dramatization, craftsmanship, nourishment innovation and physical instruction (Groffen et al., 2013).
5. **Investment:** With schools under more financial weight than any time in recent memory, an organization of AI innovation at scale is costly and not all schools will have simple access to such assets (Luehrmann, 1972).
6. **Privacy, Data & Cyber Security:** This is probably the only greatest risk of AI sending instruction so close to homely information that is required for progress. In the education situation, this test is motivated more by the method that will be managing minors' close to homely information and data. In other words, there will be a more strong representation

SOLUTIONS AND RECOMMENDATIONS

Current trend to solve the problem using artificial intelligence in education:

1. **Alternative Assessment:** Broadly speaking alternative assessment is considered an alternative to uniform, norm-referenced, various decision testing's and typically claims the following features (Brusilovsky, 1999). AI in alternative assessment helps in several ways in education few as highlights:
   a. Student participation in setting goals and criteria for assessment.
   b. Performing an assignment, making an artefact/product.
   c. Use of higher-level thinking and/or problem-solving skills.
   d. Estimating metacognitive, combined and intrapersonal aptitudes as well as intellectual products.
   e. Evaluating significant instructional events.
   f. Contextualization in a real-world application.
   g. Utilization of determined criteria, known ahead of time, which characterize measures for good performance.
2. **Constructivism:** Artificial intelligence plays an important role in constructivism. Enhancing the brain and thinking about the power of the children. AI helps to draw diagrams and other kind of fun activities based on their behaviour (Pan, Cheok, Yang, Zhu, & Shi, 2006).

3. **Critical Thinking:** AI sorts out the object analysis and evaluation issues over and judgment. In Universities and Colleges, AI helps to find out the best fit solution for a particular problem. Among different solution for a problem, AI can assist to find out the best fit solution.
4. **Foreign Language Learning:** AI Natural Language Processing helps to translate one language into another language. This could be possible due to artificial intelligence (Barson, Frommer, & Schwartz, 1993).
5. **Inquiry-Based Learning:** Due to advancement in the internet technology all the schools and institutes start taking their queries online. One can learn about the particular topic via the inquiry-based and learning-based system. Artificial intelligence enables chatbots and provides help to different students to learn (Tan, Yeo, & Lim, 2005).
6. **Multicultural Education:** Humans are multicultural, there is diversity in culture and education. Artificial intelligence helps to understand different religion languages. Students across the globe can understand and learn a different kind of languages (Ann Intili Morey, 2000).
7. **Teacher as Researcher:** In the university, Institutes and college, the teachers are acting as a researcher. Many of the students are working under the project mentors to submit their project and thesis. Artificial intelligence helps researchers to keep the record of their research, AI can help in personalized research, recommendation or research paper, news articles based on their area of interests (Learner, 2006; Santa & Santa, 1995).
8. **Technology in Teaching:** Artificial Intelligence helps in the automated Grading of student's marks, some of the routine tasks are managed by the computer chatbots to assist student education personally (Lawless & Pellegrino, 2007; Roblyer & Doering, 2006).
9. **Tools for Accessing Literature:** AI provides the tools for written literature worldwide. The preface of AI innovation is its extraordinary capacity to constantly gain from the gathered information. In this way, the better the algorithm, the more information about the topic obtained and more far-reaching the comprehensive analytics, the more exact the subsequent prediction of result takes place (Novak, Razzouk, & Johnson, 2012).

Outside literature, artificial intelligence programmed robots are as of now capable of writing scripts (Murphy, Murphy, & Arkin, 2000). Truly, Bloomberg, different news organizations and financial firms have been utilizing robot journalists to write data-driven content with artificial intelligence programmed writer that turns data into some meaningful stories, similar to Wordsmith (Van Dalen, 2012). It gives the innovation to clients to mechanize their composition utilizing rules-based formats with different situations (Sugisaka & Hazry, 2007).

CONCLUSION

Computational assistance has transformed the world in nearly every domain. Artificial Intelligence is now a part of human life. Modern humans surrounded by new technologies like automated car parking, automatically take decisions, comparisons, design new model, enhance customer service, detect fraudulent activity and understand the geography of the market and many more. The multifaceted problems have been benefited by the computational methods through monitoring, decision making and evaluation. Artificial Intelligence techniques have delivered high output in terms of efficiency, reduction in cost and time requirement in nearly all fields such as electrical, medical, bioinformatics, chemistry and information technology. Education is the process of facilitating learning, or the acquisition of knowledge, skills, values, beliefs and habits. Education plays a crucial role in the establishment and development of the country. Education is a very important part as well as social and cultural education, globally in the current scenario it also has huge data associated with it and with advancement IT technologies huge data is available for making a better decision in the education system. Artificial Intelligence in education is being felt, and the traditional approaches are shifting drastically. Education has no limits and Artificial Intelligence can support to remove boundaries. There are several challenges in education which are complex and can be benefited with the applications of Artificial Intelligence and Machine learning. In the education system, primary level and secondary education level plays an important role for development and competitiveness of the country because primary and secondary education is the base of the students where students learn different things like social and cultural education, social and cultural trends and many more. There are several issues in this level of education which can be resolved through the use of Artificial Intelligence methods. Limited studies have been done in the application of Artificial Intelligence with social and cultural education.

REFERENCES

Apple, M. W. (2013). *Educating the right way: Markets, standards, God, and inequality*. Routledge.

Ary, D., Jacobs, L. C., Irvine, C. K. S., & Walker, D. (2018). *Introduction to research in education*. Cengage Learning.

Asis, M. M. (2006). Living with migration: Experiences of left-behind children in the Philippines. *Asian Population Studies*, *2*(1), 45–67. doi:10.1080/17441730600700556

Barson, J., Frommer, J., & Schwartz, M. (1993). Foreign language learning using e-mail in a task-oriented perspective: Interuniversity experiments in communication and collaboration. *Journal of Science Education and Technology*, *2*(4), 565–584. doi:10.1007/BF00695325

Becker, B. E., & Luthar, S. S. (2002). Social-emotional factors affecting achievement outcomes among disadvantaged students: Closing the achievement gap. *Educational Psychologist*, *37*(4), 197–214. doi:10.1207/S15326985EP3704_1 PMID:23255834

Bergmann, J., & Sams, A. (2012). *Flip your classroom: Reach every student in every class every day*. International Society for Technology in Education.

Best, J. W., & Kahn, J. V. (2016). *Research in education*. Pearson Education India.

Blumenfeld, P. C., Kempler, T. M., & Krajcik, J. S. (2006). *Motivation and cognitive engagement in learning environments*. Academic Press.

Bourdieu, P., & Nice, R. (1977). *Outline of a Theory of Practice* (Vol. 16). Cambridge University Press.

Brown, R. (2000). Social identity theory: Past achievements, current problems and future challenges. *European Journal of Social Psychology*, *30*(6), 745–778. doi:10.1002/1099-0992(200011/12)30:6<745::AID-EJSP24>3.0.CO;2-O

Bruner, J. S. (1996). *The culture of education*. Harvard University Press.

Brusilovsky, P. (1999). Adaptive and intelligent technologies for web-based eduction. *Ki, 13*(4), 19-25.

Brusilovsky, P., & Peylo, C. (2003). Adaptive and intelligent web-based educational systems. *International Journal of Artificial Intelligence in Education*, *13*, 159–172.

Burton, R. R., & Brown, J. S. (1979). An investigation of computer coaching for informal learning activities. *International Journal of Man-Machine Studies*, *11*(1), 5–24. doi:10.1016/S0020-7373(79)80003-6

Chen, A. Y., Mashhadi, A., Ang, D., & Harkrider, N. (1999). Cultural issues in the design of technology-enhanced learning systems. *British Journal of Educational Technology*, *30*(3), 217–230. doi:10.1111/1467-8535.00111

Choi, E., Borkowski, M., Zakoian, J., Sagan, K., Scholla, K., Ponti, C., . . . Bielski, M. (2015). Utilizing content moderators to investigate critical factors for assessing the quality of answers on brainly, social learning Q&A platform for students: a pilot study. *Proceedings of the 78th ASIS&T Annual Meeting: Information Science with Impact: Research in and for the Community*. 10.1002/pra2.2015.145052010069

Choi, E., Munoz, R., Mukhlas, D., Balak, M., Farias, L., Jara, D., . . . Burkov, O. (2016). Understanding user motivations for asking and answering a question on brainly, online social learning network. *IConference 2016 Proceedings.*

Cole, S. A., & Shastry, G. K. (2009). *Smart money: The effect of education, cognitive ability, and financial literacy on financial market participation.* Harvard Business School Boston.

Cortese, A. D. (2003). The critical role of higher education in creating a sustainable future. *Planning for Higher Education, 31*(3), 15–22.

Csorny, L. (2013). *Careers in the growing field of information technology services.* Academic Press.

Delpit, L. (1988). The silenced dialogue: Power and pedagogy in educating other people's children. *Harvard Educational Review, 58*(3), 280–299. doi:10.17763/haer.58.3.c43481778r528qw4

Delpit, L. (2006). *Other people's children: Cultural conflict in the classroom.* The New Press.

Dewey, J. (2007). *Experience and education.* Simon and Schuster.

Doran, G. T. (1981). There'sa SMART way to write management's goals and objectives. *Management Review, 70*(11), 35–36.

Eisenberg, M. B. (2010). Information literacy: Essential skills for the information age. *DESIDOC Journal of Library and Information Technology, 28*(2), 39–47. doi:10.14429/djlit.28.2.166

Eisner, E. W. (2017). *The enlightened eye: Qualitative inquiry and the enhancement of educational practice.* Teachers College Press.

Elder, G. H. (2018). *Children of the great depression.* Routledge. doi:10.4324/9780429501739

Ercan, T. (2010). Effective use of cloud computing in educational institutions. *Procedia: Social and Behavioral Sciences, 2*(2), 938–942. doi:10.1016/j.sbspro.2010.03.130

Fägerlind, I., & Saha, L. J. (2016). *Education and national development: A comparative perspective.* Elsevier.

Faure, E. (1972). *Learning to be: The world of education today and tomorrow.* Unesco.

Friese, G. T., Pittman, J. T., & Hendee, J. C. (1995). *Studies of the use of wilderness for personal growth, therapy, education and leadership development: An annotation and evaluation*. University of Idaho, Wilderness Research Center.

Gartner, A., & Lipsky, D. K. (1987). Beyond special education: Toward a quality system for all students. *Harvard Educational Review*, *57*(4), 367–396. doi:10.17763/haer.57.4.kj517305m7761218

Glaser, R. (1984). Education and thinking: The role of knowledge. *The American Psychologist*, *39*(2), 93–104. doi:10.1037/0003-066X.39.2.93

Hofstede, G. (1986). Cultural differences in teaching and learning. *International Journal of Intercultural Relations*, *10*(3), 301–320. doi:10.1016/0147-1767(86)90015-5

Hunter, J. D. (2008). *The death of character: Moral education in an age without good or evil*. Basic Books.

Jongbloed, B., Enders, J., & Salerno, C. (2008). Higher education and its communities: Interconnections, interdependencies and a research agenda. *Higher Education*, *56*(3), 303–324. doi:10.100710734-008-9128-2

Kotsiantis, S. B. (2012). Use of machine learning techniques for educational proposes: A decision support system for forecasting students' grades. *Artificial Intelligence Review*, *37*(4), 331–344. doi:10.100710462-011-9234-x

Kruse, S. D., & Louis, K. S. (1993). *Developing Professional Community in New and Restructuring Urban Schools*. Academic Press.

Lantos, G. P. (2001). The boundaries of strategic corporate social responsibility. *Journal of Consumer Marketing*, *18*(7), 595–632. doi:10.1108/07363760110410281

Lasswell, H. D. (1948). The structure and function of communication in society. *The Communication of Ideas, 37*, 215-228.

Lawless, K. A., & Pellegrino, J. W. (2007). Professional development in integrating technology into teaching and learning: Knowns, unknowns, and ways to pursue better questions and answers. *Review of Educational Research*, *77*(4), 575–614. doi:10.3102/0034654307309921

Learner, R. A. (2006). Teacher As Researcher. Teachers Engaged in Research: Inquiry Into Mathematics Classrooms. *Grades*, *3-5*, 129.

Lehtomäki, E., Moate, J., & Posti-Ahokas, H. (2016). Global connectedness in higher education: Student voices on the value of cross-cultural learning dialogue. *Studies in Higher Education, 41*(11), 2011–2027. doi:10.1080/03075079.2015.1007943

Levinson, B. A. (1996). *The Cultural Production of the Educated Person. Critical Ethnographies of Schooling and Local Practice. SUNY Series, Power, Social Identity, and Education*. ERIC.

Levinson, B. U. (2001). *We are all equal: Student culture and identity at a Mexican secondary school, 1988–1998*. Duke University Press. doi:10.1215/9780822381075

Lickona, T. (1996). Eleven principles of effective character education. *Journal of Moral Education, 25*(1), 93–100. doi:10.1080/0305724960250110

Mahon, J., Bryant, B., Brown, B., & Kim, M. (2010). Using second life to enhance classroom management practice in teacher education. *Educational Media International, 47*(2), 121–134. doi:10.1080/09523987.2010.492677

Mandela, N. (2014). Education is the most powerful weapon which you can use to change the world. *Computer, 8*.

Marginson, S. (2006). Dynamics of national and global competition in higher education. *Higher Education, 52*(1), 1–39. doi:10.100710734-004-7649-x

Martin, F. G. (2012). Will massive open online courses change how we teach? *Communications of the ACM, 55*(8), 26–28. doi:10.1145/2240236.2240246

Meredith, J. P. (2010). Combating cyberbullying: Emphasizing education over criminalization. *Fed. Comm. LJ, 63*, 311.

Michalski, R. S., Carbonell, J. G., & Mitchell, T. M. (2013). *Machine learning: An artificial intelligence approach*. Springer Science & Business Media.

Morey, A. I. (2000). Changing higher education curricula for a global and multicultural world. *Higher Education in Europe, 25*(1), 25–39. doi:10.1080/03797720050002170

Morey, A. I. (2004). Globalization and the emergence of for-profit higher education. *Higher Education, 48*(1), 131–150. doi:10.1023/B:HIGH.0000033768.76084.a0

Morreale, S. P., & Pearson, J. C. (2008). Why communication education is important: The centrality of the discipline in the 21st century. *Communication Education, 57*(2), 224–240. doi:10.1080/03634520701861713

Murphy, R., Murphy, R. R., & Arkin, R. C. (2000). *Introduction to AI robotics*. MIT press.

Nandi, A., & Mandernach, M. (2016). Hackathons as an informal learning platform. *Proceedings of the 47th ACM Technical Symposium on Computing Science Education.*

Noddings, N. (2013). *Caring: A relational approach to ethics and moral education.* Univ of California Press.

Novak, E., Razzouk, R., & Johnson, T. E. (2012). The educational use of social annotation tools in higher education: A literature review. *The Internet and Higher Education, 15*(1), 39–49. doi:10.1016/j.iheduc.2011.09.002

Ohler, J. (2011). Digital citizenship means character education for the digital age. *Kappa Delta Pi Record, 47*(sup1), 25-27.

Owens, R. G. (1995). *Organizational behavior in education.* Academic Press.

Pan, Z., Cheok, A. D., Yang, H., Zhu, J., & Shi, J. (2006). Virtual reality and mixed reality for virtual learning environments. *Computers & Graphics, 30*(1), 20–28. doi:10.1016/j.cag.2005.10.004

Roblyer, M. D., & Doering, A. H. (2006). Integrating educational technology into teaching (Vol. 2). Pearson/Merrill Prentice Hall.

Roco, M. C., & Bainbridge, W. S. (2003). *Overview converging technologies for improving human performance. In Converging technologies for improving human performance* (pp. 1–27). Springer. doi:10.1007/978-94-017-0359-8

Russell, S. J., & Norvig, P. (2016). *Artificial intelligence: a modern approach.* Pearson Education Limited.

Sallis, E. (2014). *Total quality management in education.* Routledge. doi:10.4324/9780203417010

Santa, C. M., & Santa, J. L. (1995). Teacher as researcher. *Journal of Reading Behavior, 27*(3), 439–451. doi:10.1080/10862969509547891

Scott, S. S., Mcguire, J. M., & Shaw, S. F. (2003). Universal design for instruction: A new paradigm for adult instruction in postsecondary education. *Remedial and Special Education, 24*(6), 369–379. doi:10.1177/07419325030240060801

Seidman, I. (2013). *Interviewing as qualitative research: A guide for researchers in education and the social sciences.* Teachers College Press.

Seligman, M. E., Ernst, R. M., Gillham, J., Reivich, K., & Linkins, M. (2009). Positive education: Positive psychology and classroom interventions. *Oxford Review of Education, 35*(3), 293–311. doi:10.1080/03054980902934563

Sharp, R., Green, A., & Lewis, J. (2017). *Education and social control: A study in progressive primary education*. Routledge. doi:10.4324/9781315210179

Sivakumar, S. C., Robertson, W., Artimy, M., & Aslam, N. (2005). A web-based remote interactive laboratory for Internetworking education. *IEEE Transactions on Education*, *48*(4), 586–598. doi:10.1109/TE.2005.858393

Skrtic, T. M. (1991). *Behind special education: A critical analysis of professional culture and school organization*. Love Publishing Company.

Smith, S. C., & Piele, P. K. (2006). *School leadership: Handbook for excellence in student learning*. Corwin Press.

Stocker, M. (1979). Desiring the bad: An essay in moral psychology. *The Journal of Philosophy*, *76*(12), 738–753. doi:10.2307/2025856

Sugisaka, M., & Hazry, D. (2007). Development of a proportional control method for a mobile robot. *Applied Mathematics and Computation*, *186*(1), 74–82. doi:10.1016/j.amc.2006.05.214

Tan, S. C., Yeo, A. C. J., & Lim, W. Y. (2005). Changing epistemology of science learning through inquiry with computer-supported collaborative learning. *Journal of Computers in Mathematics and Science Teaching*, *24*(4), 367–386.

Trow, M. (2007). *Reflections on the transition from elite to mass to universal access: Forms and phases of higher education in modern societies since WWII. In International handbook of higher education* (pp. 243–280). Springer.

Tuckman, B. W., & Harper, B. E. (2012). *Conducting educational research*. Rowman & Littlefield Publishers.

Umashankar, V., & Dutta, K. (2007). Balanced scorecards in managing higher education institutions: An Indian perspective. *International Journal of Educational Management*, *21*(1), 54–67. doi:10.1108/09513540710716821

Van Dalen, A. (2012). The algorithms behind the headlines: How machine-written news redefines the core skills of human journalists. *Journalism Practice*, *6*(5-6), 648–658. doi:10.1080/17512786.2012.667268

Von Glasersfeld, E. (1998). Cognition, construction of knowledge, and teaching. In Constructivism in science education (pp. 11-30). Springer.

Wals, A. E., & Jickling, B. (2002). "Sustainability" in higher education: From doublethink and newspeak to critical thinking and meaningful learning. *International Journal of Sustainability in Higher Education*, *3*(3), 221–232. doi:10.1108/14676370210434688

Wang, R., Wiesemes, R., & Gibbons, C. (2012). Developing digital fluency through ubiquitous mobile devices: Findings from a small-scale study. *Computers & Education*, *58*(1), 570–578. doi:10.1016/j.compedu.2011.04.013

Watson, G., McKeown, N., & Casado, M. (2006). *NetFPGA: A tool for network research and education.* Paper presented at the 2nd workshop on Architectural Research using FPGA Platforms (WARFP).

Zipes, J. (2013). *When dreams came true: classical fairy tales and their tradition.* Routledge. doi:10.4324/9780203949672

Chapter 8
Intelligent Tutoring Systems for Filipino Learners:
Current Research, Gaps, and Opportunities

Rex Perez Bringula
Ateneo de Manila University, Philippines
Mercedes Rodrigo
Ateneo de Manila University

ABSTRACT

Intelligent tutoring systems (ITS) research is not a new field of study. Despite its pedagogical value, very few ITS are developed intended for Filipino learners. The dearth of ITS research in a local setting discounted the fact Filipino learners might need a different learning approach. This chapter presented the state of ITS research in the Philippines. Readers would be informed that there is a need for multidisciplinary studies relating to Filipino learners that could serve basis for the development of culturally-related ITS. It also described Filipino learners in terms of culture, and it will attempt to link these descriptions as design considerations for the development of ITS. Finally, it provided insights and directions on how to develop an ITS for Filipino learners.

INTRODUCTION

Intelligent tutoring system (ITS) is a computer- or mobile-based software which has the capabilities to teach or assist learners. It is capable of providing individualized and immediate feedback, which may be very difficult to provide in a class with varying

DOI: 10.4018/978-1-5225-7793-5.ch008

academic capabilities. It has become a helpful supplementary material for teachers, especially when they handle a large class. Students benefit from this educational technology since it adapts to their academic needs and abilities. Recently, ITS is now incorporated in mobile devices which greatly transform and challenge the traditional form of learning. Students now learn at their own phase, space, and time.

Capturing the attention of scholars and researchers in the field of education around the world, ITS has become a vibrant field of research that calls for multidisciplinary approaches. International societies (e.g., Artificial Intelligence in Education), journals (e.g., International Journal of Artificial Intelligence in Education), and numerous published articles dedicated to ITS research are indications that it is a growing and evolving field. One of the advances in this field is the cultural considerations in the design of the ITS.

Mathematics education benefitted from the applications of artificial intelligence (AI). Matsuda et al. (2012) maintain that students may learn the procedural and conceptual knowledge through a peer tutor. Likewise, Pareto (2014) states that a pedagogical agent (PA) can engage students to learn arithmetic concepts and reasoning. In addition, as revealed in a study by Bringula, Alvarez, Evangelista, and So (2017), a mobile-assisted mathematics learning system that provides different forms of hints is able to help students solve algebraic problems without the intervention of a human teacher. Thus, it is apparent that artificial intelligence advances teaching and learning mathematics.

Relatively, very few studies of ITS research in the Philippines have been conducted. While there are attempts to develop an ITS in the Philippine setting (e.g., Bringula et al., 2017; Bringula, Fosgate, Garcia, & Yorobe, 2018; Lagud & Rodrigo, 2010), very little is known on the cultural basis of ITS development. Consequently, these impede the advancement of ITS research and educational system in the Philippines. In light of these constraints, this paper intends to investigate the state of ITS and mathematics learning studies conducted in the Philippines. Specifically, this chapter aims to 1) present the current state of ITS research in the Philippines, 2) present current studies of mathematics teaching in the Philippines, 3) identify the problems arising from the current state of ITS and mathematics research in the Philippines, and 4) propose unexplored research topics as possible solutions to these gaps.

BACKGROUND

For the last 50 years, intelligent tutoring systems had been a valuable educational resource for teachers, educational institutions, and students (Kulik & Fletcher, 2016). With intelligent tutoring systems (ITS), students' specific learning needs in large classes are addressed appropriately. With ITS, students are given equal opportunities to learn with accessible educational technology. Students receive individualized feedback (Schroeder, Adesope & Gilbert, 2013) and real-time assessment which does not require the presence of a human teacher (Bringula, Basa, Dela Cruz, & Rodrigo, 2016; Green, 2011; Marion & Oluwafunmilayo, 2011). ITS supports self-regulated learners who can create their own learning space and time (Winne et al., 2006; Duffy & Azevedo, 2015). It provides a non-embarrassing learning environment since the interaction happens only between the ITS and the learners (Bringula et al., 2017). ITS is now incorporated in mobile technologies allowing learning to be more accessible and flexible (Aker, Ksoll, & Lybbert, 2012).

Most ITS (e.g., Matsuda et al., 2013; Graesser, Chipman, Haynes, & Olney, 2005; Kizilkaya & Askar, 2008) are mainly conducted in foreign settings which are culturally different from the Philippines. It has been established that there is a link between emotions and cultural orientations of a person (Scollon et al., 2004; Kim-Prieto, Fujita, & Diener, 2004; Shaver & Schwartz, 1992). Furthermore, cultural differences are attributed to test anxiety (Cassady, Mohammed, & Mathieu, 2004) and reward allocation (Fischer & Smith, 2003). For instance, a Filipino student may not feel comfortable when a pedagogical agent shows disgust or anger over the student's repeated mistakes (Bringula et al., 2018a). This is so because Filipinos are known to be "*mahiyain*" (easily embarrassed) (Lasquety-Reyes, 2016) and "*balat-sibuyas*" (too sensitive) (Selmer & De Leon, 2001).

The impact of these different personalities of Filipino learners on collaboration and learning is still unknown. It was observed that Filipino students exhibited shyness and varying degrees of engagement during a utilization of a mobile-based language assisted learning (Bringula et al., 2018b). Six groups of students consisting of 5 to 6 members on each group with different academic abilities played a collaborative game about the English language. As a collaborative game, the scores of the team depended on group efforts and individual competency. While students were eager to participate in the game, students had varying degrees of engagement because of shyness. Despite the results, the relationship between different personalities and sources of shyness, and the impact of group participation in a computer-supported collaborative learning environment and learning, are still untested hypotheses in the Philippine context.

Language is another aspect of culture. For a specific subject such as mathematics, the native language of the learners is taken into considerations (Abedi & Lord, 2001). Procedural and conceptual skills in solving mathematical problems will be challenging for students who struggle to comprehend a foreign language. Prior studies (Bautista et al., 2009; Bautista, 2010) had shown that Filipino students can solve mathematics problems when the problems are translated into their mother tongue. Thus, a culturally-aware ITS, whose overall objective is to achieve better academic performance, is important since it understands the learners and it improves the quality of human-computer interaction (Blanchard & Frasson, 2005).

MAIN FOCUS OF THE CHAPTER: STATE OF ITS RESEARCH IN THE PHILIPPINES

First Issue: Published ITS Papers in the Philippines

In order to identify the issues of ITS research in the Philippines, an exhaustive literature search was conducted. Published studies relating to ITS studies conducted in the Philippine setting were considered as well as those published papers in ITS in online databases (e.g., EbscoHost, ScienceDirect, Scopus, SpringerLink, Sage Journals, Taylor & Francis, Emerald Insight, ACM Digital Library, IEEE Digital Library, and Google Scholar) for the last 10 years (2008-2017) were considered. Journal articles and conference proceedings, together with journal publications (e.g., https://e-journals.ph) and conference proceedings of computer societies (e.g., National Conference of IT Education (NCITE) of the Philippine Society of Information Technology Educators [PSITE] and the Philippine Computing Society of the Philippines (PCSC) of Computing Society of the Philippines [CSP]) in the Philippines were included.

The state of ITS research in the Philippines were characterized in terms of number of published articles, researchers' profile (name, institution, number of published articles, name of journal publication, Filipino collaborators, foreign collaborators, and affiliations), types of ITS (e.g., pedagogical agents, intelligent games, intelligent computer-aided instructions, etc.), strategies (e.g., textual feedback, emotional feedback, synthetic facial expressions, and affect), and applications in subjects areas (e.g., mathematics, science, language, history, etc.). The phrases "*intelligent tutoring systems*", "*pedagogical agents*", "*intelligent games*", "*intelligent computer-aided instructions*" combined with keywords and phrases such as "*Filipino*", "*Filipino learners*", "*Filipino students*", "*Philippines*", and "*Manila*" were used to search for articles. The same procedures were conducted to answer the second objective with slight modifications with the keywords used (e.g., "*mathematics*" + "*Filipino*").

Our initial search results yielded 40 ITS papers (see Table 1). However, six papers were further excluded because of overlapping content (e.g., conference proceedings converted into full journal articles) or primary authors were Filipinos but the participants of the study were not Filipinos. Thus, only 33 papers were used in the analysis (Table 4). Initial search showed there were 481 papers where Philippine e-Journals had the most number of returned papers (348 papers). This is because the search algorithm of the said database was not yet refined. It displayed all the papers in the database even if they did not match the search keywords.

Ma. Mercedes Rodrigo from Ateneo de Manila University (ADMU) and her institution leads the ITS research in the Philippines. Having 19 papers with local and international collaborators, she has been constantly publishing papers throughout the 10-year period. Only five local institutions are conducting ITS research (Figure 1). After ADMU, the University of the East (UE) is the second institution with the highest number of ITS research in the Philippines.

The majority of the papers are mathematics-related (Algebra, 14 papers; scatterplot diagram, 7 papers) (Table 2). Scatterplot tutor (7 papers), Applusix (7 papers), and SimStudent (5 papers) are the most frequently used ITS. Scatterplot is an ITS that teaches students how to construct and interpret scatterplots (Rodrigo et al., 2012). Aplusix is an ITS for arithmetic or algebraic problems that include numerical calculation, expansion and simplification, factorization, solving equations, solving inequalities, and solving systems (Nicaud et al., 2004, 2007). SimStudent, a "machine-learning agent that learns cognitive skills by demonstration" (Matsuda, Cohen, Sewall, Lacerda, & Koedinger, 2007, p. 467), employs learning-by-teaching paradigm where students serve as the tutor and a pedagogical agent, named Stacy, acts as the tutee. The physical appearance of Stacy was designed based on Western features. In addition, her questions and instructions are given in English. That mathematics is the most investigated domain can be explained by the fact that many students struggle in this subject and that one-on-one human tutoring on this subject is tedious and time-consuming.

It is worth noting that local authors attempted to develop ITS (Table 2). Ateneo de Manila University, De La Salle University (DLSU), University of the East (UE), and Letran College developed nine ITS systems all together. One ITS in developed in ADMU was about teaching the Japanese language (Chung, Nagai, & Rodrigo, 2013). Researchers from DLSU developed SalinLahi III – an ITS for the Filipino language (Regalado et al., 2015). Four systems (PERL, DEITS, NumBysts, CircuITS) were developed in Letran College in Calamba. PERL aims to teach students in PERL programming (Acuna et al., 2011) while DEITS (Oruga et al., 2011), NumBysts (Rosellon et al., 2011), CircuITS (Ello et al., 2011) were ITS designed for teaching digital design concepts. PIA, Teacher AICA, and one unnamed software were developed at the University of the East. All of these systems are for teaching mathematics. With the exception of SQL tutor, only one paper on each system was published. The majority of publications are found in conference proceedings (n = 18 papers) and Lecture Notes in Computer Science (n = 12) is the most preferred venue of publication. There are more international publications (n = 19) than local publications (n = 14).

Table 1. Total number of papers based on inclusion criteria

Database	Initial Search Results	Number of Papers Meeting Inclusion Criteria
ACM Digital Library	7	1
EbscoHost	8	6
Sage	30	1
SpringerLink	65	11
Taylor & Francis	0	0
Emerald Insight	6	1
Philippine Online Journal (PHILJOL)	3	3
Philippine e-Journals	348	4
NCITE Conference Proceedings	4	4
PCSC Conference Proceedings	4	4
Philippine Computing Journal	4	4
IEEE Digital Library	2	1
TOTAL	481	40

In terms of research methodology, all papers in the study employed quantitative methods. The majority of the participants were high school students (14 papers). Only a small portion of studies were participated in by elementary students (1 paper). The age of the participants ranged from 6 to 19 while population size was from few (12 participants) to several participants (532 participants).

Figure 1. Institutions that Investigated ITS in the Philippines

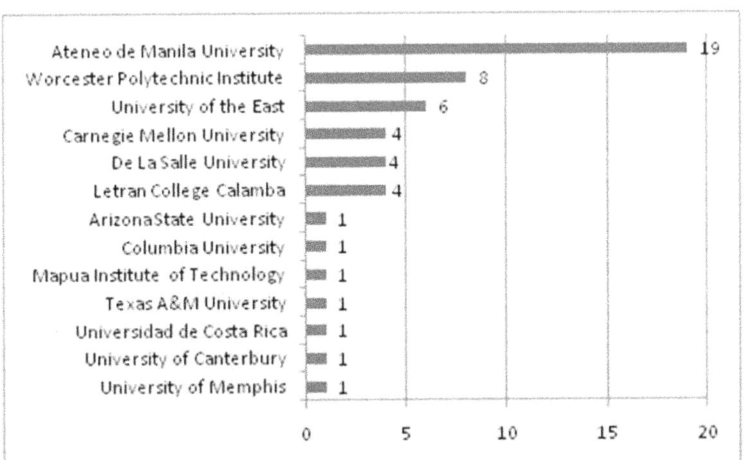

Table 2. Summary of Different ITS Studies in the Philippines

Dimension	Factor	Result
System characteristics	ITS used	n = 15 papers Scatterplot, 7 papers Applusix, 7 papers SimStudent, 5 papers
	Domain	Mathematics (Algebra, 13 papers; Scatterplot diagram, 7 papers; Laws of exponents, 1 paper), *n* = 21 papers Programming, n = 4 papers Language and reading, n = 3 papers Digital design, n = 3 papers
	Systems developed	Unnamed software for Japanese language (ADMU) SalinLahi (DLSU) PERL, NumByts, DEITS, CircuITS (Letran College) PIA, Teacher AICA, unnamed software for mathematics learning (UE)
Research methodology	Participants	Elementary students, n = 1 paper High school students, n = 14 papers College students = 9 papers
	Age	Age ranges from 6 to 19
	Research design	All quantitative papers
	Sample size	Number of participants range from 12 to 532

Table 3. Publication Venues

Publication Venues	Settings				Total
	Local	f	International	f	Total
Journal	• ANI: Letran Calamba Research Report • Philippine Computing Journal • Philippine Information Technology Journal	4 3 2	• Journal of Educational Computing Research • Teachers College Record • IEEE Transactions on Affective Computing • International Journal of Human-Computing Studies • International Journal of Web Information Systems	2 1 1 1 1	15
Conference Proceedings	• Philippine Computing Science Congress • National Conference on IT Education	3 2	• Lecture Notes in Computer Science • Advances in Mobile Computing and Multimedia	12 1	18
Total	14		19		33

Second Issue: Cultural Perspectives on Filipino Mathematics Learners

There is no single definition of culture. Nonetheless, Spencer-Oater's (2008, p. 3) definition of culture fits this study. The author defined it as "fuzzy set of basic assumptions and values, orientations to life, beliefs, policies, procedures and behavioral conventions that are shared by a group of people, and that influence (but do not determine) each member's behavior and his/her interpretations of the 'meaning' of other people's behavior." Culture is composed of explicit (e.g., language, behavior, and artifacts) and implicit (values, norms, beliefs, ideologies, and knowledge) elements (Jocano, 1999). Time, space, and event perceptions are also non-tangible elements of culture. The real life settings of these elements vary from one culture to another (Marcelino, 1990).

Culture has impact on how people learn (Jarvis, Holford, & Griffin, 1998). Filipino researchers acknowledge the importance of understanding Filipino learners in the context of its culture. In 1965, De Guzman and Varias found that one of the fears of Grades I-IV students was punishment of their teachers. Elementary students view their teachers as authoritative and important figures. Offending their teachers or not meeting their learning expectations is a sign of disrespect and of a displeasing value (De Guzman & Varias, 1965). Hence, it was advised that punishments should avoid arousal of fear; instead, they should provide extra work related to the act for which the student is being punished (Guzman & Varias, 1965).

Language, a prominent element to distinguish the cultural identity of people, is a means by which they communicate their values, perspectives, and rules of cognition (Marcelino, 1990). It is extensively investigated in mathematics learning and there are attempts to reduce the obstacle of learning mathematics by presenting the problems in Filipino or in English (Durkin & Shire, 1991; Verschaffel, Greer, & De Corte, 2000). In Philippine setting, language is indeed a factor in learning mathematics (Bernardo, 2002, 2005; Bernardo & Calleja, 2005; Bautista et al., 2009; Bautista, 2010). For example, grade 2 students were able to understand and solve arithmetic problems in their first language (Bernardo, 2002). For disadvantaged students, however, arithmetic problems written in English had to be translated into Filipino before they can answer the questions correctly (Bautista, 2010).

Cultural context of social interactions linked to academic goals and motivations has been investigated in the Philippines. As a collectivist society (Hofstede, 1980), students tend to find belongingness outside their family. Being part of a group (Bernardo & Ismail, 2010) and being able to establish secure connection with others (Mesurado, Richaud, & Mateo, 2016) are some of the characteristics of Filipino learners. Within that group, students may apply the eight levels of interaction proposed by Santiago and Enriquez (1976): *pakikitungo* (transaction/civility with), *pakikisalamuha* (interaction with), *pakikilahok* (joinining/participating with), *pakikibagay* (in conformity with/in accord with), *pakikisama* (getting along with), *pakikipag-palagayang-loob* (having rapport with), *pakikisangkot* (getting involved with), and *pakikiisa* (being one with). Mesurado et al. (2016) concluded that learning in the Philippine context is more grounded on social features. Deviating from the expected roles in these social interactions may result to "*hiya*" (shame) (Lasquety-Reyes, 2016).

Another perspective of "*hiya*" is "a feeling of inferiority, embarrassment, shyness, and alienation, which is experienced as acutely distressing' (Guthrie 1968, p. 62). This concept of "*hiya*" has a negative connotation (Jocano, 1999) since it prohibits students' academic and extra-curricular participations (Page & Zarco, 2001; Ordonez & Gandeza, 2004). Because of "*hiya*", students feel more comfortable to ask their seatmates than their teachers when clarifying ideas or instructions (Ordonez & Gandeza, 2004). Similarly, mathematics learners emphasized that a good mathematics teacher is a teacher that does not embarrass them in class (Murray, 2011; Raufelder et al., 2016).

Problems and Opportunities

This chapter intends to identify the current ITS research in the Philippines and to describe the mathematics learners in the context of Filipino culture. Identifying the gaps in ITS research in the Philippines is the first step to revolutionize the educational system in the Philippines in the era of artificial intelligence. In the first objective, our investigation leads us to the finding that ITS research is a rich research area in foreign countries. While it is evident that ITS research in the Philippines is not as mature as compared to foreign settings, it is interesting to note that there are individuals and institutions that are attempting to catch up with the trend. Published ITS studies in the Philippines can serve as baseline that could serve as springboard of locally situated ITS research.

Not surprisingly, relatively low publications, intermittent publications, and research methodological gaps (e.g., lack of mixed method studies) are the weaknesses of the existing ITS literature. These weaknesses, in turn, may have negative impact on advancing the educational pedagogy in the Philippines. Because Filipino learners are not fully understood, the advancement in theory and practice of teaching and learning through the use of artificial intelligence are not realized. Nevertheless, these gaps provide opportunities for local researchers to easily identify the possible research topics. ITS can be developed in other fields of mathematics as well as in other domains (e.g., history, sciences, language, etc.). Other foundation fields of mathematics, such as fractions and arithmetic, are still unexplored. Therefore, there is a need for further studies that would enrich the literature.

Researchers have to consider the cultural orientation of Filipino learners in the development of ITS. Development of culturally-aware ITS has been the advocacy of Blanchard and Frasson (2005) and Blanchard and Ogan (2010). Considering the collectivist culture of the Filipinos, researchers are informed that learners may be more comfortable learning as a group. This can only be achieved if "*hiya*" could be overcome by the participants. Understanding the personalities of Filipino learners and their perceptions towards engagement have to be understood in order to carry out successful interventions. This will be the primary concern of ITS researchers before engaging participants in an experiment involving collaborative learning.

Technical design of ITS is another area for improvement. It is still unclear on how to develop a pedagogical agent in terms of its behavior (e.g., gestures, textual feedback, and emotional feedback), type of companion (e.g., human, animal, cartoon), and appearance (e.g., color of the hair, eyes, skin, etc.) that are deemed appropriate for Filipino students. Similarly, the forms of appropriate reward are still unclear. Conversely, the forms of demerit without offending the Filipino students are still an open question. All of the ITS developed used a foreign language, that is, English. Thus, the content of the ITS may be delivered in the students' native language. The learning environment of the ITS based on Philippine culture is still new area of research.

SOLUTIONS AND RECOMMENDATIONS

ITS research in the Philippine is still in the infancy stage. It opens opportunities for local and foreign researchers to direct their time, efforts, and funding to explore this field. At the institutional level, higher education institutions (HEI) in the Philippines may include ITS as one of its research agenda. International and local HEI linkages may be established so that exchanges of knowledge and expertise will be beneficial to all institutions. There are institutions and individuals in the Philippines that can be tapped on this field and may be even open for research collaboration. For instance, researchers may conduct an in-depth study on the best practices of these institutions and their faculty. The results of that study could serve as basis in crafting institutional research policies.

Government funding is highly crucial in the advancement of AI research in education. In the Philippines, the Commission of Higher Education (CHED) and the Department of Science and Technology (DOST) are mandated by the government to promote research in this area. Currently, DOST and CHED include ITS research as one of its national research agenda. Both government agencies provide research funding covering this research area and encourage researchers to avail of research grants they offer.

To address the issues previously presented, a local chapter of international societies specializing AI in education could be organized. Experts from the field may be invited to conduct seminars, workshops, and trainings. Local societies may form a special interest group or an ad hoc committee that will assist researchers and monitor the status of ITS research in the Philippines. Awards or distinctions may be given to capture the interest of Filipino researchers.

It is probable that there are research projects that are not translated to publications. Since papers published in local or in-house journals are not converted to international publications, local societies may initiate trainings, research writing, and publication workshops. Also, Filipino researchers are encouraged to attend national and international conferences that offer doctoral or student consortium (e.g., International Conference on Computers in Education, International Conference on Intelligent Tutoring Systems, Future of Technology Conference). Collegial inputs and insights will significantly enhance the ITS research topics.

There is a compelling reason to include culture in the development of ITS. Multidisciplinary approach is needed considering the complexity of culture. One straightforward solution is to develop ITS whose content are delivered in the native tongue of the learners. Furthermore, a student may easily comprehend a word problem if they can easily relate to the situation and objects used. In order to materialize a culturally-aware ITS, researchers from the fields of computer science, psychology, education, linguistics, sociology, and anthropology may collaborate with one another. Furthermore, diversification of domains, participants, and methodologies are highly encouraged. It is very noticeable that most of the studies conducted of quantitative research designs. Hence, qualitative or mixed method research designs are highly desirable.

Personality traits and cultural values may be investigated before, during, and after implementation phases. Filipino students who are too sensitive or shy (or its extreme equivalents) may have different perceptions towards working with another student in a computer-supported collaborative work. The interplay of values of "*hiya*" and "*shame*" with different levels of interactions of Filipinos is not yet discovered in the context of computerized learning environment. Hence, consultations with psychologists or guidance counselors will be beneficial in developing digital punishments or deductions that are deemed appropriate for these types of students. This does not only address the design of the ITS but also the ethical dimensions. In other words, it is needed to understand the group dynamics and personality traits of Filipino students before engaging in any experiment and technical design of an ITS.

It must be noted that the methodology in collecting data of this paper has its inherent limitations. First, it is probable that there are individuals conducting ITS studies in the Philippines but do not publish their works. Hence, in order to be accounted for, it is highly encouraged that researchers present or publish their papers in national or international forums. Second, there are in-house journals that are not published online. Posting them in their institutional websites is encouraged. Lastly, the keywords used in the published articles that do not reflect the desired outcomes of this study may delimit the search results. Hence, it is recommended that Filipino researchers may include keywords that reflect the Philippine culture.

FUTURE RESEARCH DIRECTIONS

Provided that the proposed solutions are taken into actions, it is expected that there will be advancement of research policies and management in the institutions. In general, the Philippine education sector will benefit from the advancement of ITS research. It can be expected that multidiscilipinary studies will take place for the next five years. The domain of mathematics education and other fields will greatly benefit on the advancement of ITS. The influence of different forms of feedback (i.e., textual, synthetic facial expressions, and affective) on mathematics achievement is a field worth investigating. The possibility of collaboration among psychologists, anthropologists, computer scientists, and software developers may take place in order to develop a culturally-aware ITS for mathematics. Adoption studies are also expected to be carried out to determine the inhibitors and barriers of inclusion of the technology in the classroom.

CONCLUSION

This chapter intends to inform the reader the research and development of ITS in the Philippines. Issues, problems, gaps, and opportunities are provided. It is found that despite the call for research of ITS design and cultural orientation of its users, very few researchers in the Philippines responded to this research endeavor. It can be concluded that ITS research in the Philippines is not a popular field of research despite the support from the Philippine government. Nonetheless, there are individuals and institutions that specialize on this area, thus, it sparks hope that other institutions see the importance of artificial intelligence in education and will soon be engaged in this area of investigation.

The solutions proposed in this chapter clearly indicate that governmental, institutional, and individual participations are needed in the advancement of artificial intelligence in education. There is a long way in revolutionizing the Philippine education through artificial intelligence, and there will be challenges along the way of the conceptualization, policy formulation, and implementation. It will not be easy – but doable.

ACKNOWLEDGMENT

The author would like to thank Ma. Mercedes Rodrigo and the Department of Science and Technology-Engineering Research and Development for Technology for funding this study. This paper is a full version of a poster submitted in a conference.

REFERENCES

Abedi, J., & Lord, C. (2001). The language factor in mathematics tests. *Applied Measurement in Education, 14*(3), 219–234. doi:10.1207/S15324818AME1403_2

Aker, J. C., Ksoll, C., & Lybbert, T. J. (2012). Can mobile phones improve learning?: Evidence from a field experiment in Niger. *American Economic Journal. Applied Economics, 4*(4), 94–120. doi:10.1257/app.4.4.94

Bautista, D. (2010). Why do disadvantaged Filipino children find word problems in English difficult? In L. Sparrow, B. Kissane, & C. Hurst (Eds.), *Shaping the future of mathematics education: Proceedings of the 33rd annual conference of the Mathematics Education Research Group of Australasia*. Fremantle: MERGA.

Bautista, D., Mitchelmore, M., & Mulligan, J. (2009). Factors influencing Filipino children's solutions to addition and subtraction word problems. *Educational Psychology, 29*(6), 729–745. doi:10.1080/01443410903254591

Bernardo, A. B. I. (2002). Language and mathematical problem solving among bilinguals. *The Journal of Psychology, 136*(3), 283–297. doi:10.1080/00223980209604156 PMID:12206277

Bernardo, A. B. I. (2005). Language and modeling word problems in mathematics among bilinguals. *The Journal of Psychology, 139*(5), 413–425. doi:10.3200/JRLP.139.5.413-425 PMID:16285212

Bernardo, A. B. I., & Calleja, M. O. (2005). The effects of stating problems in bilingual students' first and second languages on solving mathematical word problems. *The Journal of Genetic Psychology, 166*(1), 117–129. doi:10.3200/GNTP.166.1.117-129 PMID:15782681

Bernardo, A. B. I., & Ismail, R. (2010). Social perceptions of achieving students and achievement goals of students in Malaysia and the Philippines. *Social Psychology of Education, 13*(3), 385–407. doi:10.100711218-010-9118-y

Blanchard, E. G., & Frasson, C. (2005). Making intelligent tutoring systems culturally aware: The use of Hofstede's cultural dimensions. In H. R Arabnia, & R. Joshua (Eds), *Proceedings of the 2005 International Conference on Artificial Intelligence* (pp. 644-649). Las Vegas, NV: CSREA Press.

Blanchard, E. G., & Ogan, A. (2010). Infusing cultural awareness into intelligent tutoring systems for a globalized world. In R. Nkambou, J. Bourdeau, & R. Mizoguchi (Eds.), *Advances in Intelligent Tutoring Systems* (pp. 485–505). Berlin: Springer-Verlag. doi:10.1007/978-3-642-14363-2_24

Bringula, R., Alvarez, J., Evangelista, M., & So, R. (2017). Learner-interface interactions with mobile-assisted learning in mathematics: Effects on and relationship with mathematics performance. *International Journal of Mobile and Blended Learning*, *9*(1), 34–48. doi:10.4018/IJMBL.2017010103

Bringula, R., Rodrigo, M. M. T., Ocumpaugh, J. L., Porayska-Pomsta, K., Olatunji, I., & Luckin, R. (2018b). Towards the development of a computer-based game for phonemic awareness. In *Proceedings of the 26th International Conference on Computers in Education* (pp. 657-662). Manila: Asia-Pacific Society for Computers in Education.

Bringula, R. P., Basa, R. S., Dela Cruz, C., & Rodrigo, M. M. T. (2016). Effects of prior knowledge in mathematics on learner-interface interactions in a learning-by-teaching intelligent tutoring system. *Journal of Educational Computing Research*, *54*(4), 462–482. doi:10.1177/0735633115622213

Bringula, R. P., Fosgate, I. C. O. Jr, Garcia, N. P. R., & Yorobe, J. L. M. (2018a). Effects of pedagogical agents on students' mathematics performance: A comparison between two versions. *Journal of Educational Computing Research*, *56*(5), 701–722. doi:10.1177/0735633117722494

Cassady, J. C., Mohammed, A., & Mathieu, L. (2004). Crosscultural differences in test perceptions: Women in Kuwait and the United States. *Journal of Cross-Cultural Psychology*, *35*(6), 713–718. doi:10.1177/0022022104270113

De Guzman, J. V., & Varias, R. R. (1965). *Psychology of Filipinos : studies and essays*. Manila: Vilfran Press.

Duffy, M. C., & Azevedo, R. (2015). Motivation matters: Interactions between achievement goals and agent scaffolding for self-regulated learning within an intelligent tutoring system. *Computers in Human Behavior*, *52*, 338–348. doi:10.1016/j.chb.2015.05.041

Durkin, K., & Shire, B. (Eds.). (1991). *Language in mathematical education: Research and practice*. Buckingham, UK: Open University Press.

Fischer, R., & Smith, P. (2003). Reward allocation and culture: A meta-analysis. *Journal of Cross-Cultural Psychology*, *34*(3), 251–268. doi:10.1177/0022022103034003001

Graesser, A. C., Chipman, P., Haynes, B. C., & Olney, A. (2005). AutoTutor: An intelligent tutoring system with mixed-initiative dialogue. *IEEE Transactions on Education*, *48*(4), 612–618. doi:10.1109/TE.2005.856149

Green, D. T. (2011). *Intelligent tutoring systems for skill acquisition* (Unpublished manuscript). The University of Arizona, Tucson, AZ.

Guthrie, G. (1968). The Philippine temperament. In G. Guthrie (Ed.), *Six perspectives on the Philippines* (pp. 49–84). Manila: The Bookmark, Inc.

Hofstede, G. (1980). *Culture's consequences: International differences in work-related values*. Beverly Hills, CA: Sage.

Jarvis, P., Holford, J., & Griffin, C. (1998). *The theory and practice of learning*. London: Kogan Page, Limited.

Jocano, F. L. (1999). *Management by culture: Fine-tuning modern management to Filipino culture* (revised edition). Quezon City, Philippines: Punlad Research House, Inc.

Kim-Prieto, C., Fujita, F., & Diener, E. (2004). *Culture and structure of emotional experience* (Unpublished manuscript). University of Illinois, Urbana-Champaign, IL.

Kizilkaya, G., & Askar, P. (2008). The effect of an embedded pedagogical agent on the students' science achievement. *Interactive Technology and Smart Education*, *5*(4), 208–216. doi:10.1108/17415650810930893

Kulik, J. A., & Flecher, J. D. (2016). Effectiveness of intelligent tutoring systems: A meta-analytic review. *Review of Educational Research*, *86*(1), 42–78. doi:10.3102/0034654315581420

Lagud, M. C. V., & Rodrigo, M. M. T. (2010, June). The affective and learning profiles of students using an intelligent tutoring system for algebra. In *International Conference on Intelligent Tutoring Systems* (pp. 255-263). Berlin: Springer 10.1007/978-3-642-13388-6_30

Lasquety-Reyes, J. (2016). In defense of hiya as a Filipino virtue. *Asian Philosophy*, *26*(1), 66–78. doi:10.1080/09552367.2015.1136203

Marcelino, E. P. (1990). Towards understanding the psychology of the Filipino. *Women & Therapy*, *9*(1-2), 105–128. doi:10.1300/J015v09n01_07

Marion, A. O., & Oluwafunmilayo, A. A. (2011). Design and development of an intelligent instructive system: Scholastic Tutor (St*). *Turkish Online Journal of Distance Education-TOJDE*, *12*(4), 34–44.

Matsuda, N., Cohen, W. W., Koedinger, K. R., Keiser, V., Raizada, R., Yarzebinski, E., & Stylianides, G. (2012). Studying the effect of tutor learning using a teachable agent that asks the student tutor for explanations. In M. Sugimoto, V. Aleven, Y. S. Chee, & B. F. Manjon (Eds.), *Proceedings of the International Conference on Digital Game and Intelligent Toy Enhanced Learning (DIGITEL 2012)* (pp. 25–32). Takagawa, Japan: Conference Publishing Services. 10.1109/DIGITEL.2012.12

Matsuda, N., Cohen, W. W., Sewall, J., Lacerda, G., & Koedinger, K. R. (2007). Predicting students' performance with simstudent that learns cognitive skills from observation. In R. Luckin, K. R. Koedinger, & J. Greer (Eds.), *Proceedings of the International Conference on Artificial Intelligence in Education* (pp. 467-476). Amsterdam: IOS Press.

Matsuda, N., Yarzebinski, E., Keiser, V., Raizada, R., Cohen, W. W., Stylianides, G. J., & Koedinger, K. R. (2013). Cognitive anatomy of tutor learning: Lessons learned with SimStudent. *Journal of Educational Psychology*, *105*(4), 1152–1163. doi:10.1037/a0031955

Mesurado, B., Richaud, M. C., & Mateo, N. J. (2016). Engagement, flow, self-efficacy, and eustress of university students: A cross-national comparison between the Philippines and Argentina. *The Journal of Psychology*, *150*(3), 281–299. doi:10.1080/00223980.2015.1024595 PMID:25915707

Murray, S. (2011). Secondary students' descriptions of "good" mathematics teachers. *Australian Mathematics Teacher*, *67*(4), 14–21.

Nicaud, J. F., Bouhineau, D., & Chaachoua, H. (2004). Mixing microworld and CAS features in building computer systems that help student learn algebra. *International Journal of Computers for Mathematical Learning*, *9*(2), 169–211. doi:10.1023/B:IJCO.0000040890.20374.37

Nicaud, J. F., Bouhineau, D., Mezerette, S., Andre, N. (2007). Aplusix II [Computer software].

Ordonez, R. V., & Gandeza, N. (2004). Integrating traditional beliefs and modern medicine: Filipino nurses' health beliefs, behaviors, and practices. *Home Health Care Management & Practice*, *17*(1), 22–27. doi:10.1177/1084822304268152

Page, R. M., & Zarco, E. P. (2001). Shyness, physical activity, and sports team participation among Philippine high school students. *Child Study Journal, 31*(3), 193–204.

Pareto, L. (2014). A teachable agent game engaging primary school children to learn arithmetic concepts and reasoning. *International Journal of Artificial Intelligence in Education, 24*(3), 251–283. doi:10.100740593-014-0018-8

Raufelder, D., Nitsche, L., Breitmeyer, S., Keßler, S., Herrmann, E., & Regner, N. (2016). Students' perception of "good" and "bad" teachers-Results of a qualitative thematic analysis with German adolescent. *International Journal of Educational Research, 75*, 31–44. doi:10.1016/j.ijer.2015.11.004

Santiago, C., & Enriquez, V. (1976). Tungo sa makapilipinong pananaliksik. *Sikolohiyang Pilipino: Mga Ulat at Balita, 1*(4), 3–10.

Schroeder, N. L., Adesope, O. O., & Gilbert, R. B. (2013). How effective are pedagogical agents for learning?: A meta-analytic review. *Journal of Educational Computing Research, 49*(1), 1–39. doi:10.2190/EC.49.1.a

Scollon, C. N., Diener, E., Oishi, S., & Biswas-Diener, R. (2004). Emotions across cultures and methods. *Journal of Cross-Cultural Psychology, 35*(3), 304–326. doi:10.1177/0022022104264124

Selmer, J., & De Leon, C. (2001). Pinoy-style HRM: Human resource management in the Philippines. *Asia Pacific Business Review, 8*(1), 127–144. doi:10.1080/713999124

Shaver, P. R., & Schwartz, J. C. (1992). Cross-cultural similarities and differences in emotion and its representation. In C. Z. Malatesta & C. Izard (Eds.), *Emotions in adult development* (pp. 319–338). Beverly Hills, CA: Sage.

Spencer-Oatey, H. (2008). *Culturally speaking: Culture, communication and politeness theory* (2nd ed.). London: Continuum.

Verschaffel, L., Greer, B., & De Corte, E. (2000). *Making sense of word problems*. Lisse, The Netherlands: Swets & Zeitlinger.

Winne, P. H., Nesbit, J. C., Kumar, V., Hadwin, A. F., Lajoie, S. P., Azevedo, R., & Perry, N. E. (2006). Supporting self-regulated learning with gStudy software: The Learning Kit Project. *Technology Instruction Cognition and Learning, 3*(1/2), 105–113.

ADDITIONAL READING

Bodenheimer, B., Williams, B., Kramer, M. R., Viswanath, K., Balachandran, R., Belynne, K., & Biswas, G. (2009). Construction and evaluation of animated teachable agents. *Journal of Educational Technology & Society, 12*(3), 191–205.

Bringula, R., Rodrigo, M. M. T., Ocumpaugh, J. L., Porayska-Pomsta, K., Olatunji, I., & Luckin, R. (2018). Portraits of underprivileged Filipino second language learners: Towards the development of computer-based educational game. In *Proceedings of the 26th International Conference on Computers in Education* (pp. 562-568). Manila: Asia-Pacific Society for Computers in Education.

Chambers, J., & Sprecher, J. (1983). *Computer-assisted instruction: Its use in the classroom*. Englewood Cliffs, New Jersey: Prentice-Hall Inc.

Chisholm, L. (1996). *The culture of learning and teaching in Gauteng schools: report of the Committee on the Culture of Learning and Teaching*. Johannesburg: Education Policy Unit, University of the Witwatersrand.

Corbett, A. T., & Anderson, J. R. (1992). LISP Intelligent Tutoring System Research in Skill Acquisition. In J. Larkin & R. Chabay (Eds.), *Computer assisted instruction and intelligent tutoring systems: shared goals and complementary approaches* (pp. 73–110). Englewood Cliffs, New Jersey: Prentice-Hall Inc.

Cruz-Jesus, F., Oliveira, T., & Bacao, F. (2018). The global digital divide: Evidence and drivers. *Journal of Global Information Management, 26*(2), 1–26. doi:10.4018/JGIM.2018040101

Department of Science and Technology-Engineering Research and Development for Technology. (2019). DOST-ERDT Research Agenda. Retrieved from http://erdt.coe.upd.edu.ph/research-and-development/erdt-r-d-agenda.html

Kinnebrew, J. S., & Biswas G. (2011). Modeling and measuring self-regulated learning in teachable agent environments. *Journal of e-Learning and Knowledge Society, 7*(2), 19–35.

VanLehn, K. (2011). The relative effectiveness of human tutoring, intelligent tutoring systems, and other tutoring systems. *Educational Psychologist, 46*(4), 197–221. doi:10.1080/00461520.2011.611369

KEY TERMS AND DEFINITIONS

Culturally-Aware Intelligent Tutoring System: An intelligent tutoring system that is designed based on the culture of its users.

Collectivist Society: A characteristic of a society where it values the sense of welfare of the group over one's self.

Intelligent Games: These are types of games that are adaptive to the skills and knowledge of the gamers.

Intelligent Tutoring System: A computerized educational software that is able to provide customized feedback or instructions to learners.

Pedagogical Agent: An artificially simulated human, object, or animal that assist learners in an educational software.

Synthetic Facial Expressions: Facial expressions that are emulated by pedagogical agents.

Textual Feedback: A computer-generated feedback that corrects mistakes or informs learners about their prior actions.

APPENDIX

List of Papers Qualified in the Study

Table 4. List of Papers Qualified in this Study

No.	Title
1	Acuna, P. R. D., Naredo, K. M. S., Pua, C. J. B., & Ferrera, L. (2011). PERL - Intelligent tutoring system. *Ani: Letran Calamba Research Report, 1*(1), 16.
2	Andallaza, T. C. S., & Jimenez, R. J. M. (2012). *Design of an affective agent for Aplusix* (Unpublished Undergraduate thesis). Ateneo de Manila University, Quezon City, Philippines.
3	Anglo, E. A., & Rodrigo, M. M. T. (2010). Can Affect Be Detected from Intelligent Tutoring System Interaction Data?–A Preliminary Study. In V. Aleven, J. Kay, J. Mostow (Eds.), *Intelligent Tutoring Systems* (pp. 260-262). Berlin: Springer.
4	Baker, R. S., D'Mello, S. K., Rodrigo, M. M. T., & Graesser, A. C. (2010). Better to be frustrated than bored: The incidence, persistence, and impact of learners' cognitive–affective states during interactions with three different computer-based learning environments. *International Journal of Human-Computer Studies, 68*(4), 223-241.
5	Bate, A. E. C., & Rodrigo, M. M. T. (2010). *Automatic detection of student off-task behavior while using an intelligent tutor for algebra* (Unpublished master's thesis). Ateneo de Manila University, Quezon City, Philippines.
6	Beck, J., & Rodrigo, M. M. T. (2014). Understanding wheel spinning in the context of affective factors. In S. Trausan-Matu S., K. E. Boyer, M. Crosby, & K. Panourgia (Eds), *Intelligent Tutoring Systems* (pp. 162-167). Switzerland:Springer.
7	Bringula, R. P., Basa, R., & Dela Cruz, C. (2015). Clustering learners in a learning-by-teaching intelligent tutoring system and differences in their mathematics performance. In *Proceedings of the 15th Philippine Computing Science Congress* (pp. 50-55). Davao, Philippines. Retrieved from https://drive.google.com/open?id=0BxI8feCZhWsoRI9lclhONmlUSlU&authuser=0
8	Bringula, R. P., Basa, R. S., Dela Cruz, C., & Rodrigo, M. M. T. (2016). Effects of prior knowledge in mathematics on learner-interface interactions in a learning-by-teaching intelligent tutoring system. *Journal of Educational Computing Research, 54*(4), 462-482.
9	Bringula, R. P., Belza, J. L. G., Belarmino, S. P., & Chavez, M. C. G. (2016, November). Teacher AICA: A Mobile-based Intelligent Tutoring System for Laws of Exponents. In *Proceedings of the 14th International Conference on Advances in Mobile Computing and Multi Media* (pp. 199-202). Singapore:ACM.
10	Bringula, R., De Leon, J. S., Rayala, K. J., Pascual, B. A., & Sendino, K. (2017). Effects of different types of feedback of a mobile-assisted learning application and motivation towards mathematics learning on students' mathematics performance. *International Journal of Web Information Systems, 13*(3), 241-259.
11	Bringula, R. P., Fosgate Jr, I. C. O., Garcia, N. P. R., & Yorobe, J. L. M. (2018). Effects of pedagogical agents on students' mathematics performance: A comparison between two versions. *Journal of Educational Computing Research, 56*(5), 701-722.
12	Bueno, D., Rabe, E., & Sy, B. (2011). iFeedback: An intelligent feedback API for tutoring system. In *Proceedings of the 9th National Conference on IT Education* (pp. 19-22). Palawan, Philippines:PSITE.
13	Bustos, D. M., Chua, G. L., Cruz, R. T., Santos, J. M., & Suarez, M. T. (2011, June). Gesture-based affect modeling for intelligent tutoring systems. In G. Biswas G., S. Bull, J. Kay, A. Mitrovic (Eds.), *Artificial Intelligence in Education(AIED 2011)* (pp. 426-428). Berlin:Springer.
No.	**Title**
14	Castillo, V. R. C., Villaflor, K. B. V., Rodriguez, R. L., & Rodrigo, M. M. T. (2010). Is the part greater than the whole: A comparison of affective and behavioral models derived from feature sub-sets. In *Proceedings of the 8th National Conference on IT Education* (pp. 99-105). Boracay, Aklan, Philippines:PSITE.
15	Chung, Z. T., Nagai, H., & Rodrigo, M. M. T. (2013). An intelligent tutoring system for japanese language particles with user assessment and feedback. In *AIED Workshops*. Retrieved from http://citeseerx.ist.psu.edu/viewdoc/download?doi=10.1.1.415.5425&rep=rep1&type=pdf
16	Ello, A., Fortus, M. G., Singh, M., & Rivera, V. (2011). CircuITS: Circuits intelligent tutoring system. *Ani: Letran Calamba Research Report, 1*(1), 15.

continued on following page

Table 4 Continued

No.	Title
17	Guia, T. F. G., Rodrigo, M. M. T., Dagami, M. M. C., Sugay, J. O., Macam, F. J. P., & Mitrovic, A. (2012). Modeling the affective states of students using SQL-Tutor. In S.A. Cerri, W. J. Clancey,G. Papadourakis, K. Panourgia (Eds.), *Intelligent Tutoring Systems (ITS 2012)* (pp. 634-635). Berlin:Springer.
18	Guia, T. F. G., Sugay, J. O., Rodrigo, M. M. T., Macam, F. J. P., Dagami, M. M. C., & Mitrovic, A. (2011). Transitions of affective states in an intelligent tutoring system. In *Proceedings of the 9th National Conference on IT Education* (pp. 31-35). Palawan, Philippines:PSITE.
19	Lagud, M. C. V., & Rodrigo, M. M. T. (2010). The affective and learning profiles of students using an intelligent tutoring system for algebra. In V. Aleven, J. Kay, J. Mostow (Eds.), *Intelligent Tutoring Systems* (pp. 255-263). Berlin: Springer.
20	Ong, E. C. J., & Soriano, Z. C. (2015). A conversational agent to shift students' affect state. In M. Baldoni et al. (Eds.), *Principles and Practice of Multi-Agent Systems* (pp. 86-97). Switzerland:Springer.
21	Oruga, J. E., Guevarra, P. J., Robledo, J., & Garcia, M. (2011). DEITS: Digital electronics intelligent tutoring system. *Ani: Letran Calamba Research Report, 1*(1), 16.
22	Regalado, R. V., Bo•on, M. L., Chua, N., Pi•era, R. R., & Cruz, S. R. D. (2015). Salinlahi III: An Intelligent Tutoring System for Filipino Heritage Language Learners. In H.-H. Chen, Y.-H. Tseng, Y. Matsumoto, & L. H. Wong (Eds.), *Proceedings of the 2nd Workshop on Natural Language Processing Techniques for Educational Applications* (pp. 87-93). Beijing, China:Association for Computational Linguistics.
23	Rodrigo, M. M. T., Baker, R. S., Agapito, J., Nabos, J., Repalam, M. C., Reyes, S. S., & San Pedro, M. O. C. (2012). The effects of an interactive software agent on student affective dynamics while using; an intelligent tutoring system. *IEEE Transactions on Affective Computing, 3*(2), 224-236.
24	Rodrigo, M. M. T., Baker, R. S. J. D., & Rossi, L. (2013). Student off-task behavior in computer-based learning in the Philippines: comparison to prior research in the USA. *Teachers College Record, 115*(10), 1-27.
25	Rodrigo, M. M. T., d Baker, R. S., Agapito, J., Nabos, J., Repalam, M. C., & Reyes, S. S. (2010). Comparing disengaged behavior within a cognitive tutor in the USA and Philippines. In V. Aleven, J. Kay, J. Mostow (Eds.), *Intelligent Tutoring Systems* (pp. 263-265). Berlin:Springer.
26	Rodrigo, M. M. T., Geli, R., Ong, A., Vitug, G., Bringula, R., Basa, R., & Matsuda, N. (2013). Exploring the implications of tutor negativity towards a synthetic agent in a learning-by-teaching environment. *Philippine Computing Journal, 8*, 15-20.
No.	**Title**
27	Rosellon, L. A., Abad, J. E. R., Cruz, J. J. V., & Rivera, V. (2011). NUMBYSTS (A tutorial of number-based system with game application). *Ani: Letran Calamba Research Report, 1*(1), 17.
28	San Pedro, M. O. C. Z., d Baker, R. S., & Rodrigo, M. M. T. (2011). Detecting carelessness through contextual estimation of slip probabilities among students using an intelligent tutor for mathematics. In Biswas G., S. Bull, J. Kay, A. Mitrovic (Eds.), *Artificial Intelligence in Education(AIED 2011)* (pp. 304-311). Berlin:Springer.
29	San Pedro, M. O. C. Z., Rodrigo, M. M. T., & d Baker, R. S. (2011). The relationship between carelessness and affect in a Cognitive Tutor. In S. D'Mello, A. Graesser, B. Schuller, J.C. Martin (Eds.), *Affective Computing and Intelligent Interaction (ACII 2011)* (pp. 306-315). Berlin:Springer.
30	Soriano, J. C. A., Rodrigo, M. M. T., Baker, R. S., Ogan, A., Walker, E., Castro, M. J., ... & Belmontez, R. (2012). A cross-cultural comparison of effective help-seeking behavior among students using an ITS for math. In S.A. Cerri, W. J. Clancey, G. Papadourakis, & K. Panourgia (Eds.), *Intelligent Tutoring Systems (ITS 2012)*. (pp. 636-637). Berlin:Springer.
31	Vea, L. V., Mesina, M. R. D., Toriaga, R. P., & Padla, N. J. (2013). The development and implementation of an intelligent agent that detects student's negative affect while making a computer program. In *Proceedings of the 11th National Conference on IT Education* (pp. 24-29).Camiguin, Philippines:PSITE.
32	Yarzebinski, E., Dumdumaya, C., Rodrigo, M. M. T., Matsuda, N., & Ogan, A. (2017). Regional cultural differences in how students customize their avatars in technology-enhanced learning. In E. André, R. Baker, X. Hu, M. Rodrigo, & B. du Boulay (Eds.), *Artificial Intelligence in Education (AIED 2017)* (pp. 598-601). Switzerland:Springer.
33	Yarzebinski, E., Ogan, A., Rodrigo, M. M. T., & Matsuda, N. (2015). Understanding students' use of code-switching in a learning by teaching technology. In C. Conati, N. Heffernan, A. Mitrovic, & M. Verdejo (Eds.), *Artificial Intelligence in Education (AIED 2015)* (pp. 504-513). Switzerland:Springer

Chapter 9
A New Paradigm for Acceptance of Analytics in Learning Management Systems at Jordanian Universities (JLMS)

Abdeleh Bassam Al Amoush
University of New England, Australia

Kamaljeet Sandhu
https://orcid.org/0000-0003-4624-6834
University of New England, Australia

ABSTRACT

E-learning or learning management systems (LMS) are broadly used in higher education systems. They've become a necessity to help the participants (instructors, students, and administrators) in their daily use. Learning analytics presents an auspicious approach. This chapter aims to examine the acceptance of analytics and use of an LMS at Jordanian universities. It also focuses on the factors influencing acceptance of analytics in LMS at Jordanian universities. Therefore, the chapter presents a new model for acceptance of analytics in learning management systems at Jordanian universities. It calls Jordanian learning management system (JLMS). This chapter is based on the most recent and related literature explaining various scenarios where learning management systems address learning issues in the digital environment in a way that was not possible in the previous confines of print logics.

DOI: 10.4018/978-1-5225-7793-5.ch009

INTRODUCTION

In the last few years, the use of information technology (IT) has received interest from people in every walk of life (Majdalawi, Almarabeh, & Mohammad, 2014). At the present, IT based tools are not only used for business and daily activities, but also for university education, where it is used to manage different academic activities (Denscombe, 2014). A learning analytics system (McDaniel, Fanfarelli, & Lindgren, 2017) is software that is used in administration, reporting and other training exercises (Al-Dmour, 2014). The research question is: "What are the factors for the acceptance of analytics in learning management system at Jordanian universities?" This chapter aims to identify the factors that impact on the acceptance of analytics in learning management system at Jordanian universities. This chapter also investigates the literature on LMSs in many different contexts of learning analytics and the research methodology for the study is also presented.

Learning analytics are widely used at universities for streamlining teaching and learning tasks, as they effectively manage learning tools and resources for user participants (students and teachers) (Kats, 2010). A phenomenal revolution has occurred in the university education over the past decade as a result of learning analytics, as they have been found to significantly benefit students' understanding and academic progress (Alnsour, Muhsen, Dababnah, Eljinini, & Barhoum, 2011). LMS applications are multifunctional, enabling students to have ubiquitous access to systems, watch lectures, download course materials and upload assignments online (AlQudah, 2014).

The latter provides convenience to students as never before and is conducive to study. To have efficient functioning of learning analytics, it is necessary to enable well-established links between data that is indexed by search engines, and web bots that connect and bind information together (Babić, 2012). LMS empowers users and offers a greatly enhanced user experience overall (McIntosh & Torres, 2014; Phillipo & Krongard, 2012).

A learning analytics greatly simplify learning and deliverables, such as tests, assignments and other forms of assessment, with the use of multimedia applications that incorporate team learning through dynamic, real time, documented collaboration. Some examples include the use of chat, file transfer and assessment applications. A learning analytics create new platforms for the active learner and results in greatly expanding the learning curve. To fully understand the nature and implications of different LMSs, it is vital to explore exactly what the LMS context is (Ahmad, Chinade, Gambaki, Ibrahim, & Ala, 2012). This study is based on the most recent and related literature explaining various scenarios where learning analytics address learning issues in the digital environment in a way that was not possible in the previous confines of print logics.

Research Question

To address the research question, research question (what are the factors for the acceptance of analytics in LMS at Jordanian universities?) will determine the factors that impact on the acceptance of analytics in learning management system at Jordanian universities. This will be achieved through an investigation of the impact of LMS tools within different contexts on the research participants. The results of the investigation will reveal the factors influencing LMS use by the user participants. It is anticipated that the answers to these questions might be revealed from the aspects discussed below:

The first aspect is the social and cultural issues (Hofstede, Minkov, & Hofstede, 2016), which are very important because the culture of each country will influence how the LMS is used in that country. Infrastructure is another aspect that influences LMS use and refers to the availability and accessibility of technology, such as the availability of technology like PCs and Internet connections, and the accessibility of technology like access to the Internet and access to LMS tools. These two main aspects are the factors that may influence the use of analytics in learning management system at Jordanian universities (Majadlawi, Almarabeh, & Mohammad, 2014).

There are other factors that affect the use of an LMS, such as linguistic barriers, where there may be lack of understanding of the technology languages and commands. Additionally, a well-designed learning analytics system or LMS should have a reassuring and intuitive user interface that promotes confidence among potential users. Another factor that influences LMS use is technical support and how easy the system is to use (Davis, 1989). Some managers use incentives to encourage users to dedicate time to training, and develop resources to encourage the user to use the new system (M. Al-Shboul, 2013). Finally, the lack of training for technology professionals and the interactive and synchronous collaboration tools can influence the level of use of an LMS (AlQudah, 2014; Davis, 1989).

Research Problem

The single most significant barrier mentioned by Al Bakri (2013) is the lack of understanding of how to perform online transactions and progress system workflows. There exists a perceived mistrust of electronic operations and new "process improvement" software because in Jordanian culture, people are still afraid to use new technology and do transactions online, and they prefer and trust the use of chapter instead of the electrical process. Therefore, this current research assesses the level and lack thereof of Information and Communication Technology (ICT) knowledge in the context of LMS applications in Jordanian universities and the factors influencing the level of learning analytics acceptance.

Successful LMS applications must support a five year business plan or its equivalent (Al Bakri, 2013). The implementation of an LMS should involve many processes, such as infrastructure preparation, training support, users' feedback, upgrades and updates. The author suggests that reports on performance analysis in critical areas, including recruitment and training regimens, are required to measure the progressive effectiveness of learning analytics. Unfortunately, universities in Jordan are still struggling to deliver successfully integrated LMS applications for three main reasons: the lack of users' general understanding, and their lack of familiarity and competency with technology. Consequently because of their poor computer skills, universities have not made any improvement and benefited from learning analytics. M. Al-Shboul (2013) found that there were a number of barriers hindering the successful implementation of Information Communication Technology (ICT), learning analytics and LMSs specifically.

Research Methodological Issues in Learning Analytics

This research utilises the mixed methodology research approach in both data collection and the analysis process. This is justified as the application of mixed methods will lead to greater understanding of the broad aspect in the research process (Creswell, 2013). Firstly, the use of the quantitative method, which includes a survey, should build the first impression of the issue under investigation. Secondly, the quantitative process will be enhanced by the qualitative method, where interviews will be applied to extract deeper information for further analysis. The combination of both quantitative and qualitative methodologies will be of great use to build a complete picture of the state of analytics in LMS use at Jordanian universities.

The research discovers information that would be useful to the decision makers at Jordan universities and the government, academic university professors, heads of schools, deans, and senior management of the university, and highlights the issues related to the use of analytics in LMSs in higher educational institutions and the degree of acceptance in using analytics in LMSs at Jordanian universities. The web-based survey will be posted in six universities: which are University of Jordan (UJ), Princess Sumaya University for Technology (PSUT), Philadelphia University (PU) Jordan University of Science and Technology (JUST), The Applied Science Private University (ASU) and Al al-Bayt University (AABU). Quantitative data will be obtained by interviewing the faculty members. The data collected from participants will be analysed to determine the factors by using Statistical Package for the Social Science (SPSS) statistics software, version 17.0 and the partial least square modelling technique developed by Professor Wynne Chin (Chin, 1995).

1. Qualitative Interviews

The interviews will be conducted among the research participants within Jordanian universities (six universities) to extract information. The researcher will collect qualitative data from interviews and then refine the quantitative data questionnaire, which will then be used for the survey. It will also adopted to obtain qualitative and quantitative data in order to develop and refine concepts identified from the literature for inclusion in the conceptual model and the survey instrument and examine the acceptance of the Jordanian Learning Management System Model (JLMS) at Jordanian universities. It will formulate the quantitative survey questions and discover the findings obtained from the survey (Creswell, 2013; Yin, 1981).

2. Quantitative Questionnaire

The survey method will be adopted to find quantitative data in order to identify the concepts from the literature for inclusion in the conceptual model and the quantitative instrument and also to formulate the quantitative questions. According to Eriksson and Kovalainen (2015, p. 56) the quantitative research is " more prone to structured, standardized and abstracted modes of collecting and analyzing empirical data". The greatest number of researchers rely on quantitative methods, while fewer researchers depend on qualitative methods because of the long time needed for quantitative research (Venkatesh, 1999). Moreover, business research books typically introduce quantitative research because it provides rigorous results. However, qualitative research provides a suspicious affair results (Eriksson & Kovalainen, 2015).

Valid results will be obtained from the quantitative research (survey method). In this chapter, the survey method will be applied on six different types of universities: the University of Jordan (UJ), Jordan University of Science and Technology (JUST) and Al al-Bayt University (AABU) are a government universities, Princess Sumaya University for Technology (PSUT) is a semi- government university (government and private university), and Philadelphia University (PU) and The Applied Science Private University (ASU) are a private universities. These universities will cover all types of universities in Jordan, and will present real figures from different aspects.

Lack of Analytics in LMS Research in Jordanian Universities

Researchers found that there is a lack of analytics in LMS research in developing countries such as Jordan. They undertook minor research in specific faculty in their university to highlight the adoption of analytics in LMS. AlQudah (2014) conducted a study on 80 instructors at the University of Jordan (UJ) and found a lack of technical support for using analytics in LMS in their university because of the shortage of expert staff to handle new technology from both the management side and the users side. Accepting new technology software is difficult, because users are afraid to use new technology, preferring the old and traditional ways (Al Musawi, Ambusaidi, Al-Balushi, & Al-Balushi, 2015; Alnsour et al., 2011; Majadlawi et al., 2014; McDaniel et al., 2017).

Alnsour et al. (2011) conducted a survey on 86 students at Isra University (IU) in Jordan and recommended creating a guide for students to use analytics in LMS, and received encouragement from the management of the university. Majdalawi et al. (2014) conducted a questionnaire survey on 240 students at the University of Jordan (UJ), and found that the attitude towards using analytics in LMS is a direct determinant of behaviour intention.

Aims of the Chapter

The aims of this chapter are to:

1. Investigate the acceptance and use of analytics in LMS at Jordanian universities.
2. Research the extant literature to support the success of academic performance enhancements and benefits to users of analytics in LMS.
3. Focus on the factors influencing acceptance of analytics in LMS at Jordanian universities.
4. Collect and analyse qualitative data (i.e. interviews and case studies) and quantitative data (i.e. surveys, PLS model technique for PLS model development and testing) (Loehlin & Beaujean, 2017).
5. Test and measure the new model for analytics in LMS use at Jordanian universities.
6. Report on the data findings about the discovery of new knowledge for analytics in LMS at Jordanian universities.

Study Context: Jordanian Universities

The chapter will be conducted in the context of Jordanian universities. It will particularly focus on six main universities in Jordan: the University of Jordan (UJ) (www.ju.edu.jo), which is the oldest government university in Jordan, Princess Sumaya University for Technology (PSUT) (www.psut.edu.jo), which is a mixed university system (government and private), and Philadelphia University (PU) (www.philadelphia.edu.jo), which is one of the private universities in Jordan. Jordan University of Science and Technology (JUST) (www.just.edu.jo), which is one of the public universities in Jordan. The Applied Science Private University (ASU) (www.asu.edu.jo), which is one of the private universities in Jordan. The last university is Al al-Bayt University (AABU) (www.aabu.edu.jo), which is one of the public universities in Jordan. These six different types of universities represent the major universities in Jordan. The following are some details of these universities from which the research data will be collected.

The aim of the current chapter is to investigate the acceptance and use of analytics in LMS at Jordanian universities. It also focuses on the factors influencing acceptance of analytics in LMS at Jordanian universities. The research problem was clearly presented along with the required data collection and analysis procedures. These have formulated the research methodological aspects including the conceptual framework underpinning the research. The research questions that will be answered throughout this current study is: What are the factors for the acceptance of analytics in LMS at Jordanian universities?

The research context shown earlier was the Jordanian universities: University of Jordan (UJ), Princess Sumaya University for Technology (PSUT), Philadelphia University (PU), Jordan University of Science and Technology (JUST), The Applied Science Private University (ASU) and Al al-Bayt University (AABU). The research context covers both a private university, such as (PU, ASU) and the government sector, for instance, (UJ, JUST and AABU). The third context is half government and half private sector, as for PSUT. Learning management systems in general will be discussed, followed by a discussion of Jordanian universities in particular. The gap in literature of using an analytics in LMS at Jordanian universities and the conceptual research model will also be presented.

LMS Use and Acceptance in the Jordan Universities

The following literature review analyses research on the most significant benefits, obstacles, implications and effects of analytics in LMS use in Jordanian universities. The review explores the most pertinent issues and aspects of the introduction of analytics in LMSs at Jordanian universities today. Moreover, the suppositions regarding the key outcomes of analytics in LMS integration are the result of a thorough investigation of its influence on the academic process.

EL-Seoud, Al-Khasawneh, and Awajan (2007), surveyed 160 students from PSUT who were participating in web based learning to determine if and how the digital medium enhances the education process in Jordan at university level. The findings identify and highlight issues regarding students' ability to comprehend and retain the content and knowledge of the subject matter. Additionally, students overwhelmingly preferred the web-based version of the course over the traditional classroom style. The study also reveals how the use of a web-based format, tools and automatic standardised grading functionality considerably reduces the concerns of faculty members in relation to assessing students consistently and fairly.

Majdalawi et al. (2014) surveyed 240 UJ students about factors they perceive affect students' ability to learn when using an LMS at university. This study also raises important issues about UJ students using the popular "Moodle" LMS. Students are now comfortable and familiar with the LMS software and workflow. University students almost unanimously deemed "Moodle" very useful therefore heightening the awareness and support of academic decision makers. As a result of student progress, responses and feedback, the adoption and integration of the LMS continues to increase.

This study highlights how some academic faculties benefited more than others, and reveals inconsistent results for the LMS integration success rate. It appears that faculties where students typically possess a high level of computer literacy seamlessly integrated LMS, whereas those such as the arts and social sciences are not exploiting any of the benefits of LMS. These findings illustrate the need for all students to be well versed, competent and comfortable using technology.

Almarabeh (2014) undertook a study on 180 UJ students and found that those most fluent with the LMS software were considerably more likely to leverage and benefit. Students' attitude, including their perceptions and overall view of the LMS, was ultimately the most critical factor affecting the successful integration of the innovative learning landscape. For example, if students harboured negative preconceptions about the LMS they generally failed to successfully implement and/or integrate the LMS. In contrast, those who were excited, typically IT and technology savvy students, embraced and consequently evolved in a large way by integrating the LMS. The researcher impresses the need for all faculty personnel learning and supporting each other's transition from a print-based, traditional learning model to a digital context. If the LMS content is not comprehensible to all users as intended the message is lost in the medium and is never imparted. Even scholarly, highly intelligent people are essentially illiterate if they are not able to use the LMS software properly and absorb the data presented in this new topology and form.

AlQudah (2014) study involved 80 instructors from different UJ faculties, and points out that technical support further influences the ease and transition of faculty members transitioning to the LMS. He also references additional studies where results support his theories and recommendations.

M. Khasawneh (2015) undertook a study on academic stuff in Jordanian universities and found that there are four factors indicated for the Perceived Behavioral Control which are: self-efficacy (SE), Technology Facilitating Condition (TFC), Resources Facilitating Condition (RFC) and Government Facilitating Condition (GFC). He found also that facilitating condition and self-efficacy have positively affected the behavioral intention to use ICT in the higher educational system among academic staff. Additionally, a significant relationship between the academic member stuff and perceived behavioral control towards using the technology in the Jordanian educational system. The study also reveals the adoption of technologies status is in a very early stages comparing between the developing countries such as Jordan and other developed countries in North America and Europe.

The current state of LMS applications in Jordan universities has not been widely studied researchers, because there are differences in using and exploiting LMS tools between the faculties departments and users. There are a considerable number of studies that focused on the state of technology in Jordan in the educational context; however, their focus is on the level of technology in general, rather than LMS applications in particular. Therefore, this research study will fill this gap in the literature. The following table is a summary of prior studies on analytics in LMS at Jordanian universities.

Factors for the Acceptance of Analytics in LMS at Jordanian Universities

The Technology Acceptance Model (TAM) (Davis, 1989; Venkatesh, 1999) has usually been used to examine the acceptance of a new technology. In this chapter, a research model is based on the TAM to investigate the acceptance of using analytics in LMSs at Jordanian universities. The component of technical support will be incorporated through the TAM model, and serves as an extension to TAM. This is conducted in order to measure the acceptance of using analytics in LMSs at Jordanian universities. The research model will explain the system usage of applying analytics in LMSs at Jordanian universities. It consists of concepts that will be refined in relation to the Jordanian Learning Management System (JLMS) and include technical support, perceived usefulness (PU) and perceived ease of use (PEOU) (Venkatesh & Davis, 2000).

Information technology infrastructure (IT infrastructure) and the Jordanian culture, which are the main element factors that directly affect the acceptance of analytics in LMS at Jordanian universities, followed by perceived usefulness and perceived ease of use of the LMS. After that will be tested and discussed the acceptance of using LMS and make sure it will continue use of analytics in LMS at Jordanian universities.

1. Information Technology (IT) Infrastructure for Analytics in LMSS at Jordanian Universities

IT infrastructure for analytics in LMSs at Jordan refers to the availability of technology in the country in general, and in universities in particular, such Internet connections, computers and LMS tools (AlQudah, 2014). Many developing countries are still struggling with lack of IT infrastructure, and this chapter highlights this factor as being one of the main factors influencing the acceptance of analytics in LMS at

Table 1. Summary of Prior Studies in the Acceptance of Analytics in LMS at Jordanian Universities

Author(s) / Year	Study design	Research aims	Sample	Data collection	Main findings
Atoum, Issa **Otoom, Ahmed** **Ali, Amer Abu** 2017	International Journal of Information, Business and Management	To implement the National Information Assurance and Cyber Security Strategy (NIACSS) of Jordan	Not mentioned	Case study	Results are demonstrated to NITC directors and security managers. They have made a consensus on the applicability of the HCS-IF to implement the CSS of Jordan. They had suggested a need for further analysis in the fields of human resources and change management which are outside the scope of our research.
Rana El Bahsha and Mohammad I. Daoud 2016	Proceedings of the 35th Annual IEEE International Conference on Computer Communications	Contributes to the ongoing efforts to expand the use of open-source e-learning tools in higher education institutes. To evaluate the effectiveness of the Moodle-based e-learning system	46 engineering students in German Jordanian University, Jordan	Questionnaire based study	Moodle is mainly used as an online repository to access course materials. The interactive learning tools of Moodle are not effectively utilized. The students demonstrated a positive perspective towards expanding the use of Moodle in the learning process. These results suggest expanding the use of Moodle in the educational process, particularly by employing its interactive learning tools to achieve an effective and interactive learning environment (El-Bahsh & Daoud, 2016).
Mohammad Khasawneh 2015	Procedia - Social and Behavioral Sciences	to examine the potential prominent factors related to the usage of ICT in the public universities among the academic staff	Academic staff only, Not mentioned the number of the research study	Case study	The findings show that self-efficacy (SE), and facilitating condition (FC) have positively affected the Behavioral Intention (BI) to use ICT in the higher educational system among academic staff. There is also a significant relationship between academic staff's perception of technology characteristics and their Perceived Behavioral Control (PBC) towards using the technology in the educational system. There is insufficient knowledge regarding ICT adoption in the less developed countries and in the Arab regions particularly. The adoption of technologies in the Arab regions in comparison to other countries in North America, Europe, and other developing countries is still at its very early stages. Adoption and usage of ICT in the Arab regions at this stage has not been fully researched by practitioners or academia in the region. Many countries in these regions are still lagging far behind the developed countries in terms of the acceptance of technologies, and many organizations in these regions are not yet ready to accept the ICT. There are four factors indicated for the Perceived Behavioral Control (self-efficacy, Technology Facilitating Condition, Resources Facilitating Condition and Government Facilitating Condition)
Ayman Ahmed AlQudah 2014	European Scientific Journal	To identify staff attitudes towards Moodle.	80 instructors	Survey & Interview	Technical support has a positive effect on the perceived usefulness of The instructors significantly tend to like Moodle and see using it is a good idea. The instructors' answers is because they lack computer skills, unlike the IT department. This leads to the difficulty most staff face and making Moodle easy would be an issue. Also, this may relate to resistance to issues of change.

continued on following page

Table 1. Continued

Author(s) / Year	Study design	Research aims	Sample	Data collection	Main findings
Almarabeh, Tamara 2014	iJET, journal article	To examine students' perception of E-learning at the University of Jordan	180 students	Survey	The students of the University of Jordan are highly qualified to use E-learning system and have sufficient awareness of benefits of this system. The results revealed that the perceived usefulness and perceived ease of use are factors that directly affect students' attitudes toward using E-learning system, whereas the perceived usefulness is the strongest and most significant determinant of students' attitude towards using.
Majdalawi, Yousef Kh. Almarabeh, Tamara Mohammad, Heba 2014	Life Science Journal	To examine how students receive and how they use Moodle platform. Additional external variables were also adopted: GPA, academic year, and faculty.	240 Students	Questionnaire	The students of the University of Jordan are highly qualified to use Moodle and have sufficient awareness of benefits of this system. The results revealed that the perceived usefulness and perceived ease of use are factors that directly affect students' acceptance toward using Moodle, noting that the attitudes of students for using Moodle because of the perceived ease of use and not because of the perceived usefulness which invites the decision makers in the university to increase the awareness of the importance and usefulness of Moodle and other ICT tools. Type of the faculty is an important factor that effect on perceived ease of use and perceived usefulness which means the decision makers in the University of Jordan must give more attention to the students in humanities faculties to increase their skills in using computer and internet in their courses and increase their awareness about the benefits of the Learning Management Systems.
Muhannad Al-Shboul 2013	International Education Studies	To investigate the degree of E-Learning integration at the University of Jordan. to identify potential factors related to the use of e-Learning tools by faculty members (users and non-users) at this University	1314 faculty members	Paper based survey	Offer more training sessions in the use of e-Learning tools Offer workshops concerning the technical issues in using e-Learning tools Reduce teaching loads to make more time available for employing e-Learning tools Offer rewards and incentives for using e-Learning tools Offer adequate encouragement and support concerning the use of e Learning tools such as establishing or activating faculty development programs that focus on the use of e-Learning tools

continued on following page

Table 1. Continued

Author(s) / Year	Study design	Research aims	Sample	Data collection	Main findings
Khasawneh, Mohammad MF Ibrahim, Huda 2012	Knowledge Management International Conference (KMICe)	to present the differences between academic staffs' demographic characteristics and the usage of common technologies such as computers, Internet, mobile phone, and personal digital assistant (PDA) that affects their adoption and usage of ICT in the teaching and learning process.	500 academic staff	quantitative technique survey	An empirical research on the usage of technologies by academic staff in Jordanian public universities. It gives benefits to the higher education system and the universities in Jordan to improving the teaching and learning process by utilizing ICT services in the teaching system. The study also gives the higher education leaders a full image about the current status of ICT usage in the teaching system. Pointed out that academicians in Jordanian universities like to use ICT services in the educational system more than Knowledge Management International Conference (KMICe) 2012, Johor Bahru, Malaysia, 4 – 6 July 2012 482 others in their teaching and learning process. Barriers that face the academicians to use the educational technologies. There is a significant relationship between academic staff's demographic characteristics and their use of common technologies that affect their intention to use ICT in the educational system (M. M. Khasawneh & Ibrahim, 2012).
Alnsour, Ayman Muhsen, Zahraa Dababnah, Maher Eljinini, Mohammad Barhoum, Khalil Ali 2011	IJCSNS International Journal of Computer Science and Network Security	To introduce the e-learning system to all Isra University students. To support the understanding of the overall learning process, learning motivation, legitimatize application of knowledge, and a challenge for improving the teaching behaviours.	86 undergraduate students	Survey	Increases the student's motivation to read and search for this e-learning system, due to the fact that it does save a lot of time. Organize and manage different concurrent classes for a particular course.
Muneer Mahmood Abbad, David Morris and Carmel de Nahlik 2010	International Review of Research in Open and Distance Learning	To investigates and identifies some of the major factors affecting students' adoption of an E-learning system in a university in Jordan.	486 undergraduate students	Survey	Students who are frequent and/or heavy users of the Internet are more likely to use eLearning systems. Students who are confident in their ability to master an e-learning system, without help, are more likely to become users. Students are reassured by the availability of back-up technical support. Students believe that an e-learning system will be more useful to them if it is easy to use.
EL-Seoud, S. A., Al-Khasawneh, B., & Awajan, A. (2007)	Case Study	To better explain the need for web based courses. To measure the degree of acceptance of such method among the different users.	160 student	Survey	The online course management system was used to make available the course syllabus, the class assignment rubrics (guidelines plus evaluation criteria), and the weekly class agenda. The calendar tool was employed to inform students about on-campus events, conferences, and other resources that we thought might be of interest to the students. E-mail and bulletin board tools were used for communication between instructor and students, students and instructor, and students and students. Students could monitor their progress by accessing their grades for every activity that had a grade associated with it. Reading quizzes, class surveys, and final course evaluation were also made available online.

Jordan universities. According to Samak and Tawfik (2017), the Jordanian Ministry of Education made a five-year plan to establish IT infrastructure for public schools. This plan will be useful to identify the amount, methods and types of infrastructure used in the schools.

According to Khwaldeh, Al-Hadid, and Masa'deh (2017), the infrastructure for analytics in LMS at Jordanian universities needs to improve and suit the demands of users (students, instructors and administration users). The chapter highlighted some users' infrastructure needs, such as deaf and the blind users, which means there is a gap in the IT infrastructure that needs to be identified and improved to be usable for all users (students and stuff).

Donation from developed countries and organisations are being used to help upgrade the IT infrastructure for analytics in LMSs at Jordanian universities from the old infrastructure to a new platform infrastructure; however, because of other obstacles like refugees from the border country and Jordan's lack of financial resources, the improvement is slow, which means that there is a lack of infrastructure, especially in the education sectors.

IT infrastructure for analytics in LMSs at Jordanian universities positively affects the acceptance of analytics in LMS through perceived use and perceived ease of use. Two hypotheses (H) were formulated regarding IT infrastructure for analytics in LMSs as follows:

H1: IT infrastructure for LMSs has a positive effect on perceived usefulness for the LMS; and

H3: IT infrastructure for LMSs has a positive effect on perceived ease of use for the LMS.

2. Culture in Jordan

Cultural factors affect the use of analytics in LMS tools at Jordanian universities. The unique culture in Jordan is a very important factor that influences the use of analytics in LMSs in different ways, and this chapter focuses on this factor through perceived use and perceived ease of use. According to Cho and Berge (2002), the most influential factors regarding the adoption and deployment of analytics in LMS are the culture and norms of those working in higher education faculties. Therefore, pedagogical issues and the lack of technology professional training are affecting the acceptance of analytics in LMS.

Many researchers highlight culture as one of the most significant factors affecting the acceptance of analytics in using LMSs at Jordanian universities. A limitation in the studies done in Jordan universities is that they do not reflect the real number of users, and to be accurate, the sample size should represent all types of users (Abdullateef, Elias, Mohamed, Zaidan, & Zaidan, 2016; M. Al-Shboul, 2013; Al Musawi et al., 2015; Atoum, Otoom, & Ali, 2017; Khwaldeh et al., 2017).

According to M. Al-Shboul (2013), “We need to spread the culture of using e-Learning technology to enhance the quality of learning”. The university management advised that more focus on user training is needed and the university culture needs to be more open to new technology to improve the quality of teaching and learning. With reference to Abbad, Morris, and De Nahlik (2009, p. 19) “Cultures that are more focused on oral traditions may be less engaged with e-learning”. Management should work more on user training so the users can accept and enjoy the new technology and look forward to new updates. According to Varis and Al-Agtash (2008, p. 74) “As a relevant factor in the dissemination of values and in the formation of society’s thinking, the media are responsible for disseminating local culture and the events that occur in the world”. The media today is a very important player in local social life and improving the use of any new technology. It’s the key player in changing user culture and improving positively any new technology.

In this chapter, a significant relationship exists between the influence of culture and the perceived usefulness and perceived ease of use of adopting analytics in LMS at Jordanian universities. There is a need to confirm this prediction with respect to the location (Jordanian universities) through this research. The relationship between cultural influence and the use of analytics in LMS is hypothesised in this research as follows:

H2: Culture has a positive effect on perceived ease of use for the LMS; and
H4: Culture has a positive effect on perceived usefulness for the LMS.

3. Perceived Usefulness of Analytics in LMS

The perceived usefulness of analytics in LMS is defined as the degree to which the user believes that using the LMS tool would improve their learning performance (Davis, 1989). It is “the degree to which a person believes that using a particular system could enhance their job performance” and “it is the extent to which an individual believes that using the system enhances his/her performance” (Saadé & Bahli, 2005, pp. 217-240). According to Davis (1989, p. 320) “People tend to use or not use an application to the extent they believe it will help them perform their job better. We refer to this first variable as perceived usefulness”.

In the TAM, Davis (1989) suggests two determinants of computer usage: PU (perceived usefulness) and PEOU (perceived ease of use). Later, other investigators and researchers extended the TAM model to combine additional variables that could account for extra variance in computer usage technology (Gefen & Straub, 1997;

Venkatesh & Davis, 2000). The advantage paradigm from behavioural decision theory is relevant to perceived usefulness and perceived ease of use (Beach & Mitchell, 1978).

The benefits of the hypotheses of IT infrastructure and culture are to encourage users (students, instructors and management) to accept any new technology and work on it to gain all the advantages and improve the quality of learning. The IT infrastructure and culture in Jordan are very important factors affecting the acceptance of any new technology to accept, including the use of analytics in LMSs at Jordanian universities (M. Al-Shboul, 2011; M. A. Al-Shboul & Alsmadi, 2010; Alnsour et al., 2011; AlQudah, 2014).

This chapter highlights the perceived usefulness on analytics in LMS tools from the IT infrastructure and the culture in Jordan context to show the attention of acceptance using analytics in LMS at Jordan universities. The relationship between perceived usefulness and the acceptance of analytics in LMS to adopt LMS is hypothesised as follows:

H5: Perceived usefulness in accepting an analytics in LMS has a positive effect on acceptance of analytics in LMS.

4. Perceived Ease of Use of an Analytics in LMS

The perceived ease of use of an analytics in LMS is defined as the degree to which the user believes that using the LMS will be free of effort (Davis, 1989). It can be described as "the degree to which a person believes that using a particular system is free of effort. Previous research has demonstrated that individuals are more likely to use a new technology if they perceive that it is easy to use" (Saadé & Bahli, 2005, pp. 101-132).

Davis (1989) shows that ease of use had a direct effect on perceived usefulness. Many studies on the TAM also provided strong experimental support for a positive relationship between perceived usefulness and perceived ease of use. The TAM shows that perceived ease of use and perceived usefulness have a direct effect on acceptance of using a new technology (Adams, Nelson, & Todd, 1992; Szajna, 1996; Venkatesh & Davis, 2000). Venkatesh (1999) discovered that "facilitating conditions and external control served as anchors that users employ to inform perceived ease of use about information technology" as cited in (Abbad et al., 2009, p. 167). According to Williams (2002), an important factor in determining the acceptance of technology such as an LMS is the availability of "technical support".

Both IT infrastructure and culture are very important factors that affect ease of use of an analytics in LMS. According to M. Al-Shboul (2013) IT infrastructure and culture are key players in enhancing the quality of learning. IT infrastructure should be able to support and accept any technology and software tools without obstacles. Poor infrastructure will cost any organisation money and time in activating the new tools or new technology software.

It is hypothesised that IT infrastructure and culture affect the perceived ease of use an analytics in LMS positively and negatively. Good infrastructure makes any new software easy to apply and use. With regard to culture, knowledge of the culture where a new software will be applied will allow the new technology to be easy for the uses to use for the users to use (students, instructors and managements) (Al-Dmour, 2014; AlQudah, 2014).

Perceived ease of use of an analytics in LMS shows the intention a user has to make use of a technology under a given behaviour. It was predicted that users' behavioural intention to adopt LMS has an encouraging influence on acceptance of analytics in LMS.

H6: Perceived ease of use of an analytics in LMS has a positive effect on acceptance for analytics in the LMS.

5. Acceptance of an Analytics in LMS

The Technology Acceptance Model (TAM) "has become well-established as a robust, powerful, and parsimonious model for predicting user acceptance" (Venkatesh & Davis, 2000, p. 19). A large number of researchers have adopted the TAM to test and examine the acceptance of new technologies like personal computers (Igbaria, Zinatelli, Cragg, & Cavaye, 1997).

Davis (1989, p. 335) indicates that: "the possibility of dysfunctional impacts generated by information technology emphasizes that user acceptance is not a universal goal and is actually undesirable in cases where systems fail to provide true performance gains. Although there has been a growing pessimism in the field about the ability to identify measures that are robustly linked to user acceptance, the view taken here is much more optimistic. User reactions to computers are complex and multifaceted. But if the field continues to systematically investigate fundamental mechanisms driving user behaviour, cultivating better and well measures and critically examining alternative theoretical models, sustainable progress is within reach".

To accept a new system, hypotheses for both perceived usefulness and perceived ease of use should be examined (Davis, 1989). The model reflects these hypotheses to measure the acceptance of new software for any organisation, especially Jordanian universities, and it will then be possible to see if it is appropriate to use this new software in these universities. The model can then be used for all universities in Jordan. The outcome will influence the continued use of analytics in LMS software in Jordanian universities in general (Almarabeh, 2014).

Figure 1. Conceptual framework for Jordanian Learning Management System Model (JLMS)

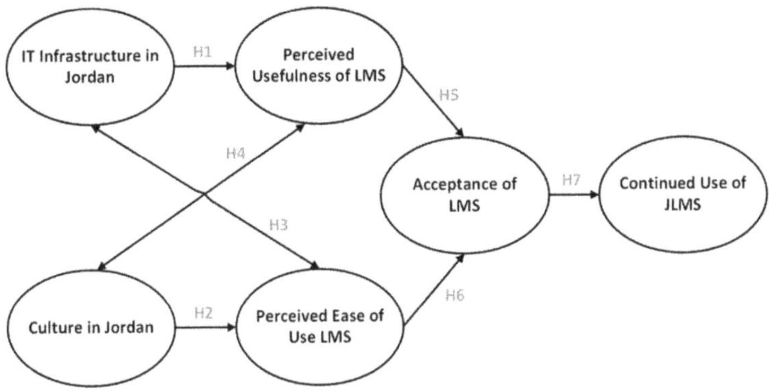

Acceptance of an analytics in LMS shows the perceived usefulness and perceived ease of use of an analytics in LMS under a given behaviour for continued use of analytics in LMSs at Jordanian universities.

H7: Acceptance of an analytics in LMS has a positive effect on continued use of analytics in the LMS.

Conceptual Constructs and the Research Model

The chapter utilises the Technology Acceptance Model (TAM) as a framework to address all the relevant issues around the LMS context. In this research, we propose a model, based on the extension of the Technology Acceptance Model (TAM) (Davis, 1989) that will be applied, tested and examined for the discovery of new information and understanding of the Jordanian Learning Management System model (JLMS). The following is a review and definition of this framework with critical perspectives.

The literature review highlighted many hypotheses affect that suggest the acceptance of analytics in LMS is subject to complex relations between variables. The following hypotheses were proposed:

Summarizing Hypotheses

H1: IT infrastructure characteristics positively affect perceived usefulness of an LMS
H2: Cultural characteristics positively affect perceived ease of use of an LMS
H3: IT infrastructure characteristics positively affect perceived ease of use of an LMS
H4: Cultural characteristics positively affect perceived usefulness of an LMS

H5: Perceived usefulness of LMS characteristics positively affect acceptance of an LMS
H6: Perceived ease of use of LMS characteristics positively affect acceptance of the LMS
H7: Acceptance of an LMS characteristics positively affects continued use of the JLMS

A number of issues can affect users' decision to accept LMS tools of choice, and Jordan is one of the developing countries that experience problems such as lack of network connectivity, slow system response and social cultural issues. In this research, the many factors that affect acceptance and rate of adoption are used to understand how they influence the diffusion rate of LMS tools as innovative instructional delivery tools. Therefore, we investigate behavioural intent to use LMS tools by employees, based on attitude, relative advantage, complexity and compatibility (Mkhize, Mtsweni, & Buthelezi, 2016).

Significance of the Study

The chapter presents information that will be useful to decision makers in Jordanian universities and highlight the issues related to using analytics in LMS in higher education and demonstrate the degree of acceptance of analytics in LMSs at Jordanian universities. In this part of study, the focus will be on six different universities: University of Jordan (UJ), Princess Sumaya University of Technology (PSUT), Philadephia University (PU), Jordan University of Science and Technology (JUST), The Applied Science Private University (ASU) and Al al-Bayt University (AABU). It will highlight the current status of each of them regarding the use of LMS in higher educational teaching. The chapter investigates the following aspects:

1. Current use of analytics in LMSs at Jordanian universities
2. Factors influencing the acceptance of analytics in LMS applications at Jordanian universities
3. Attitudes of participants using LMS applications
4. Participants knowledge of LMS applications.

According to Feeney (2001), LMSs are becoming important for university education. Adoption of LMS tools becomes for both intuitional aim and for a source of data upon which to estimate performance. Kim (2008) indicates that faculty workload is the main factor influencing faculty participation in an LMS (distance education). Most importantly, universities in Jordan are still struggling to deliver successful integrated LMS applications, particularly in engineering and computer science. As a result, most of these universities may not be able to achieve their specified goals in terms of applying LMS applications.

Summary and Findings

Learning Management Systems (LMS's) are the latest innovative trend facilitated by the prorogation of Information Technology allowing learning capabilities previously not thought possible. The literature review has demonstrated various learning analytics strategies and their uses. Online learning is an innovative way of acquiring knowledge that is making life easier for all individuals involved in learning analytics. This chapter has summarised the viewpoints of other researchers and authors. It has also discussed some of the latest technologies that can be adopted for the learning analytics process like digital libraries. Insight the LMS applications were also mentioned.

Additionally, the TAM model was explained, including the research limitations and the LMS application in higher educational sectors at Jordanian universities. The literature reviewed the LMS facilities used in the Jordanian universities mentioned. The research problem was clearly presented along with the required data collection and analysis procedures. These have formulated the research methodological aspects including the conceptual framework underpinning the research. A new model has created to improve using of analytics in LMS at Jordanian universities, and this model will help the ministry of higher education Jordan to improve using learning management tool for all the Jordanian universities.

REFERENCES

Abbad, M. M., Morris, D., & De Nahlik, C. (2009). Looking under the bonnet: Factors affecting student adoption of e-learning systems in Jordan. *The International Review of Research in Open and Distributed Learning*, *10*(2). doi:10.19173/irrodl.v10i2.596

Abdullateef, B. N., Elias, N. F., Mohamed, H., Zaidan, A., & Zaidan, B. (2016). An evaluation and selection problems of OSS-LMS packages. *SpringerPlus*, *5*(1), 1. doi:10.118640064-016-1828-y PMID:27064567

Adams, D. A., Nelson, R. R., & Todd, P. A. (1992). Perceived usefulness, ease of use, and usage of information technology: A replication. *Management Information Systems Quarterly*, *16*(2), 227–247. doi:10.2307/249577

Ahmad, S. A., Chinade, U. B., Gambaki, A. M., Ibrahim, S., & Ala, N. A. (2012). The need for MOODLE as a learning management system in Nigerian Universities: Digesting University Utara Malaysia Learning Zone as a case study. *Academic Research International*, *2*(3), 444.

Al Bakri, A. (2013). An Overview of Information and Communication Technology (ICT) in Jordan: Review the Literature of Usage, Benefits and Barriers. *International Journal of Internet and Distributed Systems*, *1*(02), 9–15. doi:10.4236/ijids.2013.12002

Al-Dmour, R. (2014). *An integration model for identifying the determinants of the adoption and implementation level of HRIS applications and Its effectiveness in business organisations in Jordan.* Academic Press.

Al Musawi, A., Ambusaidi, A., Al-Balushi, S., & Al-Balushi, K. (2015). Effectiveness of E-Lab Use in Science Teaching at the Omani Schools. *TOJET: The Turkish Online Journal of Educational Technology, 14*(1).

Al-Shboul, M. (2011). Potential Use of Course Management Systems in Higher Education Institutions in Jordan. *Online Submission*, *8*(2), 220–232.

Al-Shboul, M. (2013). The Level of E-Learning Integration at the University of Jordan: Challenges and Opportunities. *International Education Studies*, *6*(4). doi:10.5539/ies.v6n4p93

Al-Shboul, M. A., & Alsmadi, I. (2010). Challenges of Utilizing E-Learning Systems in Public Universities in Jordan. *iJET, 5*(1), 4-10.

Almarabeh, T. (2014). Students' Perceptions of E-learning at the University of Jordan. *iJET, 9*(3), 31-35.

Alnsour, A., Muhsen, Z., Dababnah, M., Eljinini, M. A., & Barhoum, K. A. (2011). Implementing Moodle as a Tool to develop the Isra University e-learn system. *IJCSNS International Journal of Computer Science and Network Security*, *11*, 120–124.

AlQudah, A. A. (2014). Accepting Moodle by academic staff at the University of Jordan: Applying and extending TAM in technical support factors. *European Scientific Journal*, *10*(18).

Atoum, I., Otoom, A., & Ali, A. A. (2017). Holistic Cyber Security Implementation Frameworks: A Case Study of Jordan. *International Journal of Information, Business and Management*, *9*(1), 108.

Babić, S. (2012). Factors that influence academic teacher's acceptance of e-learning technology in blended learning environment. *E-Learning-Organizational Infrastructure and Tools for Specific Areas*, 3-18.

Beach, L. R., & Mitchell, T. R. (1978). A contingency model for the selection of decision strategies. *Academy of Management Review*, *3*(3), 439–449. doi:10.5465/amr.1978.4305717

Chin, W. W. (1995). Partial least squares is to LISREL as principal components analysis is to common factor analysis. *Technology Studies*, *2*(2), 315–319.

Cho, S. K., & Berge, Z. L. (2002). Overcoming barriers to distance training and education. *USDLA Journal*, *16*(1), 16–34.

Creswell, J. W. (2013). *Research design: Qualitative, quantitative, and mixed methods approaches*. Sage Publications.

Davis, F. D. (1989). Perceived usefulness, perceived ease of use, and user acceptance of information technology. *Management Information Systems Quarterly*, *13*(3), 319–340. doi:10.2307/249008

Denscombe, M. (2014). *The good research guide: for small-scale social research projects*. UK: McGraw-Hill Education.

El-Bahsh, R., & Daoud, M. (2016). Evaluating the use of Moodle to achieve effective and interactive learning: A case study at the German Jordanian University. *Proceedings of the 35th Annual IEEE International Conference on Computer Communications*.

El-Seoud. (2007). *Using Web-Based Course to Enhance Educational Process at Jordan Universities – A Case Study*. PSUT.

Eriksson, P., & Kovalainen, A. (2015). Qualitative methods in business research: A practical guide to social research. *Sage (Atlanta, Ga.)*.

Feeney, D. R. (2001). *Rates of adoption in a university course management system*. West Virginia University.

Gefen, D., & Straub, D. W. (1997). Gender differences in the perception and use of e-mail: An extension to the technology acceptance model. *Management Information Systems Quarterly*, *21*(4), 389–400. doi:10.2307/249720

Hofstede, G. J., Minkov, M., & Hofstede, G. (2016). *Allemaal andersdenkenden: omgaan met cultuurverschillen*. Business Contact.

Igbaria, M., Zinatelli, N., Cragg, P., & Cavaye, A. L. (1997). Personal computing acceptance factors in small firms: A structural equation model. *Management Information Systems Quarterly*, *21*(3), 279–305. doi:10.2307/249498

Kats, Y. (2010). *Learning Management System Technologies and Software Solutions for Online Teaching: Tools and Applications: Tools and Applications*. IGI Global.

Khasawneh, M. (2015). Factors influence e-learning utilization in Jordanian universities-academic staff perspectives. *Procedia: Social and Behavioral Sciences, 210*, 170–180. doi:10.1016/j.sbspro.2015.11.356

Khasawneh, M. M., & Ibrahim, H. (2012). *Technology to enhance learning: The Jordanian experience*. Academic Press.

Khwaldeh, S. M., Al-Hadid, I., Masa'deh, R. e., & Alrowwad, A. (2017). The Association between E-Services Web Portals Information Quality and ICT Competence in the Jordanian Universities. *Asian Social Science, 13*(3), 156. doi:10.5539/ass.v13n3p156

Kim, M. (2008). Factors influencing the acceptance of e-learning courses for mainstream faculty in higher institutions. *International Journal of Instructional Technology and Distance Learning, 5*(2), 29–44.

Loehlin, J. C., & Beaujean, A. A. (2017). *Latent variable models: An introduction to factor, path, and structural equation analysis*. Taylor & Francis.

Majadlawi, Y., Almarabeh, T., & Mohammad, H. (2014). Factors affecting students' usage of learning management system at The University of Jordan. *Life Science Journal, 11*(6), 666–671.

Majdalawi, Y. K., Almarabeh, T., & Mohammad, H. (2014). *Factors Affecting Students' Usage of Learning Management System at the University of Jordan*. Academic Press.

McDaniel, R., Fanfarelli, J. R., & Lindgren, R. (2017). Creative Content Management: Importance, Novelty, and Affect as Design Heuristics for Learning Management Systems. *IEEE Transactions on Professional Communication, 60*(2), 183–200. doi:10.1109/TPC.2017.2656578

McIntosh, J., & Torres, M. I. (2014). *Learning Management Systems: Revisiting Learning Management Systems at the University Level*. The University of Tampa.

Mkhize, P., Mtsweni, E. S., & Buthelezi, P. (2016). Diffusion of Innovations Approach to the Evaluation of Learning Management System Usage in an Open Distance Learning Institution. *The International Review of Research in Open and Distributed Learning, 17*(3). doi:10.19173/irrodl.v17i3.2191

Phillipo, J., & Krongard, S. (2012). *Learning Management System*. LMS.

Saadé, R., & Bahli, B. (2005). The impact of cognitive absorption on perceived usefulness and perceived ease of use in on-line learning: An extension of the technology acceptance model. *Information & Management*, *42*(2), 317–327. doi:10.1016/j.im.2003.12.013

Samak, A., & Tawfik, Z. (2017). *Exploration of Jordanian English Language Teachers' Attitudes*. Skills, and Access as Indicator of Information and Communication Technology Integration in Jordan.

Szajna, B. (1996). Empirical evaluation of the revised technology acceptance model. *Management Science*, *42*(1), 85–92. doi:10.1287/mnsc.42.1.85

Varis, T., & Al-Agtash, S. (2008). *Ubiquitous ICT for sustainable education and cultural literacy*. Citeseer.

Venkatesh, V. (1999). Creation of favorable user perceptions: Exploring the role of intrinsic motivation. *Management Information Systems Quarterly*, *23*(2), 239–260. doi:10.2307/249753

Venkatesh, V., & Davis, F. D. (2000). A theoretical extension of the technology acceptance model: Four longitudinal field studies. *Management Science*, *46*(2), 186–204. doi:10.1287/mnsc.46.2.186.11926

Williams, P. (2002). The learning web: The development, implementation and evaluation of internet-based undergraduate materials for the teaching of key skills. *Active Learning in Higher Education*, *3*(1), 40–53. doi:10.1177/1469787402003001004

Yin, R. K. (1981). The case study crisis: Some answers. *Administrative Science Quarterly*, *26*(1), 58–65. doi:10.2307/2392599

Chapter 10
The Wit-Learning Methodology as a Means for Research Skills Acquisition: A Longitudinal Assessment

Luis Ibarra
https://orcid.org/0000-0002-7290-3001
Tecnologico de Monterrey, Mexico

Arturo Soriano
https://orcid.org/0000-0003-3299-9851
Tecnologico de Estudios Superiores de Ixtapaluca, Mexico

Pedro Ponce
Tecnologico de Monterrey, Mexico

Arturo Molina
Tecnologico de Monterrey, Mexico

ABSTRACT

The present blistering modernization, epitomized by artificial intelligence, demands engineering graduates to address holistic, fast-changing, and even unknown problems. Thus, skills development, such as self-learning, is gaining importance against the traditional educational approach. To this regard, the wit-learning methodology was designed to stimulate the research skills during a course, supported on the similitude of the research endeavor with the desired engineers' profile. It stands out from other proposed alternatives targeting the students' capabilities that do not focus on research skills or misses their quantitative evaluation. In this chapter, the wit-learning methodology is presented together with its assessment regarding

DOI: 10.4018/978-1-5225-7793-5.ch010

research skills acquisition, using direct and indirect measurements. Notably, it was verified to help improve the research skills through three criteria: the improvement of the students' research reports, the increased students' agreement to researchers while evaluating research reports, and their understanding of the research goals and processes.

INTRODUCTION

The rapid technological development and the accentuated availability of IT commodities shape an uncertain future. The versatility of artificial intelligence (AI) not only finds application in everyday services such as interaction in social networks and chatbots, it directly impacts the value chains of corporations and organizations and, in the end, is redefining the value of work of many people. In this way, the interaction of the AI in the individual life of a worker exhibits, in the words of Abeles (2016), even a threat to his identity and his sense of well-being. One might think that professional practice would be exempt from such a risk; however, applications of AI are present in areas related to high-level thinking such as learning, emotion evaluation, and disease detection (Wright & Schultz, 2018; Williams, 2019). That locates AI, according to the interpretation of Abeles (2016), as a competitive entity similar to a community capable of filling job vacancies traditionally occupied by the original population.

This panorama imposes new considerations on a sophisticated space of work opportunities *per se* and has motivated research regarding the incorporation of AI into professional practice. The consulted literature agrees that, although the AI is already modifying businesses, it has not conclusively affected the current work environment (Morikawa, 2017; Fountaine et al., 2019); however, a definitive growth is expected. In this sense, the current concerns about professions lie in their foreseen relevance and in the type of preparation necessary to face the future. In this regard, Wright & Schultz (2018) present a framework to identify the activities that most likely and promptly face an AI labor disruption. In that work, three axes with antipodal linguistic scales are identified, namely: (1) social or non-social, (2) skilled or unskilled and (3) non-routine or routine based. A routine based non-social activity that does not demand skill will, according to Wright & Schultz (2018), be more easily and promptly undertaken by AI.

Interestingly, the activities that are further away from such "absorption" are activities such as scientific practice and surgical care. It is foreseen that mid-level jobs will disappear, giving rise to specialized or low-level activities, focusing the latter on services (Wright & Schultz, 2018). The same authors point out that skilled jobs could even benefit from the exhaustive automation provided by the AI, polarizing society in terms of economic compensation. A similar situation occurs between big, global organizations with investment capacity against small companies (Morikawa, 2017). This gap impacts society from an ethical point of view, not abandoned by current research. Full discussions can be found in (Wright & Schultz, 2018) and the references therein, regarding the holistic meaning of work for the individual. Similarly, higher education is urged to aim at educating high-skilled professionals (Williams, 2019), now required not to be technically proficient but also competent toward the modernization mentioned above, capable to face such a holistic and changing environment proactively and being prepared for future, unpredicted problems.

As asserted by Chan et al. (2017), accreditation bodies, employers, engineering students, and teachers have recently placed their attention in *generic skills* which are defined by the same authors as "skills, abilities and attributes which are fundamental in helping students to acquire, construct, and apply knowledge" and are "generic to different learning situations." This implies a change in the way engineering programs are designed, taught, and evaluated, and points directly to skills acquisition rather than knowledge transmission. Such point of view is familiar to many researchers who state that the graduates require analyzing and synthesizing capabilities, be critical thinkers, and autonomously find solutions for the daily problems (Brew & Mantai, 2017; Huet, 2018; Williams, 2019). Similarly, Clements & Joswick (2018) state that "twenty-first-century skills are focused on creativity, ingenuity, critical thinking, and the like," affirming that persevering at problem-solving, producing extended chains of reasoning, and communicating effectively orally and in writing are decidedly expected.

In order for the engineering practice to become compelling, the traditional approach to engineering courses' teaching is not enough. Knowledge facilitation or transmission is necessary but not sufficient against contingency; as a result, many teaching techniques and engineering programs have turned toward the generation of skills or capabilities (Williams, 2019). As stated by the American National Research Council (Rijst, 2017), "The meaning of 'knowing' has shifted from being able to remember and repeat information to being able to find and use it;" in addition, current approaches also insist on the *generation* of knowledge (Clements & Joswick, 2018) as a requirement. The main aim of such effort is to guarantee that the graduates' capabilities are not fortuitous, or exclusively dependent on each's given skills. Indeed, the expectancy is to provide some certainty about the ability of all graduates to fit into the aforementioned professional environment. Then, there are two key concepts to deal with; namely, skills and uncertainty. However, what type of skills would address uncertainty? Alternatively, *how can a teaching methodology enable undergraduate students to acquire skills, necessary for tackling holistic, ongoing, or unknown scenarios*?

This chapter introduces a methodology specifically designed for answering the above question. It was first proposed in (Ponce, Ibarra, Mata, & Molina, 2019) as a means to deal with thorough engineering courses by stating that *research skills* would effectively help graduates when dealing with future engineering problems. That specific set of skills was the focus of the proposed learning technique because the research endeavor finds many similitudes with the expected, future engineering practice. For instance, inquiry, self-learning, objectivity, and methodological proficiency are some of the "assets" to add to the graduate professional toward the generation of specialized workers as presented above. Also, many studies have found that "true" learning is strengthened through research, inquiry, and discovery (Huet, 2018); similarly, Clements & Joswick (2018) assert that "to understand is to invent," framing the inventive as the verification of understanding. Then, the introduced technique appealed to make the students undergo a similar "proof" of understanding while performing research-like activities.

As the development of research skills and self-learning capabilities is not a natural process in undergraduate students, there has been a recent interest on directing students to do research and inquiry through different teaching techniques (Healey & Jenkins, 2009). Current expectations are that the students become capable of addressing current, ongoing, and even undetermined future problems in their fields, as commented by (Serra Toledo et al., 2013). It is clear that this outcome has not been pursued or encouraged directly through traditional teaching and learning methodologies, thereby motivating the development of different, novel approaches, including research-based learning (Huet, 2018). It is essential to notice that there is not a definitive research-based teaching methodology, and every proposal pursues different objectives which, however, find their main aim and relevance in the paradigm change commented before. There is not even a homologated perception of research-based learning among educators, and the perceived benefits are also different (Brew & Mantai, 2017). Then, it is stated the need for finding how research-based learning should be driven to verify and maximize its intended benefits, mainly through direct evidence (Rijst, 2017).

The technique used in this study, referred to hereafter as *Wit Learning* (WL), lies on a foundation of bringing research methodology to the classroom, supported by reports prepared under the teacher's supervision and double-blind peer evaluations, as recommended in (Tomkins, Zhang, & Heavlin, 2017). Its main aim is to make students *assimilate*, rather than learn, the research methodology. Besides this learning technique was evaluated before, as shown in (Ponce et al., 2019), the objective was to test if students became critical, objective, and propositional as indicators of research abilities, but research skills were not formally defined nor measured, so its benefits could not be highlighted or compared. Then, the second purpose of this chapter is to determine whether or not WL benefits the building of research skills and, if so, how much these skills improved as a result (this chapter extends the work of Ibarra, Soriano, Ponce, & Molina (2019) in this sense).

However, measuring research skills is not an easy task. The measurement instruments must provide evidence of the students' progress and achievements (Chan, Zhao & Luk, 2017). Evidence is classified as direct or indirect; for example, a student's written work and rubric evaluations are considered direct evidence because they point to skills development. On the other hand, interviews and questionnaires are considered as indirect evidence (and not as reliable) due to the use of reflections, perceptions, or secondary evidence in the forming of conclusions (Chan et al., 2017; Maki, 2010).

Accordingly, the curse used pre-semester and post-semester surveys that could quantify the students' perceptions about research by measuring the numerical changes in their responses that would account for perception shifts (similar to that presented by Feldon, Maher, Hurst, & Timmerman (2015)). It is important to note that the "correct" answer to each question of the survey was never provided/suggested to the students, so the numerical shifts in perceptions would be the result of WL and not from studying or memorizing research methodology as a separate topic, thus isolating WL as the origin of such perceptions. In this case, the survey results are compared to the opinions of skilled researchers to check for perceptional alignment as evidence of the students' understanding of the research process and its motivation, accompanied by quantitative information from the rubric reports in order to have direct evidence to compare the results.

The rubric was also prepared to assess each part of the research process separately, aiming to quantify the students' improvement on specific skills, enabling direct comparison with the perception alignment. The assessment consisted of a numeric comparison of results from the rubrics completed by the students and those by a senior researcher (the teacher) over the same projects, as described by Kishbaugh et al. (2012). Both rubrics were expected to become similar as the semester progressed. Also, the evaluation provided by the teacher was tracked along the semester to check for students' practical improvement when preparing their research reports.

The structure of this chapter is as follows: the Background section introduces the WL technique; the Methodology section comprises the survey process schematic and the students' progress tracking, comprised by direct rubric evidence and the teachers' observations. The results of the longitudinal study are available in the Results section, whereas a discussion about the findings and additional steps regarding WL assessment are in the Solutions and Recommendations section. Finally, the conclusions are presented in their section.

BACKGROUND

Motivation and Current Issues

Making undergraduate students to face research-based courses is not as irregular as it may sound. Even if their professional life may be unrelated to research, research skills could provide advantages in their everyday practice, considering the changes imposed, for instance, by AI. Then, the objective of research-based techniques is not to develop researchers but to grow a specific set of skills that could cope with future professional requirements. Apart from the professional approach, it has been pointed out by Poincaré (1984) that the pursuit of science settles a moral ground where truth is sought and nourished. Similarly, such a disinterested search of truth, as a "training of the intellect," according to Haverhals (cited in Huet, 2018), encompasses a transformation of society from below and from within.

In the same line, it is essential to mention the work of Williams (2019), who identifies the primary skills and abilities students should have to face the challenges imposed by AI. The author states that communication, collaboration, initiative, and adaptability are principal competencies in this sense, even matching employers' preferences. Other competencies such as social/cultural, critical thinking, problem-solving, and creativity are reported to be present throughout literature as necessary to tackle the AI-imposed environment. Lastly, the author points out that the learning process should pursue *authentic learning*, intended to develop students as whole persons with rounded educations; it comprises the following learning elements: ill-defined problems, sustained investigation, multiple sources and perspectives, collaboration, reflection, interdisciplinary perspective, integrated assessment, polished products, and multiple interpretations and outcomes. Such an approach finds many similitudes to the research practice.

Incorporating research-based courses is then beneficial in higher education as a means to "build" integral professionals. However, there is no unique way to include research activities as part of the undergraduate curricula, and many efforts have been made to test similar proposals and measure their benefits. Although the acquisition of skills and the referred "professional integrity" may be subjective, the past application of research-based teaching techniques have delivered some clear directives to propose, test, measure, and compare different proposals. To this matter, a short presentation of the work of Rijst, (2017) is used below to provide context and frame the proposal subject of this chapter.

Different approaches, such as inquiry-based, research-intensive, and research-based learning techniques, have been applied to furnish a course where research is the central axis of student's activities. As has been repeatedly commented so far, the expectancy of such courses is not only to transfer specialized knowledge, but, as pointed out by Rijst, (2017), to develop students' cognition, skills, and attitudes: "a lived epistemological experience of what it means to construct knowledge." Rijst states that such benefits would only be possible if the research opportunities are "well" incorporated into the course's learning activities, and "well" supervised by the teaching staff. In Rijst's work, "well" is an implication of an emphasis on seeking conceptual/cognitive change among students by profoundly involving them in research activities so "they own their research" (ownership and autonomy); such perspective is similar to that of Rodenbusch (cited in Huet, 2018), who states that research-based courses are better than research internships.

In words of Healey (cited in Rijst, 2017), research-based courses are intended to enhance the depth of learning and understanding, this implies reaching the procedural and meta-cognitive knowledge, according to the Bloom's revised taxonomy. It lays, of course, over solid bases of factual and conceptual knowledge; however, it aims to its application, analysis, evaluation, and creation (Rijst, 2017). Therefore, students learn by engaging in solving real-world problems, using prior knowledge as a foundation for new knowledge, observing new knowledge demonstrations, having an opportunity to apply such knowledge, and, finally, integrating such knowledge into their world (Rijst, 2017). This process coincides with the perspective of Huet (2018), who couple them with the principles of assimilation and accommodation. Accordingly, the benefits associated with research-based learning are, at least, related to cognitive skills; namely, problem-solving and critical-thinking skills.

Other works have identified the benefits coming from research/discovery-based learning like that by Clements & Joswick (2018). The authors directly pointed to the differences arising from letting the students identify and state the problem, rather than only solving it. They state that the interplay between both activities is directly related to the development of conceptual knowledge. Similarly, the same study questioned the role of immediate directive guidance and found it relevant only in the attitudinal context, concluding that inquiry may be more efficacious if done before directive instruction. On the other hand, such guidance was found to be beneficial if restricted to provide conceptual constraints or activity's modifications; however, "the teacher must make use of carefully planned feedback to make these exercises meaningful over time and to build personal sense-making" (Clements & Joswick, 2018).

Finally, Rijst (2017) provides some recommendations to perform and report experiments related to research-based learning. It seems not to be enough experimental designs or longitudinal assessments of students' achievements. Conceptual change is, to this author, only speculatively addressed as no study shows a direct correlation between the research-based technique and the referred change. Some of the difficulties in dealing with such a complex setup point to the need for a hybrid testing approach, comprised of direct and indirect evidence: "... direct and indirect evidence can supplement each other. While the former tells what students have learned, the latter is more related to students' attitudes and beliefs along their process of learning" (Chan et al., 2017).

Wit Learning

Due to the uncertainty of how future problems are to be addressed, the proposed technique recognizes the need to provide the students with research skills so that that future issues could be tackled and, perhaps, be dealt with effectively (Missingham, Shah, & Sabir, 2018). WL as a methodology contemplates that the future solvers of involved, modern challenges would benefit from research skills that enable them to identify and state the problem at hand, to be self-sustainable in acquiring the requisite knowledge, to be able to propose a potential solution, to look at such proposals critically, and, finally, to generate new knowledge.

Although this proposal finds its roots in the paper by Ponce et al. (2019), it was not directly intended to build research skills. Such proposal aimed to teach thorough ongoing topics, trying to provide students with an overall view of the subject in question, taking advantage of students' own motivation to dig around central concepts depending on their interests or expertise area. The main idea was to incentivize critical-thinking, objectivity, and academic formality as indirect triggers of future self-learning and self-motivated inquiry. In order to do so, a research-publishing process including peer-review evaluation was replicated along the course, taking the agreement between the students and the teacher's rubrics as a metric: their gradual similitude would account for a change of students' viewpoint of academic quality.

The proposed technique looked forward to addressing the complexity of a specific subject (the smart grid in this case). It was impossible for a traditional course to cover all the essential aspects in the given time, so the main aim was to let different teams depart from central concepts and find the associated problems hindering the power grid modernization. In this way, each team would hand a differentiated paper around the same sub-topic which, during the peer-review, was made available to the other teams; hence, covering specific content outside the classroom and enabling the teams' reports quality improvement by comparing their works. As everybody used the same rubric, and there were sanctions regarding rubrics' disagreement (variance analysis), students were expected to be committed with the evaluation process and to weigh others' work effectively. Indeed, the assigned grades were statistically analyzed, so that (i) the project report's grade is the result of a weighted sum of the teacher's and students' grades; (ii) a penalty is assigned to the team when one of its members is detected to grade inconsistently (accomplished by a variance analysis of all the team members grades); and (iii) a numerical incentive is awarded to the team delivering "the best report," as conferred by all the graders.

Each project was required to follow a specific format/structure of a research paper and a detailed rubric which directly assesses methodological skills. Then, each project went through a double-blind peer-review process, where the students and the teacher used the rubric to assign a score to each section of the project and then give an overall grade. For instance, in a class of 20 students having five teams with four members, each team would write one report, which would be graded by the teacher and four other classmates. The assigned reviewers are sorted by the teacher to guarantee that a single team has access to all or most of the reports and that an individual student reviews at least one report of each team during the semester. The peer review distribution and rubric make it possible that all the proposals are shared among the groups so that each team can identify the strengths and weaknesses of the reports to understand their quality (Kishbaugh et al., 2012). More importantly, each team is exposed to the other teams' problem statements and solution proposals, potentially providing to all the students a broad panorama of the covered technical material. Also, the teacher supplies detailed, written feedback for each report, covering the issues that each team should address to improve their grade (Feldon et al., 2015).

The process was repeated through eight projects during one semester, each dealing with a specific sub-topic. Each team was carefully advised to guarantee the variety of the addressed problems, and the peer-review was meticulously planned to distribute the handed papers evenly among students and along the semester. The written/verbal feedback provided by the teacher (a skilled researcher) was detailed and exhaustive, trying to ensure improvement, understood as matching the rubric's criteria. In this way, students became used to work around a self-motivated problem, stating a potential solution, suggesting a validating methodology, and running any needed test to obtain results and conclusions: indeed, they performed research departing from central concepts and known tools. As students were encouraged to use their prior knowledge (they were senior students), the diversity of the reports was enlarged, the inquiry intensified, and the reports' quality progressively enhanced.

After applying the above technique a few times, the authors of (Ponce et al., 2019) observed students' changes related to their academic performance. They noticed that students were behaving differently at other courses, being critical about their work and others'. Their grades improved and became confident with their writing and reporting skills. Some graduated students commented that their employers conceived them as formal, capable, autonomous, and proactive; those students made special mentions to the methodology used during the smart-grid class. Although those outcomes could be reasonably related to the applied methodology, an explanation was not available. However, the research-based learning literature associates such changes with the generation of research-skills or generic-skills as seen above; thus, the association of the proposed technique with the generation of such skills was addressed in (Ibarra et al., 2019).

This proposal exhibits one fundamental characteristic: Instead of the teachers providing a defined, delimited problem to the students as the project's input, the students are required to state a problem in their areas of experience, the solution of which could come from the technical material covered in class. As the advisor during this problem-statement phase, the teacher assures that there are academic relevance and variety of content in the problems selected by the student teams. In order for the students to link the covered material with a potential solution to a self-selected problem, they need to use their wits to develop a proposal for a practical solution; hence, the name, "wit learning."

According to the classification proposed by Healey (2005), WL is a proper *research-based* learning methodology for teams; from the classification of Brew & Mantai (2017), it is a *wholistic* approach within courses. Both classifications imply the following: students are a central part of the research generation/evaluation process, they *own* their research in the words of Rijst (2017), and are guided by the teacher through the evaluation provided about their work and their classmate's work. There is a focus on conceptual/cognitive change, incentivizing the learning's deepening. WL fully incorporates the recommendations found in research-based learning literature presented above.

METHODOLOGY

Surveying Research Skills

To effectively address research perceptions, a precise definition of research is needed. For this purpose, the research process shares standard features with several disciplines and can be defined as "*a systematic, methodologically controlled, and transparent process, which needs to be reflected on and which is aimed at generating new knowledge*" (Böttcher & Thiel, 2018). This definition broadens to five areas of skills; namely, in reviewing the state of research, methodological skills, skills in reflecting on research findings, communication skills, and content knowledge (Missingham et al., 2018; Willison & O'Regan, 2007). A survey was designed to address the first four of those areas.

Skilled researchers designed the proposed survey in the form of statements to which the student responders agreed or disagreed. Thereby, the survey became an instrument to check whether or not the students shared an opinion with the skilled researchers and to what degree. Each question was answered using a Likert scale to obtain the degree of agreement to each statement. Each question was scored through the selection of eleven values ranging from *strongly disagree* to *agree strongly* (Derrick & White, 2017). To reduce the tendency towards acquiescence in the responses, the survey designers restated half of the items to imply the opposite assertion, thus reducing the tendency to have a positive bias.

The survey consisted of 28 statements; nine regarding methodological skills (MS), six about reviewing the state of research (SR); seven addressing communication skills (CS), and six about reflecting on the research (RR). Some example statements are reproduced below, translated from Spanish to English by the authors.

The methodological skills (MS) involve the appropriate use of the research method, the problem statement, and the definition of objectives with their associated validations. The survey checked if the student agreed on the method's worth and process. For instance, two examples of MS statements are, "*A true research problem cannot be entirely solved at once: the solution proposal specifies the approach taken to address, not to solve the problem fully,*" and "*The subject of study is omitted during the problem statement because it is addressed later in the results section.*"

The statements regarding the state of research (SR) pointed to the effectiveness and legitimacy of the sources, the referencing, the value of prior work, and the students' discrimination about sources and data. The recognition of early studies and their importance is captured in the following example: "*Prominent researchers are so ahead in their expertise area than they do not need to list references.*"

Communication skills (CS) statements mostly concentrated on the presentation of results by focusing on the worth of the information and data, the use of tables and graphs, and the expected academic formality of the report. An example statement included in the survey is, "*New knowledge should be rapidly shared. Academic formalities mostly delay and hinder research overall.*"

Finally, research reflection (RR) addressed the limitations of the methodology and the multidisciplinary nature of research. It mainly dealt with the use and purpose of research considering social, environmental, and ethical implications. An example of RR statements is, "*Addressing any problem is possible by following a clear methodology; it does not depend on the knowledge one may have regarding the problem.*" Another example is, "*Quantitative methods can yield concrete results; qualitative ones cannot.*"

These statements were provided through a digital survey which randomized all the 28 statements, and only one statement was shown at once, avoiding any association or thematic grouping. The students were explicitly instructed to answer the survey only based on their beliefs, being told, "There are no correct or wrong answers," and a fixed grade was assigned after survey completion. The students were tracked through their university ID for the sake of the longitudinal test. The same mechanism was used to repeat the surveying at the end of the semester.

Each answer was then processed as $s \times r$, where s is the numerical representation between 0 and 10 of the value selected by the student, and r is a 1 or a -1, according to the researchers' agreement or disagreement with the statement, respectively. After multiplying by r, the resulting score will be positive if the researcher and the student agreed or negative otherwise. Then, the answers were averaged both statement-wise (QW) and student-wise (SW). These values were later compared as $f_i - f_j$, where f_i is the value taken from the end-of-semester (EOS) survey and f_j is the value from the beginning-of-semester (BOS) survey. The obtained fields were normalized, considering the absolute maximum value of both EOS and BOS and separately for QW and SW. This metric showed an equally weighed relative evolution of the research perception, so it is possible not only to analyze its improvement but also to make comparisons of both statements and students.

Students' Progress Tracking

In addition to survey information, direct evidence (Maki, 2010) was also acquired to have a stronger comparison reference frame. As introduced above, both the students and the teacher used the same rubric to accomplish the evaluation. This rubric was very detailed and addressed each part of the report concerning the expected research requirements (Kishbaugh et al., 2012). It has been already reported by Ponce et al. (2019) that the students' evaluations became progressively similar to those of the teacher as the semester advanced, indicating a closer alignment with a skilled researcher.

In that study (Ponce et al., 2019), the comparison considered the average evaluation values of only the final grade. As a consequence, it was not possible to measure the improvement areas in terms of research skills as the semester progressed (Healey & Jenkins, 2009). Then, the rubric fields were grouped, depending on the evaluated skill. Although the reports were requested to include a literature review, the rubric barely weighed it because many students commonly complain about the complexity of the available scientific material and their time availability, so the *skills in reviewing the state of research* could not be directly observed.

However, the rubric fields can be still grouped in the remaining three skills; namely, methodological skills, skills in reflecting on research findings, and communication skills. Rubric inputs were normalized to a [0, 10] interval, and an absolute difference (teacher minus students' grades) was calculated for every field and every project. Each category was statistically analyzed as follows: All the differences as calculated above in related fields, for example, methodological skills, were box-plotted for each project. The expected outcome was a mean and a variance reduction through time toward the eighth project, indicating congruence between the students' and the teacher's criteria in each category.

Also, the teacher reported that the projects improved as the semester proceeded. This effect also validates skills acquisition and should be measured. In this case, the teacher's rubrics were analyzed, and the average grades assigned to all teams in the eight projects were calculated. The overall tendency of the grades would be expected to increase because this represents the evaluation of the skilled researcher about the quality of the students' reports.

For the sake of clarity, a schematized rubric representation is shown in Table 1, the different areas comprising research skills are placed next to the category field on the table. It is noteworthy that the rubric follows the expected structure of the written report, so the subjectivity associated with the report contents' location is minimized, showing where the evaluator should find, and what to consider, about each expected outcome. It can be seen that the highest scores are assigned to the "methodology" and the "results" sections, trying to make students focus over those report's sections. Table 1 shows the "elements to evaluate" field with the questions and assertions that the evaluator is supposed to weight for each category; however, the actual rubric is comprised of six guiding statements that help the evaluator to grade from 0 to 100, depending on the associated rubric's statement.

Case Study

A longitudinal study was proposed, comprised of the full application of the WL methodology and the surveys of students' perception of research at the beginning and the end of the semester. The learning methodology itself had direct evidence outputs, namely, rubric grades, covering three of the four research skills of interest, whereas the survey provided indirect data about the evolution of the students' perception of research. However, this evolution was measured for all four areas of interest in skills. Even though the survey statements and the rubric fields can be classified under the same research skills, each addressed each skill differently.

Briefly, the survey statements yield an abstract, conceptual approach to research, whereas the rubric fields assess the detailed, practical requirements of a research project. The partnership of these two approaches is desired as a means to measure skills building. Discordance between these tests would be accounted for by the direct memorizing of research methodology concepts or an apparent imitation of others' work.

It is noteworthy that none of the students in this project previously had been enrolled in a research methodologies course, nor any similar course, and that they had not performed research activities in their bachelor program before the project began. Also, the teacher did not provide direct answers or opinions about the survey statements: feedback to the students was general and did not explain research methodologies in detail. Therefore, the students in the project began with a "blank slate" regarding research methodologies and had not tested their research skills,

Table 1. Schematic view of the rubric's criteria

Category	Subcategory	Score	Elements to Evaluate
Title (CS)	Is it related to the report's contents?	2%	• Clarity • Content-related • Keywords appearance
Problem statement (CS)	During the abstract	3%	• Is it an actual problem? • Objectives-related • Clarity • Validity
	During the introduction	4%	• Explained thoroughly • Content-related • Coherence
Problem justification (CS)	During the abstract	2%	• Is the problem's importance highlighted? • Does its solution seem necessary?
	During the introduction	4%	• Is the justification related to the proposed solution? • Is it convincing?
How has the problem been previously solved? (CS)	During the abstract	1%	• Alternatives/Attempts • Are they relevant? • Are they related to the proposed solution? • Is the need for new solutions highlighted?
	During the introduction	2%	• Are alternatives explained? • Are they confronted with the proposed solution?
Solution statement (MS)	During the abstract	2%	• Clarity • Objectives-related • Are the most important results highlighted?
	During the introduction	4%	• Thorough explanation • Objectives-related • Is it aware of other solutions?
Methodology (MS)	Solution description	10%	• Are the used methods explained thoroughly? • Is the experimentation detailed? • Is this in line with the proposed solution?
	Validity	10%	• Can the methodology verify the proposed solution? • Is the solution enough to attain the set objectives?
	Complexity (different from entangled or intricate)	5%	• General • Modular • Verifiable • Complete
Results	Format (RR)	2%	• Are all the results clear and visible? • Do they match the expected format?
	Effectiveness (RR)	15%	• Objectives-related • Is the analysis facilitated by the results presentation? • Is the important information highlighted?
	Analysis (MS)	17%	• Deepness • Does it come entirely from the presented results? • Can conclusions be posed from it?
Conclusions (RR)	Pertinence	15%	• Concise • Objectives-related • Problem closure • Are these entirely related with the results' analysis?
	Clarity	2%	• Not redundant • Precise

Figure 1. An example view of the spreadsheet used to fill the rubric

Rubric														TOTAL
Who is being evaluated:														23.6%
Category	Description													SubT
	Score		100		80		60		40		20		0	
Results and analysis	34%													23.6%
Format	2%	0	All the figures, graphs, tables, text, etc. can be understood and match the expected format	1	Like the one on the left, but the format is not met	1	There are details that cannot be seen, incongruences (e.g. incorrect units)	0	Many of the results are not understandable or are illegible	0	Most of the results are not understandable or are illegible	0	It is not understandable at all	1.4
Effectiveness	15%	0	The analysis can come directly from the results' presentation - Important information is clearly provided to the reader	1	The analysis is facilitated from the results' presentation but their connection to the objectives is not direct	0	Analysis is not facilitated from the results' presentation, but there is somehow association with the objectives	0	There is no clear cocnnection with the objectives	0	Results are presented inadequately and the relation with the objectives is missing	0	Results' presentation is entirely inadequate	12
Analysis	17%	0	The analysis directly comes from the results and the cited references - They point directly to the conclusions	1	The analysis directly comes from the results - some data do not point to the conclusions	0	The analysis seems shallow	1	The analysis is shallow	0	The analysis does not come from the results or do not point to the conclusions	0	There is no analysis at all	10.2

which only could have been associated with fortuitous events during their studies or by self-provision if they had had any exposure.

This methodology was tested in the undergraduate "Smart-Grid" course, as in (Ponce et al., 2019) during the fall semester of 2018 at Tecnológico de Monterrey, in Mexico City. The course has a duration of 16 weeks and is part of the mechanical engineering curricula. Nineteen senior students were enrolled, so five teams were made, four with 4 participants and one with 3. The students decided their teams. The final course grade was determined by averaging the grades of 8 projects. The grades were obtained by following the described peer-review technique.

All the students participated in both BOS and EOS surveys. It is important to note that all of the students but one were in the last semester of their bachelor program.

RESULTS

Independently from the starting point of the students, this longitudinal study aimed to detect changes in their perceptions about research. It was expected that the students would become more aligned with the perceptions of skilled researchers about research as an effect of the WL methodology. Therefore, according to the data values, the differences between EOS and BOS surveys were expected to be positive. It is noteworthy that zero change would imply not a right/wrong perception, but no change along the semester.

Figure 2(a) shows the results from a statement-wise perspective, grouped by their related research-skills categories. There is an overall improvement throughout 26 categories and descending performance in only two. Those that descended,

Figure 2. Measured improvement

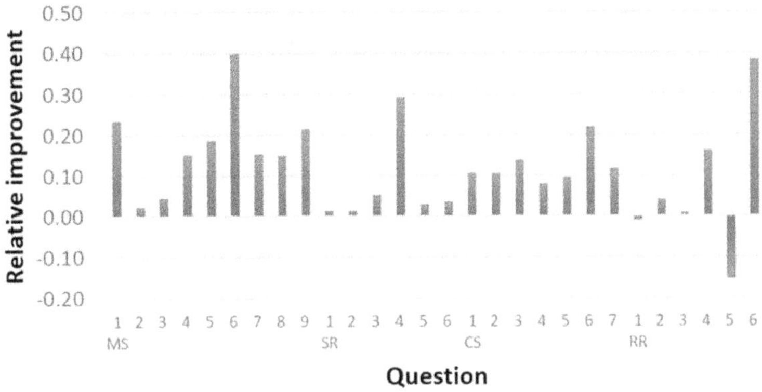

(a) Per-statement improvement

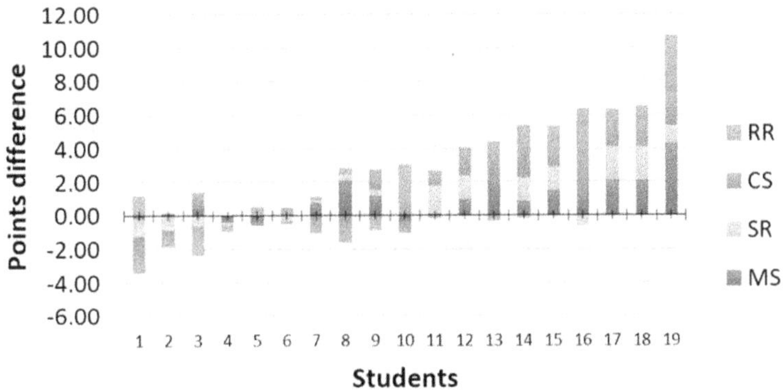

(b) Per-student improvement

specifically statements 1 and 5 inside RR, were: (1) "A researcher seeks the truth, and will become recognized once successful," and (5) "Quantitative methods can yield concrete results; qualitative ones cannot."

The intent of statement (1) was to make a wrong assertion about research capabilities and the concept of truth. Its relative difference was almost zero; it is still worth noticing because research implies continuing improvement and ever-perfectible, iterative attempts toward the truth as one of its major pillars. It is possible that engineering students took this statement as reasonable due to their habituated, highly pragmatical means and their "problem-solving" assumptions. In this case, WL seems not to help understand this concept, perhaps due to the self-selection of the problem statement; i.e., triggered more by engineering pragmatism than scientific inquiry.

On the other hand, statement (5) mistakenly demeans qualitative methods in favor of quantitative ones. This negative result may be due to engineering students' propensity to rely on quantitative evidence as a standard requirement. As said before, these enrolled students were alien to research methodologies; moreover, the rubric specifically asks for methodological validation, which is usually numerical in engineering practice.

It is also relevant to address the heterogeneous nature of every group. Students do not have the same competencies, and their performances differ. Whereas results in Figure 2(a) show the averaged performance of all the students, Figure 2(b) shows their improvements in the four assessed research skills. Results are sorted to provide a direct, visual impression of the points difference between EOS and BOS.

In terms of individual development, the acquisition of research skills depends on the active participation of each student inside his or her team (Afdal & Spernes, 2018). WL anticipates the acquisition of abilities in a structured and progressive way, hence requiring the students to *do* something (Clements & Joswick, 2018). The results of each student differ, as is shown in Figure 2(b), where 13 of 19 students present an improvement. Even though the students' participation involves a team project and the evaluation of other projects, the students decide how much to participate inside their team. This can account for the differences found in Figure 2(b); nevertheless, homogeneous improvement cannot be expected, mainly because their performance is not directly measured and becomes obscured by the overall teamwork.

Regarding direct rubric data, three skills were assessed and box plotted. The boxplot shows relevant statistical information about a dataset; in particular, it provides a quick visual representation of data dispersion. In this case, each project and skill were box-plotted; they were subsequently grouped by skill in order to compare the differences in grades longitudinally. Figure 3 shows all three skills; explicitly, the statistical behavior of MS, CS, and RR are shown in Figure 3(a), Figure 3(b), and Figure 3(c), respectively. Differences are computed as the absolute value in the rubric fields in a 0 to 10 interval.

All plots in Figure 3 depict the statistical behavior of the grading differences in time. Due to the natural ordering of the projects throughout the semester, it was expected a dispersion-decreasing trend in time. Figure 3 shows that the dispersion decreased for every assessed skill. It is essential to consider that a monotonically decreasing variability would be hardly attained, mainly due to two reasons: (i) students' evolution and behavior cannot be expected to be homogeneous, and (ii) the numeric evaluation may easily differ even for similar rubric selections.

In order to directly observe the overall behavior of rubric data, the average difference was plotted in Figure 4(a). The outliers were removed before averaging. There is a decreasing trend in differences for all the evaluated areas and overall

Figure 3. Statistical analyses of the differences between students' and teacher's grades in the eight projects, classified according to the specific assessment areas of the report (MS, CS, and RR)

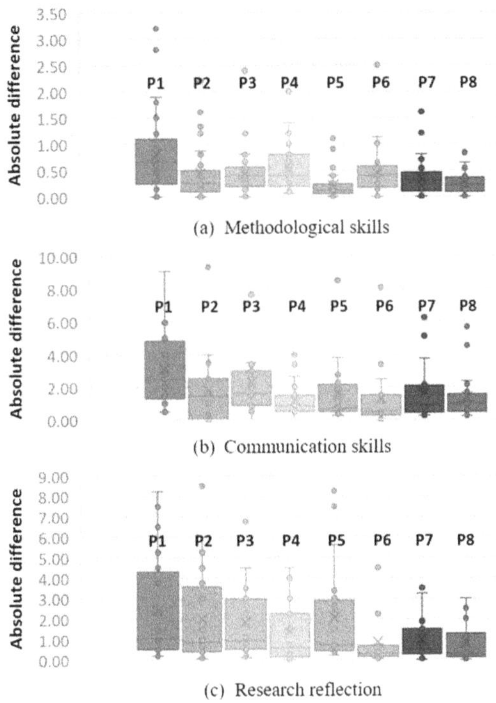

decreasing behavior as well. This effect has been already reported in (Ponce et al., 2019) and confirms the alignment of the student-researcher grade assignments.

It is important to note that there is an average difference increase between P6 and P7. As stated before, all the enrolled students but one, were taking their last semester of the bachelor program, and the deadline of P7 overlapped with their final engineering project presentation (similar to a thesis defense). Besides, P8 also overlapped with the final exams. This effect has been already reported in (Ponce et al., 2019) as an issue of time availability among students, which, however, does not create a significant concern in this project.

Similarly, Figure 4(b) shows the average grade among teams assigned by the skilled researcher to each project as a measurement of improvement: the grade was acquired directly from rubric data. There is a trend of improvement until the sag at P7. This result was expected due to the schedule overlapping mentioned above. This also demonstrates the researcher's grading consistency; a quality problem

Figure 4. Rubric analysis for the eight projects

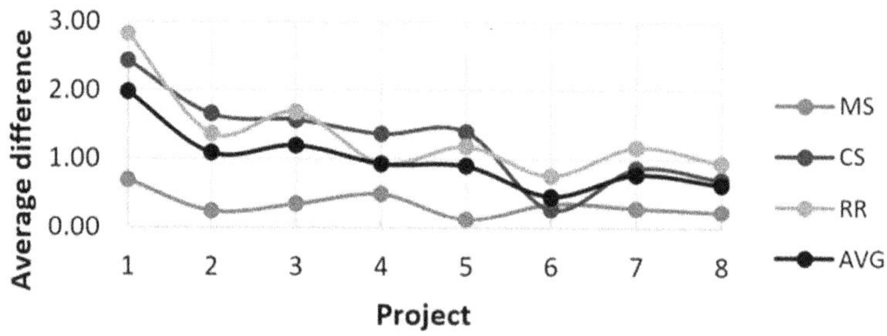

(a) The average difference between grades assigned by students and expert researcher (the teacher)

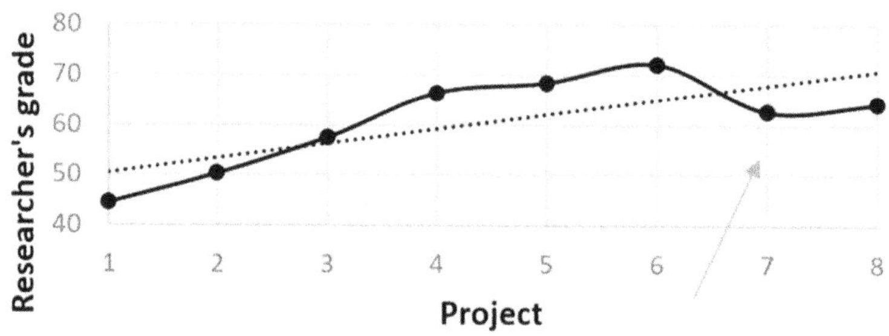

(b) Researcher's grade

appeared when students were stressed and busy. A similar expectation occurs in the peer-review process.

Direct and indirect data are consistent: students' perception about research became more aligned with that of experienced researchers through time, and the evaluation results found in the surveys also revealed the progressive alignment of the students to the same standards of research held by the teacher. This implies that the student became more aware of what a research project was supposed to stand for, and he or she modified their perceptions about research. The research skills of the students improved in practice, as reflected in the evaluation processes and, abstractly, in the improvement between the BOS and EOS surveys.

SOLUTIONS AND RECOMMENDATIONS

Although the apparent benefits of WL are considerable, there are some issues to consider regarding the difficulties around its implementation, hindering its potential replication. The following observations and recommendations come from informal opinions, acquired by directly talking with the students and the teacher.

Students seem stressed and irritated along the semester. Firstly, they are not used to the methodology, and their first grades are usually low (see Figure 4). On the other hand, the Mexican education system does not usually request written reports from students, so their writing skills are not as expected by a researcher. Secondly, students comply that WL is very time-consuming outside classes; they declared that the WL course was the most demanding among all the activities they had during the semester. Finally, they felt confronted with the received feedback. As it is very detailed, students typically take the number of comments as an indication of incompetence, even if such comments recall the same few general errors, and future efforts are foreseen as hopeless. Also, the students' perception about their time/effort in preparing a report and the obtained grade and feedback seem not to be congruent.

The above-presented observations are more recurrent at the beginning of the course, and different opinions arise getting closer to the end of the semester. Students were observed to "show off" with peers not enrolled in the WL course about their newly acquired skills and demeaned other past and current courses as lenient and unchallenging. On a more positive tone, some of the students took advantage of the WL methodology and improved their performance in other parallel courses. The other teachers better perceived the students' overall work, and their grades increased. In specific cases, already graduated students that were enrolled in the WL smart grid course commented on the preference their bosses had over them, entailing the WL course as an asset directly related with such an outcome.

The teacher, on the other hand, reported that the advisory and feedback were very time-consuming. Also, the commented students' irritation was noticeable during most interactions, making the course rigid and unpleasant. Indeed, the institutional evaluation used to score the teacher was not as good as in regular courses. However, the teacher comments that it is worth it overall, mostly because the reports' quality is noticeably improved and his perception about the students' evolution gives a sense of sheer satisfaction. Similarly, top students got back in touch for further technical advisory, asking for graduate programs or a recommendation letter, suggesting recognition.

Besides confrontation and perceptions, the implementation of WL is very time-consuming for both sides. On the side of the students' opinion, it is complicated to disassociate the WL learning curve from the course because preparing them to conduct research would be contradictory regarding the aims of WL. On the side of the teacher, feedback must be detailed, implying thorough revisions. Conclusively, the time needed to undergo a WL course needs to be somehow optimized; there are two recommendations as follows. Firstly, the teacher must be used to the WL technique, or at least confident with the use of the rubric; secondly, following WL courses may progressively boost the students' capacity to prepare reports, manage their time, work in teams, and others. Another recommendation is to provide a broad perspective of the WL benefits to the students at the very beginning of the course, perhaps using some success examples to trigger their motivation and make the whole process not to seem arbitrary or unnecessary.

It has been already reported by Rijst (2017) that research-based learning is time-consuming for teachers, and that special attention is necessary to the students' achievements in both, the research skills and the course content. Similarly, the teacher is required to be an active researcher who, based on the same study, implies for the teacher a perceived competition between teaching and research time. The recommendation, in this sense, is to share with the teacher the WL benefits, framing them as tools to identify new talent and to incentivize students' high-level of thinking capabilities. Other foreseen obstacles in encouraging researchers to adopt WL and similar research-based techniques can be consulted in the work of Brew & Mantai (2017).

FUTURE RESEARCH DIRECTIONS

It is essential to highlight some of the areas of opportunity identified during this project meriting further research. Briefly, there are three issues to discuss; namely, the surveyed research reflections (RR), the length of the study, and its comparison with a traditional course.

First, it is not possible to provide conclusive remarks about the surveyed RR. As shown in Figure 2(a), its relative improvement is not generalized among its statements. Therefore, it is necessary to encourage the use of qualitative methods and, more importantly, to address the idea of "perfectible" research by suggesting and advising scientific-oriented projects. It is reasonable that both issues are area-dependent, i.e., more related to the engineering profile of the students than with the WL methodology. Testing the methodology in different areas of knowledge would shed some light on this issue.

Although the improvements regarding the average difference of grades and the quality of the reports are confirmed, such as in (Ponce et al., 2019), the length of the semester and the schedule overlapping hinder a more extended assessment of WL. Both grading differences and researcher grades exhibit a clear trend, but their final, steady value (if any), its limits, and the effect of disturbances cannot be known. It would be highly beneficial to test WL in earlier semesters, assessing the same students through a lengthier experiment. It would also be beneficial to test the application of WL in consecutive courses to evaluate, in words of Brew & Mantai (2017), whether WL entirely copes with the requirements of a *wholistic* technique.

Finally, a supporting study of a control group would be very beneficial for the current findings. In this case, the study was planned to be longitudinal to check perception changes, whereas a different study might seek noise or perception persistence in a non-WL course. The expectancy is that perception shifts may occur but noisily, i.e., that not a discernible trend is found, revealing that WL can be definitively accounted for the presented perception shifts.

A FINAL NOTE ON TEACHING TOWARD AI INTEGRATION

Despite the conflicts that the incorporation of AI can cause at a social and cultural level, it is necessary to study, anticipate, and prepare for the changes that will be imposed on organizational structures. That is, their integration into working life is imminent, making tacit a new professional paradigm for which higher education must be prepared. It is essential to recognize that this integration does not observe negative consequences in its entirety and that it foresees, among others, the following benefits: the non-subordination of the individual to alienating jobs, the specialization and empowerment of human capacity, the efficient performance of processes, and the acceleration of activities that result in public welfare. Although the economic environment directs its attention to the generation of value and subsequent displacement of jobs, the incorporation of the AI would also open new yet unknown positions (Williams, 2019).

In this spirit, the presented perspective of students as "integral" professionals is very compelling and must be ensured. To this regard, Guilherme (2019) detects excessive technologization as a hindrance in the development of students and elaborates mainly over the necessity of human interaction during the learning process. This author states that learning goes much beyond the efficiency or market sake, affirming that education is directly connected to the psychological, social, and political facets of the human being, so needed for the presented context. In this sense, teachers cannot be reduced to mere facilitators of the learning process, rather than someone with an expertise who has something to teach others (Guilherme, 2019). It is noteworthy that the application of AI itself as a teaching-learning tool is presented in the same study.

Finally, for effectively understanding AI and avoid misconceptions, it is imperative to have a complete vision of it and its potentials. The work of Kaplan & Haenlein (2019) is an obligatory reference to have a clear context, avoiding an outright alarmist approach or a futuristic euphoria about it. For this chapter, it is vital to rescue some final notes of the work above: "Machines and AI systems, first and foremost, require control by humans. Even the smartest AI systems can make foolish mistakes [...] not accounting the fact that AI systems can be deliberately hacked [...] AI systems are only as smart as the data used to train them since they are, in their essence, nothing more than fancy curve-fitting machines [...] What is often forgotten is that humans are used to thinking on a human level while a digital system would think on a digital level" (Kaplan & Haenlein, 2019).

CONCLUSION

This chapter has introduced the WL methodology. It incorporates many of the recommendations made in the research-based learning literature, seeking for the development of students' cognition, skills, and attitudes toward an uncertain future professional practice, imposed by disruptive technologies such as AI. A special effort is made to enhance the depth of learning and understanding by interplaying the statement of a research problem and a solution proposal and its pursual. This time, the WL technique was applied and tested, and the new results confirmed past findings regarding students' critical thinking and the improvement of their reports' quality in terms of research requirements. It can be then confirmed that, as other research-based techniques, WL could be associated with the generation of procedural and meta-cognitive skills. Results show that the WL technique can be directly associated with the acquisition of research skills in two senses. Firstly, the students align with the criteria of a skilled researcher in both, the rubric evaluation and their perspective about research, entailing the conceptual and practical agreement with a researcher. Secondly, they handle better reports as the semester goes by, implying an improvement in the identification and statement of problems, a refined proposal of a potential solution, the solution's methodological testing, and an enhanced reporting ability of the results.

Apart from the confirmation described above, this longitudinal study over WL found that both the practical and abstract conceptual aspects of research were acquired by the students as a direct effect of the WL technique application, improving as the semester progressed. These claims come from the combination of direct and indirect data which were acquired independently, finding congruence in both.

Specifically, WL can be directly associated with the development of methodological and communication skills. It also shows improvements in the skills associated with the state of the research review and reflecting about research on a practical level; this could not be conclusively shown for the perceptual viewpoint. Overall, students showed an increasing agreement with skilled researchers in both their perspective about research and their evaluation criteria, hence, improving their research skills in general. Such an outcome poses a promising milestone in the search for authentic learning and the generation of skills recognized as drivers toward an AI-integrated future.

The WL technique is still in need of analysis and further enhancement regarding the time spent to apply it, as well as the perceived difficult challenge it imposes over the students. Future studies should address the informally observed benefits and drawbacks.

ACKNOWLEDGMENT

We want to thank the students of the fall 2018 “Smart-Grid” course at Tecnológico de Monterrey for participating in this study. Their willingness to improve is the prime mover of this research.

The authors would also like to acknowledge the financial and the technical support of Writing Lab, TecLabs, Tecnologico de Monterrey, Mexico, in the production of this work.

This research was supported by the CONACYT SENER Fund for Energy Sustainability [Agreement: S0019201401]. It is a product of the Project 266632 “*Laboratorio Binacional para la Gestión Inteligente de la Sustentabilidad Energética y la Formación Tecnológica*” [“Bi-National Laboratory on Smart Sustainable Energy Management and Technology Training”].

REFERENCES

Abeles, T. P. (2016). Send in the robots. *On the Horizon*, *24*(2), 141–144. doi:10.1108/OTH-07-2015-0031

Afdal, H. W., & Spernes, K. (2018). Designing and redesigning research-based teacher education. *Teaching and Teacher Education*, *74*, 215–228. doi:10.1016/j.tate.2018.05.011

Böttcher, F., & Thiel, F. (2018). Evaluating research-oriented teaching: A new instrument to assess university students’ research competences. *Higher Education*, *75*(1), 91–110. doi:10.100710734-017-0128-y

Brew, A., & Mantai, L. (2017). Academics’ perceptions of the challenges and barriers to implementing research-based experiences for undergraduates. *Teaching in Higher Education*, *22*(5), 551–568. doi:10.1080/13562517.2016.1273216

Chan, C. K. Y., Zhao, Y., & Luk, L. Y. Y. (2017). A Validated and Reliable Instrument Investigating Engineering Students’ Perceptions of Competency in Generic Skills. *Journal of Engineering Education*, *106*(2), 299–325. doi:10.1002/jee.20165

Chan, R. Y., Chan, C. K. Y., Lau, C., Liang, J., Huang, H., Cao, Q., & Tahernia, M. (2017). Direct evidence of engineering students' generic skills learning: From research to practice in an undergraduate course in information engineering. *2017 IEEE Frontiers in Education Conference (FIE)*, 1–5.

Clements, D. H., & Joswick, C. (2018). Broadening the horizons of research on discovery-based learning. *Instructional Science*, *46*(1), 155–167. doi:10.100711251-018-9449-1

Derrick, B., & White, P. (2017). Comparing Two Samples from an Individual Likert Question. *International Journal of Mathematics and Statistics*, *18*(3), 1–13.

Feldon, D. F., Maher, M. A., Hurst, M., & Timmerman, B. (2015). Faculty Mentors', Graduate Students', and Performance-Based Assessments of Students' Research Skill Development. *American Educational Research Journal*, *52*(2), 334–370. doi:10.3102/0002831214549449

Fountaine, T., McCarthy, B., & Saleh, T. (2019, July 1). Building the AI-Powered Organization. *Harvard Business Review*. Retrieved from https://hbr.org/2019/07/building-the-ai-powered-organization

Guilherme, A. (2019). AI and education: The importance of teacher and student relations. *AI & Society*, *34*(1), 47–54. doi:10.100700146-017-0693-8

Healey, M. (2005). Linking Research and Teaching to Benefit Student Learning. *Journal of Geography in Higher Education*, *29*(2), 183–201. doi:10.1080/03098260500130387

Healey, M., & Jenkins, A. (2009). *Developing undergraduate research and inquiry*. York: Higher Education Academy.

Huet, I. (2018). Research-based education as a model to change the teaching and learning environment in STEM disciplines. *European Journal of Engineering Education*, *43*(5), 725–740. doi:10.1080/03043797.2017.1415299

Ibarra, L., Soriano, A., Ponce, P., & Molina, A. (2019). Research Skills Enhancement through a Research-Based Wit-Learning Methodology. *20th International Conference on Research and Education in Mechatronics (REM)*, 1–7. 10.1109/REM.2019.8744093

Kaplan, A., & Haenlein, M. (2019). Siri, Siri, in my hand: Who's the fairest in the land? On the interpretations, illustrations, and implications of artificial intelligence. *Business Horizons*, *62*(1), 15–25. doi:10.1016/j.bushor.2018.08.004

Kishbaugh, T. L., Cessna, S., Horst, S. J., Leaman, L., Flanagan, T., Neufeld, D. G., & Siderhurst, M. (2012). Measuring beyond content: A rubric bank for assessing skills in authentic research assignments in the sciences. *Chemistry Education Research and Practice*, *13*(3), 268–276. doi:10.1039/C2RP00023G

Maki, P. L. (2010). *Assessing for Learning: Building a Sustainable Commitment Across the Institution* (2nd ed.). Sterling, VA: Stylus Publishing.

Missingham, D., Shah, S., & Sabir, F. (2018). Student Engineers Optimising Problem Solving and Research Skills. *Journal of University Teaching & Learning Practice*, *15*(4), 1–17.

Morikawa, M. (2017). Firms' expectations about the impact of ai and robotics: Evidence from a survey. *Economic Inquiry*, *55*(2), 1054–1063. doi:10.1111/ecin.12412

Poincaré, H. (1984). La moral y la ciencia. In E. de Gortari (Ed.), *Filosofia De La Ciencia* (pp. 269–283). UNAM.

Ponce, P., Ibarra, L., Mata, O., & Molina, A. (2019). How to develop research skills among undergraduate engineering students to tackle current ongoing topics? A Smart-Grid case study. *International Journal of Electrical Engineering Education*; Advance online publication. doi:10.1177/0020720918816004

Serra Toledo, R., Pérez, I. A., Herrera Rodríguez, R., Magalhães, D. S. F., Muramatsu, M., Soga, D., & Zottola Pareja, D. (2013). Physical contribution to the development of research skills in engineering students. *Revista Brasileira de Ensino de Física*, *35*(4), 1–8.

Tomkins, A., Zhang, M., & Heavlin, W. D. (2017). Reviewer bias in single- versus double-blind peer review. *Proceedings of the National Academy of Sciences of the United States of America*, *114*(48), 12708–12713. doi:10.1073/pnas.1707323114 PMID:29138317

van der Rijst, R. (2017). The Transformative Nature of Research-Based Education: A Thematic Overview of the Literature. In *Research-Based Learning* (pp. 3–22). Case Studies from Maastricht University. doi:10.1007/978-3-319-50993-8_1

Williams, P. (2019). Does competency-based education with blockchain signal a new mission for universities? *Journal of Higher Education Policy and Management*, *41*(1), 104–117. doi:10.1080/1360080X.2018.1520491

Willison, J., & O'Regan, K. (2007). Commonly known, commonly not known, totally unknown: A framework for students becoming researchers. *Higher Education Research & Development, 26*(4), 393–409. doi:10.1080/07294360701658609

Wright, S. A., & Schultz, A. E. (2018). The rising tide of artificial intelligence and business automation: Developing an ethical framework. *Business Horizons, 61*(6), 823–832. doi:10.1016/j.bushor.2018.07.001

KEY TERMS AND DEFINITIONS

Accreditation Bodies: Institutions devoted to the evaluation, ranking, and certification of higher-education programs and the institutions that offer them.

Capabilities: Set of holistic abilities, skills, aptitudes, and attitudes that determine what a person can do and to what extent.

Cognitive Change: A modification in the means and processes through which a person understands, acquires knowledge, or build abstract structures from experience.

Epistemology: In a broad sense, the theory of knowledge. Deals with what knowledge is, how is it acquired, and how is it validated.

Meta-Cognitive Knowledge: Refers to the understanding of the cognitive process and the usage of such knowledge toward some purposeful use.

Peer Review: An evaluation process of contributed material where the participating authors perform the revision among each other.

Perceptual Change: A modification in the means and processes through which a person interprets his/her experiences, and the consequent meaning obtained from them.

Procedural Knowledge: The ability of identifying the processes followed to attain an objective.

Compilation of References

Abadi, M., Agarwal, A., Barham, P., Brevdo, E., Chen, Z., Citro, C., . . . Ghemawat, S. (2015). *TensorFlow: Large-scale machine learning on heterogeneous systems*. Software available from tensorflow. org: http://tensorflow. org

Abbad, M. M., Morris, D., & De Nahlik, C. (2009). Looking under the bonnet: Factors affecting student adoption of e-learning systems in Jordan. *The International Review of Research in Open and Distributed Learning, 10*(2). doi:10.19173/irrodl.v10i2.596

Abdullateef, B. N., Elias, N. F., Mohamed, H., Zaidan, A., & Zaidan, B. (2016). An evaluation and selection problems of OSS-LMS packages. *SpringerPlus, 5*(1), 1. doi:10.118640064-016-1828-y PMID:27064567

Abedi, J., & Lord, C. (2001). The language factor in mathematics tests. *Applied Measurement in Education, 14*(3), 219–234. doi:10.1207/S15324818AME1403_2

Abeles, T. P. (2016). Send in the robots. *On the Horizon, 24*(2), 141–144. doi:10.1108/OTH-07-2015-0031

Abiyev, R. H., Sadikoğlu, G., & Abiyeva, E. (2015). Fuzzy Evaluation of Job Satisfaction of Hotel Employees. *The 2015 World Congress in Computer Science, Computer Engineering, and Applied Computing*.

Adam, C., & Gaudou, B. (2016). BDI agents in social simulations: A survey. *The Knowledge Engineering Review, 31*(3), 207–238. doi:10.1017/S0269888916000096

Adams, D. A., Nelson, R. R., & Todd, P. A. (1992). Perceived usefulness, ease of use, and usage of information technology: A replication. *Management Information Systems Quarterly, 16*(2), 227–247. doi:10.2307/249577

Afdal, H. W., & Spernes, K. (2018). Designing and redesigning research-based teacher education. *Teaching and Teacher Education, 74*, 215–228. doi:10.1016/j.tate.2018.05.011

Aguilar, J., Valdiviezo, P., Cordero, J., & Sánchez, M. (2015, January). Conceptual Design of a Smart Classroom Based on Multiagent Systems. *Proceedings on the International Conference on Artificial Intelligence (ICAI)*, 471.

Ahmad, R., & Kamaruddin, S. (2012). An overview of time-based and condition-based maintenance in industrial application. *Computers & Industrial Engineering*, *63*(1), 135–149. doi:10.1016/j.cie.2012.02.002

Ahmad, S. A., Chinade, U. B., Gambaki, A. M., Ibrahim, S., & Ala, N. A. (2012). The need for MOODLE as a learning management system in Nigerian Universities: Digesting University Utara Malaysia Learning Zone as a case study. *Academic Research International*, *2*(3), 444.

Aker, J. C., Ksoll, C., & Lybbert, T. J. (2012). Can mobile phones improve learning?: Evidence from a field experiment in Niger. *American Economic Journal. Applied Economics*, *4*(4), 94–120. doi:10.1257/app.4.4.94

Al Bakri, A. (2013). An Overview of Information and Communication Technology (ICT) in Jordan: Review the Literature of Usage, Benefits and Barriers. *International Journal of Internet and Distributed Systems*, *1*(02), 9–15. doi:10.4236/ijids.2013.12002

Al Musawi, A., Ambusaidi, A., Al-Balushi, S., & Al-Balushi, K. (2015). Effectiveness of E-Lab Use in Science Teaching at the Omani Schools. *TOJET: The Turkish Online Journal of Educational Technology, 14*(1).

Al-Dmour, R. (2014). *An integration model for identifying the determinants of the adoption and implementation level of HRIS applications and Its effectiveness in business organisations in Jordan.* Academic Press.

Alimisis, D. (2013). Educational robotics: open questions and new challenges. *Themes in Science & Technology Education, 6*(1), 63-71. Retrieved from https://files.eric.ed.gov/fulltext/EJ1130924.pdf

Almarabeh, T. (2014). Students' Perceptions of E-learning at the University of Jordan. *iJET, 9*(3), 31-35.

Alnsour, A., Muhsen, Z., Dababnah, M., Eljinini, M. A., & Barhoum, K. A. (2011). Implementing Moodle as a Tool to develop the Isra University e-learn system. *IJCSNS International Journal of Computer Science and Network Security*, *11*, 120–124.

AlQudah, A. A. (2014). Accepting Moodle by academic staff at the University of Jordan: Applying and extending TAM in technical support factors. *European Scientific Journal*, *10*(18).

Al-Shboul, M. A., & Alsmadi, I. (2010). Challenges of Utilizing E-Learning Systems in Public Universities in Jordan. *iJET, 5*(1), 4-10.

Al-Shboul, M. (2011). Potential Use of Course Management Systems in Higher Education Institutions in Jordan. *Online Submission*, *8*(2), 220–232.

Al-Shboul, M. (2013). The Level of E-Learning Integration at the University of Jordan: Challenges and Opportunities. *International Education Studies*, *6*(4). doi:10.5539/ies.v6n4p93

Anderson, J. R., Corbett, A. T., Koedinger, K. R., & Pelletier, R. (1995). Cognitive tutors: Lessons learned. *Journal of the Learning Sciences*, *4*(2), 167–207. doi:10.120715327809jls0402_2

Anderson, J. R., Matessa, M., & Lebiere, C. (1997). ACT-R: A theory of higher level cognition and its relation to visual attention. *Human-Computer Interaction, 12*(4), 439–462. doi:10.120715327051hci1204_5

Andriessen, J., & Sandberg, J. (1999). Where is education heading and how about AI? *International Journal of Artificial Intelligence in Education, 10*, 130–150.

Annis, L. F. (1983). The processes and effects of peer tutoring. *Human Learning: Journal of Practical Research & Applications*, *2*(1), 39–47.

Antonietti, A. (2001). Problem based learning--A research perspective on learning interactions. *The British Journal of Educational Psychology*, *71*, 344.

Apple, M. W. (2013). *Educating the right way: Markets, standards, God, and inequality*. Routledge.

Ary, D., Jacobs, L. C., Irvine, C. K. S., & Walker, D. (2018). *Introduction to research in education*. Cengage Learning.

Asheghan, M. M., & Míguez, J. (2016). Stability analysis and robust control of heart beat rate during treadmill exercise. *Automatica*, *63*, 311–320. doi:10.1016/j.automatica.2015.10.027

Asis, M. M. (2006). Living with migration: Experiences of left-behind children in the Philippines. *Asian Population Studies*, *2*(1), 45–67. doi:10.1080/17441730600700556

Atkinson, R. C. (1968). Computerized instruction and the learning process. *The American Psychologist*, *23*(4), 225–239. doi:10.1037/h0020791 PMID:5647875

Atmatzidou, D., Demetriadis, S., & Nika, P. (2018). How does the degree of guidance support students' metacognitive and problem-solving skills in educational robotics? *Journal of Science Education and Technology*, *27*(1), 70–85. doi:10.100710956-017-9709-x

Atoum, I., Otoom, A., & Ali, A. A. (2017). Holistic Cyber Security Implementation Frameworks: A Case Study of Jordan. *International Journal of Information, Business and Management*, *9*(1), 108.

Azevedo, R., Witherspoon, A. M., Chauncey, A., Burkett, C., & Fike, A. (2009). MetaTutor: A metacognitive tool for enhancing self-regulated learning. In *Proceedings of the AAAI Fall Symposium on Cognitive and Metacognitive Educational Systems* (pp.14-19). Menlo Park, CA: Association for the Advancement of Artificial Intelligence (AAAI) Press.

Babić, S. (2012). Factors that influence academic teacher's acceptance of e-learning technology in blended learning environment. *E-Learning-Organizational Infrastructure and Tools for Specific Areas*, 3-18.

Baker, R. S., & Inventado, P. S. (2014). Educational data mining and learning analytics. In *Learning analytics* (pp. 61–75). New York, NY: Springer.

Barmaki, R., & Hughes, C. E. (2015). Providing real-time feedback for student teachers in a virtual rehearsal environment. *Proceedings of the 2015 ACM on International Conference on Multimodal Interaction,* 531-537. 10.1145/2818346.2830604

Barr, A., Beard, M., & Atkinson, R. C. (1976). The computer as a tutorial laboratory: The Stanford BIP project. *International Journal of Man-Machine Studies*, *8*(5), 567–596. doi:10.1016/S0020-7373(76)80021-1

Barson, J., Frommer, J., & Schwartz, M. (1993). Foreign language learning using e-mail in a task-oriented perspective: Interuniversity experiments in communication and collaboration. *Journal of Science Education and Technology*, *2*(4), 565–584. doi:10.1007/BF00695325

Bartlett, J. D., O'Connor, F., Pitchford, N., Torres-Ronda, L., & Robertson, S. J. (2017). Relationships between internal and external training load in team-sport athletes: Evidence for an individualized approach. *International Journal of Sports Physiology and Performance*, *12*(2), 230–234. doi:10.1123/ijspp.2015-0791 PMID:27194668

Bautista, D. (2010). Why do disadvantaged Filipino children find word problems in English difficult? In L. Sparrow, B. Kissane, & C. Hurst (Eds.), *Shaping the future of mathematics education: Proceedings of the 33rd annual conference of the Mathematics Education Research Group of Australasia*. Fremantle: MERGA.

Bautista, D., Mitchelmore, M., & Mulligan, J. (2009). Factors influencing Filipino children's solutions to addition and subtraction word problems. *Educational Psychology*, *29*(6), 729–745. doi:10.1080/01443410903254591

Beach, L. R., & Mitchell, T. R. (1978). A contingency model for the selection of decision strategies. *Academy of Management Review*, *3*(3), 439–449. doi:10.5465/amr.1978.4305717

Beck, J., Stern, M., & Haugsjaa, E. (2005). *Applications of AI in education*. Retrieved from http://citeseerx.ist.psu.edu/viewdoc/download?doi=10.1.1.87.405&rep=rep1&type=pdf

Becker, B. E., & Luthar, S. S. (2002). Social-emotional factors affecting achievement outcomes among disadvantaged students: Closing the achievement gap. *Educational Psychologist*, *37*(4), 197–214. doi:10.1207/S15326985EP3704_1 PMID:23255834

Bergmann, J., & Sams, A. (2012). *Flip your classroom: Reach every student in every class every day*. International Society for Technology in Education.

Bernardo, A. B. I. (2002). Language and mathematical problem solving among bilinguals. *The Journal of Psychology*, *136*(3), 283–297. doi:10.1080/00223980209604156 PMID:12206277

Bernardo, A. B. I. (2005). Language and modeling word problems in mathematics among bilinguals. *The Journal of Psychology*, *139*(5), 413–425. doi:10.3200/JRLP.139.5.413-425 PMID:16285212

Bernardo, A. B. I., & Calleja, M. O. (2005). The effects of stating problems in bilingual students' first and second languages on solving mathematical word problems. *The Journal of Genetic Psychology*, *166*(1), 117–129. doi:10.3200/GNTP.166.1.117-129 PMID:15782681

Bernardo, A. B. I., & Ismail, R. (2010). Social perceptions of achieving students and achievement goals of students in Malaysia and the Philippines. *Social Psychology of Education*, *13*(3), 385–407. doi:10.100711218-010-9118-y

Best, J. W., & Kahn, J. V. (2016). *Research in education.* Pearson Education India.

Biagetti, G., Crippa, P., Falaschetti, L., Orcioni, S., & Turchetti, C. (2015). A rule based framework for smart training using sEMG signal. In *Intelligent Decision Technologies* (pp. 89–99). Cham: Springer. doi:10.1007/978-3-319-19857-6_9

Biswas, G., Jeong, H., Kinnebrew, J. S., Sulcer, B., & Roscoe, R. (2010). Measuring self-regulated learning skills through social interactions in a teachable agent environment. *Research and Practice in Technology Enhanced Learning*, *5*(2), 123–152. doi:10.1142/S1793206810000839

Blanchard, E. G., & Frasson, C. (2005). Making intelligent tutoring systems culturally aware: The use of Hofstede's cultural dimensions. In H. R Arabnia, & R. Joshua (Eds), *Proceedings of the 2005 International Conference on Artificial Intelligence* (pp. 644-649). Las Vegas, NV: CSREA Press.

Blanchard, E. G., & Ogan, A. (2010). Infusing cultural awareness into intelligent tutoring systems for a globalized world. In R. Nkambou, J. Bourdeau, & R. Mizoguchi (Eds.), *Advances in Intelligent Tutoring Systems* (pp. 485–505). Berlin: Springer-Verlag. doi:10.1007/978-3-642-14363-2_24

Bloom, B. S. (1984). The 2 sigma problem: The search for methods of group instruction as effective as one-to-one tutoring. *Educational Researcher*, *13*(6), 4–16. doi:10.3102/0013189X013006004

Blumenfeld, P. C., Kempler, T. M., & Krajcik, J. S. (2006). *Motivation and cognitive engagement in learning environments.* Academic Press.

Boril, J., Jirgl, M., & Jalovecky, R. (2016, September). Use of flight simulators in analyzing pilot behavior. In *IFIP International Conference on Artificial Intelligence Applications and Innovations.* Springer. 10.1007/978-3-319-44944-9_22

Börzel S., & Frochte, J. (2019). Case Study On Model-based Application of Machine Learning Using Small CAD Databases for Cost Estimation. *Proceedings of KDIR 2019.*

Böttcher, F., & Thiel, F. (2018). Evaluating research-oriented teaching: A new instrument to assess university students' research competences. *Higher Education*, *75*(1), 91–110. doi:10.100710734-017-0128-y

Bourdieu, P., & Nice, R. (1977). *Outline of a Theory of Practice* (Vol. 16). Cambridge University Press.

Brabazon, T. (2016). *The University of Google: Education in the (post) information age.* Routledge. doi:10.4324/9781315551838

Brew, A., & Mantai, L. (2017). Academics' perceptions of the challenges and barriers to implementing research-based experiences for undergraduates. *Teaching in Higher Education*, *22*(5), 551–568. doi:10.1080/13562517.2016.1273216

Bringula, R., Rodrigo, M. M. T., Ocumpaugh, J. L., Porayska-Pomsta, K., Olatunji, I., & Luckin, R. (2018b). Towards the development of a computer-based game for phonemic awareness. In *Proceedings of the 26th International Conference on Computers in Education* (pp. 657-662). Manila: Asia-Pacific Society for Computers in Education.

Bringula, R. P., Basa, R. S., Dela Cruz, C., & Rodrigo, M. M. T. (2016). Effects of prior knowledge in mathematics on learner-interface interactions in a learning-by-teaching intelligent tutoring system. *Journal of Educational Computing Research, 54*(4), 462–482. doi:10.1177/0735633115622213

Bringula, R. P., Fosgate, I. C. O. Jr, Garcia, N. P. R., & Yorobe, J. L. M. (2018a). Effects of pedagogical agents on students' mathematics performance: A comparison between two versions. *Journal of Educational Computing Research, 56*(5), 701–722. doi:10.1177/0735633117722494

Bringula, R., Alvarez, J., Evangelista, M., & So, R. (2017). Learner-interface interactions with mobile-assisted learning in mathematics: Effects on and relationship with mathematics performance. *International Journal of Mobile and Blended Learning, 9*(1), 34–48. doi:10.4018/IJMBL.2017010103

Brinson, J. R. (2015). Learning outcome achievement in non-traditional (virtual and remote) versus traditional (hands-on) laboratories: A review of the empirical research. *Computers & Education, 87*, 218–237. doi:10.1016/j.compedu.2015.07.003

Brown, L. E., & Kauchak, D. (2013). *Educational advances in Artificial Intelligence*. Association for the Advancement of Artificial Intelligence. doi:10.1609/aimag.v34i4.2508

Brown, R. (2000). Social identity theory: Past achievements, current problems and future challenges. *European Journal of Social Psychology, 30*(6), 745–778. doi:10.1002/1099-0992(200011/12)30:6<745::AID-EJSP24>3.0.CO;2-O

Bruner, J. S. (1996). *The culture of education*. Harvard University Press.

Brunskill, E., Garg, S., Tseng, C., Pal, J., & Findlater, L. (2010). Evaluating an adaptive multi-user educational tool for low-resource environments. In *Proceedings of the IEEE/ACM International Conference on Information and Communication Technologies and Development* (pp. 13-16). New York, NY: ACM.

Brusilovsky, P. (1999). Adaptive and intelligent technologies for web-based eduction. *Ki, 13*(4), 19-25.

Brusilovsky, P., & Peylo, C. (2003). Adaptive and intelligent web-based educational systems. *International Journal of Artificial Intelligence in Education, 13*, 159–172.

Budai, T., & Kuczmann, M. (2018). Towards a Modern, Integrated Virtual Laboratory System. *Acta Polytechnica Hungarica, 15*(3), 14.

Burton, E., Goldsmith, J., Koenig, S., Kuipers, B., Mattei, N., & Walsh, T. (2017). Ethical considerations in Artificial Intelligence courses. *AI Magazine, 38*(2), 22–34. doi:10.1609/aimag.v38i2.2731

Burton, R. R., & Brown, J. S. (1979). An investigation of computer coaching for informal learning activities. *International Journal of Man-Machine Studies, 11*(1), 5–24. doi:10.1016/S0020-7373(79)80003-6

Canfield, W. (2001). ALEKS: A Web-based intelligent tutoring system. *Mathematics and Computer Education, 35*(2), 152.

Carbonell, J. R. (1970a). *Mixed-initiative man-computer instructional dialogues (No. BBN-1971).* Cambridge, MA: Bolt, Beranek, and Newman.

Carbonell, J. R. (1970b). AI in CAI: An artificial-intelligence approach to computer-assisted instruction. *IEEE Transactions on Man-Machine Systems, 11*(4), 190–202. doi:10.1109/TMMS.1970.299942

Cassady, J. C., Mohammed, A., & Mathieu, L. (2004). Crosscultural differences in test perceptions: Women in Kuwait and the United States. *Journal of Cross-Cultural Psychology, 35*(6), 713–718. doi:10.1177/0022022104270113

Castle, R. (in press). Shadowing a police officer: How to be unobtrusive while solving cases in spectacular fashion. *Professional Writers' Journal.*

Cen, H., Koedinger, K., & Junker, B. (2006). Learning factors analysis–a general method for cognitive model evaluation and improvement. In *Proceedings of the International Conference on Intelligent Tutoring Systems* (pp. 164-175). Berlin: Springer. 10.1007/11774303_17

Chan, R. Y., Chan, C. K. Y., Lau, C., Liang, J., Huang, H., Cao, Q., & Tahernia, M. (2017). Direct evidence of engineering students' generic skills learning: From research to practice in an undergraduate course in information engineering. *2017 IEEE Frontiers in Education Conference (FIE)*, 1–5.

Chan, C. K. Y., Zhao, Y., & Luk, L. Y. Y. (2017). A Validated and Reliable Instrument Investigating Engineering Students' Perceptions of Competency in Generic Skills. *Journal of Engineering Education, 106*(2), 299–325. doi:10.1002/jee.20165

Chen, A. Y., Mashhadi, A., Ang, D., & Harkrider, N. (1999). Cultural issues in the design of technology-enhanced learning systems. *British Journal of Educational Technology, 30*(3), 217–230. doi:10.1111/1467-8535.00111

Chen, B., Wan, J., Shu, L., Li, P., Mukherjee, M., & Yin, B. (2018). Smart Factory of Industry 4.0: Key Technologies, Application Case, and Challenges. *IEEE Access: Practical Innovations, Open Solutions, 6*, 6505–6519. doi:10.1109/ACCESS.2017.2783682

Cheng, L. (2018, Jan. 15). Beauty in the machine. *Time Magazine,* 26.

Cheng, T. M., Savkin, A. V., Celler, B. G., Su, S. W., & Wang, L. (2008). Nonlinear Modelling and Control of Human Heart Rate Response During Exercise With Various Work Load Intensities. *IEEE Transactions on Biomedical Engineering, 55*(11), 2499–2508. doi:10.1109/TBME.2008.2001131

Chen, M., Mao, S., & Liu, Y. (2014). Big data: A survey. *Mobile Networks and Applications, 19*(2), 171–209. doi:10.100711036-013-0489-0

Chi, M., VanLehn, K., Litman, D., & Jordan, P. (2011). An evaluation of pedagogical tutorial tactics for a natural language tutoring system: A reinforcement learning approach. *International Journal of Artificial Intelligence in Education, 21*(1-2), 83–113.

Chin, W. W. (1995). Partial least squares is to LISREL as principal components analysis is to common factor analysis. *Technology Studies, 2*(2), 315–319.

Choi, E., Borkowski, M., Zakoian, J., Sagan, K., Scholla, K., Ponti, C., . . . Bielski, M. (2015). Utilizing content moderators to investigate critical factors for assessing the quality of answers on brainly, social learning Q&A platform for students: a pilot study. *Proceedings of the 78th ASIS&T Annual Meeting: Information Science with Impact: Research in and for the Community.* 10.1002/pra2.2015.145052010069

Choi, E., Munoz, R., Mukhlas, D., Balak, M., Farias, L., Jara, D., . . . Burkov, O. (2016). Understanding user motivations for asking and answering a question on brainly, online social learning network. *IConference 2016 Proceedings.*

Cho, S. K., & Berge, Z. L. (2002). Overcoming barriers to distance training and education. *USDLA Journal, 16*(1), 16–34.

Chung, M. H., & Miller, J. (2011). Do we live in a box of crayons? Looking at multicultural metaphors written by teachers. *Multicultural Education, 18*(4), 39.

Chu, S. K. W., Reynolds, R. B., Tavares, N. J., Notari, M., & Lee, C. W. Y. (2017). *Twenty-first century skills education in Switzerland: An example of project-based learning using Wiki in science education. In 21st Century Skills Development Through Inquiry-Based Learning* (pp. 61–78). Singapore: Springer. doi:10.1007/978-981-10-2481-8_4

Clements, D. H., & Joswick, C. (2018). Broadening the horizons of research on discovery-based learning. *Instructional Science, 46*(1), 155–167. doi:10.100711251-018-9449-1

Cole, S. A., & Shastry, G. K. (2009). *Smart money: The effect of education, cognitive ability, and financial literacy on financial market participation.* Harvard Business School Boston.

Colombo, A. W., Karnouskos, S., Shi, Y., Yin, S., & Kaynak, O. (2016). Industrial Cyber–Physical Systems. *Proceedings of the IEEE, 104*(5), 899–903. doi:10.1109/JPROC.2016.2548318

Constantinescu, V., & Patrascu, M. (2017). Route encoding in evolutionary control systems for emergency vehicles. In *ITS Telecommunications (ITST), 2017 15th International Conference on.* IEEE. 10.1109/ITST.2017.7972216

Cook, S. B., Scruggs, T. E., Mastropieri, M. A., & Casto, G. C. (1985). Handicapped students as tutors. *The Journal of Special Education, 19*(4), 483–492. doi:10.1177/002246698501900410

Corbett, A. T., & Anderson, J. R. (1994). Knowledge tracing: Modeling the acquisition of procedural knowledge. *User Modeling and User-Adapted Interaction, 4*(4), 253–278. doi:10.1007/BF01099821

Cortese, A. D. (2003). The critical role of higher education in creating a sustainable future. *Planning for Higher Education*, *31*(3), 15–22.

Crawley, E. F., Malmqvist, J., Lucas, W. A., & Brodeur, D. R. (2011). *The CDIO Syllabus v2. 0: An Updated Statement of Goals for Engineering Education. In Proceedings of the 7 th Intl. CDIO conference*. Copenhagen: University of Demark.

Creswell, J. W. (2013). *Research design: Qualitative, quantitative, and mixed methods approaches*. Sage Publications.

Cross, J. (2004). An Informal History of E-Learning. *On the Horizon*, *12*(3), 103-110.

Crowe, S. (2018). *10 biggest challenges in robotics*. Retrieved from https://www.therobotreport.com/10-biggest-challenges-in-robotics/

Csorny, L. (2013). *Careers in the growing field of information technology services*. Academic Press.

Cunha-Pérez, C., Arevalillo-Herráez, M., Marco-Giménez, L., & Arnau, D. (2018). On incorporating affective support to an intelligent tutoring system: An empirical study. *IEEE Revista Iberoamericana de Tecnologias del Aprendizaje*, *13*(2), 63–69. doi:10.1109/RITA.2018.2831760

D2L Cooperation. (2018). *The Future of Work and Learning in the Age of the 4th Industrial Revolution.* Developed in Partnership with Colleges and Institutes Canada (CICAN).

Davis, F. D. (1989). Perceived usefulness, perceived ease of use, and user acceptance of information technology. *Management Information Systems Quarterly*, *13*(3), 319–340. doi:10.2307/249008

De Guzman, J. V., & Varias, R. R. (1965). *Psychology of Filipinos : studies and essays*. Manila: Vilfran Press.

De Vicente, A., & Pain, H. (2002, June). Informing the detection of the students' motivational state: an empirical study. In *International Conference on Intelligent Tutoring Systems* (pp. 933-943). Berlin: Springer. 10.1007/3-540-47987-2_93

Delpit, L. (1988). The silenced dialogue: Power and pedagogy in educating other people's children. *Harvard Educational Review*, *58*(3), 280–299. doi:10.17763/haer.58.3.c43481778r528qw4

Delpit, L. (2006). *Other people's children: Cultural conflict in the classroom*. The New Press.

Denscombe, M. (2014). *The good research guide: for small-scale social research projects*. UK: McGraw-Hill Education.

Derrick, B., & White, P. (2017). Comparing Two Samples from an Individual Likert Question. *International Journal of Mathematics and Statistics*, *18*(3), 1–13.

Dewey, J. (2007). *Experience and education*. Simon and Schuster.

Doran, G. T. (1981). There'sa SMART way to write management's goals and objectives. *Management Review*, *70*(11), 35–36.

Dorf, R. C., & Bishop, R. H. (2011). *Modern control systems*. Pearson.

Drigas, A. S., & Ioannidou, R. (2012). Artificial Intelligence in special education: A decade review. *International Journal of Engineering Education*, *28*(6), 1366–1372.

Dubois, D., Lorini, E., & Prade, H. (2017). The Strength of Desires: A Logical Approach. *Minds and Machines*, *27*(1), 199–231. doi:10.100711023-017-9426-5

Duffy, M. C., & Azevedo, R. (2015). Motivation matters: Interactions between achievement goals and agent scaffolding for self-regulated learning within an intelligent tutoring system. *Computers in Human Behavior*, *52*, 338–348. doi:10.1016/j.chb.2015.05.041

Dumais, S. T. (2004). Latent semantic analysis. *Annual Review of Information Science & Technology*, *38*(1), 188–230. doi:10.1002/aris.1440380105

Durkin, K., & Shire, B. (Eds.). (1991). *Language in mathematical education: Research and practice*. Buckingham, UK: Open University Press.

Eisenberg, M. B. (2010). Information literacy: Essential skills for the information age. *DESIDOC Journal of Library and Information Technology*, *28*(2), 39–47. doi:10.14429/djlit.28.2.166

Eisner, E. W. (2017). *The enlightened eye: Qualitative inquiry and the enhancement of educational practice*. Teachers College Press.

El-Bahsh, R., & Daoud, M. (2016). Evaluating the use of Moodle to achieve effective and interactive learning: A case study at the German Jordanian University. *Proceedings of the 35th Annual IEEE International Conference on Computer Communications*.

Elder, G. H. (2018). *Children of the great depression*. Routledge. doi:10.4324/9780429501739

El-Seoud. (2007). *Using Web-Based Course to Enhance Educational Process at Jordan Universities – A Case Study*. PSUT.

Emara, M., Tscholl, M., Dong, Y., & Biswas, G. (2017). Analyzing students' collaborative regulation behaviors in a classroom-integrated open ended learning environment. In B. K. Smith, M. Borge, E. Mercier, & K. Y. Lim (Eds.), *Making a difference: Prioritizing equity and access in CSCL, 12th International Conference on Computer Supported Collaborative Learning (CSCL)* (*vol. 1*, pp. 319-326). Philadelphia, PA: International Society of the Learning Sciences.

Ercan, T. (2010). Effective use of cloud computing in educational institutions. *Procedia: Social and Behavioral Sciences*, *2*(2), 938–942. doi:10.1016/j.sbspro.2010.03.130

Eriksson, P., & Kovalainen, A. (2015). Qualitative methods in business research: A practical guide to social research. *Sage (Atlanta, Ga.)*.

Ernst, J., & Monroe, M. (2004). The effects of environment-based education on students' critical thinking skills and disposition toward critical thinking. *Environmental Education Research*, *10*(4), 507–522. doi:10.1080/1350462042000291038

Ersoy, M., & Gies, S. (Eds.). (2017). *Fahrwerkhandbuch: Grundlagen–Fahrdynamik–Fahrverhalten–Komponenten–Elektronische Systeme–Fahrerassistenz–Autonomes Fahren–Perspektiven*. Springer-Verlag. doi:10.1007/978-3-658-15468-4

Esteva, A., Robicquet, A., Ramsundar, B., Kuleshov, V., DePristo, M., Chou, K., ... Dean, J. (2019). A guide to deep learning in healthcare. *Nature Medicine*, *25*(1), 24–29. doi:10.103841591-018-0316-z PMID:30617335

Etzioni, A., & Etzioni, O. (2017). Should Artificial Intelligence be regulated? *Issues in Science and Technology*, *33*(4), 32–36. Retrieved from https://papers.ssrn.com/sol3/papers.cfm?abstract_id=2993506

Etzioni, O., & Schoenick, C. (2018). Artificial Intelligence: What educators need to know. Two AI researchers lay out what you need to know about Artificial Intelligence. *Education Week*, *37*(16), 28–29. Retrieved from https://www.edweek.org/ew/articles/2018/01/10/artificial-intelligence-what-educators-need-to-know.html

Fägerlind, I., & Saha, L. J. (2016). *Education and national development: A comparative perspective*. Elsevier.

Faggella, D. (2017). *Examples of Artificial Intelligence in education*. Retrieved from https://www.techemergence.com/examples-of-artificial-intelligence-in-education/

Faure, E. (1972). *Learning to be: The world of education today and tomorrow*. Unesco.

Feeney, D. R. (2001). *Rates of adoption in a university course management system*. West Virginia University.

Feldon, D. F., Maher, M. A., Hurst, M., & Timmerman, B. (2015). Faculty Mentors', Graduate Students', and Performance-Based Assessments of Students' Research Skill Development. *American Educational Research Journal*, *52*(2), 334–370. doi:10.3102/0002831214549449

Fischer, R., & Smith, P. (2003). Reward allocation and culture: A meta-analysis. *Journal of Cross-Cultural Psychology*, *34*(3), 251–268. doi:10.1177/0022022103034003001

Fister, I. Jr, Ljubič, K., Suganthan, P. N., Perc, M., & Fister, I. (2015). Computational intelligence in sports: Challenges and opportunities within a new research domain. *Applied Mathematics and Computation*, *262*, 178–186. doi:10.1016/j.amc.2015.04.004

Fitzgerald, J., Larsen, P. G., & Verhoef, M. (Eds.). (2014). Collaborative Design for Embedded Systems. Academic Press. doi:10.1007/978-3-642-54118-6

Forbus, K. D., Usher, J. M., Lovett, A. M., Lockwood, K., & Wetzel, J. (2008). CogSketch: Open-domain sketch understanding for cognitive science research and for education. *SBM*, *8*, 159–166.

Fountaine, T., McCarthy, B., & Saleh, T. (2019, July 1). Building the AI-Powered Organization. *Harvard Business Review*. Retrieved from https://hbr.org/2019/07/building-the-ai-powered-organization

Freedman, R., Ali, S. S., & McRoy, S. (2000). Links: What is an intelligent tutoring system? *Intelligence, 11*(3), 15–16. doi:10.1145/350752.350756

Friese, G. T., Pittman, J. T., & Hendee, J. C. (1995). *Studies of the use of wilderness for personal growth, therapy, education and leadership development: An annotation and evaluation*. University of Idaho, Wilderness Research Center.

Frochte, J., Lemmen, M., & Schmidt, M. (2018). Seamless Integration of Machine Learning Contents in Mechatronics Curricula. In *2018 19th International Conference on Research and Education in Mechatronics (REM)* (pp. 75-80). IEEE. 10.1109/REM.2018.8421794

Gadanidis, G. (2017). Artificial Intelligence, computational thinking, and mathematics education. *The Information Journal of Information and Learning Technology, 34*(2), 133–139. doi:10.1108/IJILT-09-2016-0048

Galkin, D. W., Parkin, R. M., Safaric, R., & Czarnecki, C. A. (1998). Visualisation, Simulation and Control of a Robotic System using Internet Technology. *Proc. of the 5th International Workshop on Advanced Motion Control*, 399-404.

Galway, L. P., Corbett, K. K., Takaro, T. K., Tairyan, K., & Frank, E. (2014). A novel integration of online and flipped classroom instructional models in public health higher education. *BMC Medical Education, 14*(1), 181. doi:10.1186/1472-6920-14-181 PMID:25169853

Gao, Y., & Wu, X. (2015). User Acceptance of Learning Technology: The Case of Using Moodle. *International Journal of Learning: Annual Review, 21*.

Gartner, A., & Lipsky, D. K. (1987). Beyond special education: Toward a quality system for all students. *Harvard Educational Review, 57*(4), 367–396. doi:10.17763/haer.57.4.kj517305m7761218

Gefen, D., & Straub, D. W. (1997). Gender differences in the perception and use of e-mail: An extension to the technology acceptance model. *Management Information Systems Quarterly, 21*(4), 389–400. doi:10.2307/249720

Glaser, R. (1984). Education and thinking: The role of knowledge. *The American Psychologist, 39*(2), 93–104. doi:10.1037/0003-066X.39.2.93

Gomes, C., Thule, C., Broman, D., Larsen, P. G., & Vangheluwe, H. (2017). *Co-simulation: State of the art.* Retrieved from http://arxiv.org/abs/1702.00686

Gose, B. (2016). When the teaching assistant is a robot: Faculty members experiment with Artificial Intelligence in the classroom. *The Chronicle of Higher Education.* Retrieved from https://www.chronicle.com/article/When-the-Teaching-Assistant-Is/238114

Graesser, A. C., Chipman, P., Haynes, B. C., & Olney, A. (2005). AutoTutor: An intelligent tutoring system with mixed-initiative dialogue. *IEEE Transactions on Education, 48*(4), 612–618. doi:10.1109/TE.2005.856149

Graesser, A. C., & D'Mello, S. (2012). Emotions during the learning of difficult material. In B. Ross (Ed.), *Psychology of learning and motivation* (Vol. 57, pp. 183–225). Cambridge, MA: Academic Press. doi:10.1016/B978-0-12-394293-7.00005-4

Green, D. T. (2011). *Intelligent tutoring systems for skill acquisition* (Unpublished manuscript). The University of Arizona, Tucson, AZ.

Greenwood, C. R., Delquadri, J. C., & Hall, R. V. (1989). Longitudinal effects of class wide peer tutoring. *Journal of Educational Psychology*, *81*(3), 371–383. doi:10.1037/0022-0663.81.3.371

Guilherme, A. (2019). AI and education: The importance of teacher and student relations. *AI & Society*, *34*(1), 47–54. doi:10.100700146-017-0693-8

Gustafson, S. M., & Gustafson, D. A. (2016). *Artificial Intelligence*. Retrieved from https://www.accessscience.com/content/artificial-intelligence/053300

Guthrie, G. (1968). The Philippine temperament. In G. Guthrie (Ed.), *Six perspectives on the Philippines* (pp. 49–84). Manila: The Bookmark, Inc.

Haber, M. G., Mazzotti, V. L., Mustian, A. L., Rowe, D. A., Bartholomew, A. L., Test, D. W., & Fowler, C. H. (2016). What works, when, for whom, and with whom: A meta-analytic review of predictors of postsecondary success for students with disabilities. *Review of Educational Research*, *86*(1), 123–162. doi:10.3102/0034654315583135

Habib, M. K. (2001). Collaborative Telecontrol and Integrative User Interface Merging Reality with Virtuality. *IEEE-RAS 2nd International Conference on Humanoid*, 367-376.

Habib, M. K. (2006). Telecooperation Through Shared & Integrated Distributed and Collaborative Intelligent Environments Supporting Mixed Realities. *International SICE-ICCAS Conference*, 2639-2643.

Habib, M. K. (2008). Distributed Teleoperation and Collaborative Environment for Robotics E-Learning and Cooperation. *IEEE International Conference on Industrial Informatics (INDIN 2008)*, 1358-1363. 10.1109/INDIN.2008.4618315

Hall, M., Frank, E., Holmes, G., Pfahringer, B., Reutemann, P., & Witten, I. H. (2009). The WEKA data mining software: an update. *ACM SIGKDD Explorations Newsletter, 11*(1), 10-18.

Healey, M. (2005). Linking Research and Teaching to Benefit Student Learning. *Journal of Geography in Higher Education*, *29*(2), 183–201. doi:10.1080/03098260500130387

Healey, M., & Jenkins, A. (2009). *Developing undergraduate research and inquiry*. York: Higher Education Academy.

Heffernan, N. T., & Koedinger, K. R. (2002). An intelligent tutoring system incorporating a model of an experienced human tutor. In *Proceedings of the International Conference on Intelligent Tutoring Systems* (pp. 596-608). Berlin: Springer. 10.1007/3-540-47987-2_61

Henry, H. R., Tawfik, A. A., Jonassen, D. H., Winholtz, R. A., & Khanna, S. (2012). "I know this is supposed to be more like the real world, but...": Student perceptions of a PBL implementation in an undergraduate materials science course. *Interdisciplinary Journal of Problem-based Learning*, *6*(1), 5. doi:10.7771/1541-5015.1312

Hertzberg, J., Lingemann, K., & Nüchter, A. (2012). *Mobile Roboter: Eine Einführung aus Sicht der Informatik*. Springer-Verlag. doi:10.1007/978-3-642-01726-1

Hircca, N. (2017). The Influence of Hands on Physics Experiments on Scientific Process Skills According to Prospective Teachers' Experiences. *European Journal of Physics Education*, *4*(2), 6–14.

Hofstede, G. (1980). *Culture's consequences: International differences in work-related values*. Beverly Hills, CA: Sage.

Hofstede, G. (1986). Cultural differences in teaching and learning. *International Journal of Intercultural Relations*, *10*(3), 301–320. doi:10.1016/0147-1767(86)90015-5

Hofstede, G. J., Minkov, M., & Hofstede, G. (2016). *Allemaal andersdenkenden: omgaan met cultuurverschillen*. Business Contact.

Huet, I. (2018). Research-based education as a model to change the teaching and learning environment in STEM disciplines. *European Journal of Engineering Education*, *43*(5), 725–740. doi:10.1080/03043797.2017.1415299

Hunter, J. D. (2008). *The death of character: Moral education in an age without good or evil*. Basic Books.

Hussain, R., & Zeadally, S. (2019). Autonomous Cars: Research Results, Issues, and Future Challenges. *IEEE Communications Surveys and Tutorials*, *21*(2), 1275–1313. doi:10.1109/COMST.2018.2869360

Hwang, G. J. (2014). Definition, framework and research issues of smart learning environments-a context-aware ubiquitous learning perspective. *Smart Learning Environments, 1*(4).

Ibarra, L., Soriano, A., Ponce, P., & Molina, A. (2019). Research Skills Enhancement through a Research-Based Wit-Learning Methodology. *20th International Conference on Research and Education in Mechatronics (REM)*, 1–7. 10.1109/REM.2019.8744093

Igbaria, M., Zinatelli, N., Cragg, P., & Cavaye, A. L. (1997). Personal computing acceptance factors in small firms: A structural equation model. *Management Information Systems Quarterly*, *21*(3), 279–305. doi:10.2307/249498

Intelligent Tutoring Systems. (2018). In *Wikipedia*. Retrieved from https://en.wikipedia.org/wiki/Intelligent_tutoring_system#Limitations

Ionescu, T. C., & Patrascu, M. (2018). *Control systems for time delay processes*. Bucharest: Politehnica Press.

Jacobs, R. (1997). Control model of human stance using fuzzy logic. *Biological Cybernetics*, *77*(1), 63–70. doi:10.1007004220050367 PMID:9309863

Jarke, M., Neumann, B., Vassiliou, Y., & Wahlster, W. (1989). KBMS requirements of knowledge-based systems. In *Foundations of knowledge base management* (pp. 381–394). Berlin: Springer. doi:10.1007/978-3-642-83397-7_17

Jarvis, P., Holford, J., & Griffin, C. (1998). *The theory and practice of learning*. London: Kogan Page, Limited.

Jocano, F. L. (1999). *Management by culture: Fine-tuning modern management to Filipino culture* (revised edition). Quezon City, Philippines: Punlad Research House, Inc.

Jongbloed, B., Enders, J., & Salerno, C. (2008). Higher education and its communities: Interconnections, interdependencies and a research agenda. *Higher Education*, *56*(3), 303–324. doi:10.100710734-008-9128-2

Jony, A. I., Rahman, M. S., & Islam, Y. M. (2017). ICT in higher education: Wiki-based reflection to promote deeper thinking levels. *International Journal of Modern Education and Computer Science*, *9*(4), 43–49. doi:10.5815/ijmecs.2017.04.05

Kaplan, A., & Haenlein, M. (2019). Siri, Siri, in my hand: Who's the fairest in the land? On the interpretations, illustrations, and implications of artificial intelligence. *Business Horizons*, *62*(1), 15–25. doi:10.1016/j.bushor.2018.08.004

Kats, Y. (2010). *Learning Management System Technologies and Software Solutions for Online Teaching: Tools and Applications: Tools and Applications*. IGI Global.

Kevin, P. M. (2012). *Machine learning: a probabilistic perspective*. Academic Press.

Khan, B. H. (2005). *Managing E-Learning Strategies – Design, Delivery, Implementation and Evaluation*. Bangladesh: Information Science Publisher. doi:10.4018/978-1-59140-634-1

Khasawneh, M. M., & Ibrahim, H. (2012). *Technology to enhance learning: The Jordanian experience*. Academic Press.

Khasawneh, M. (2015). Factors influence e-learning utilization in Jordanian universities-academic staff perspectives. *Procedia: Social and Behavioral Sciences*, *210*, 170–180. doi:10.1016/j.sbspro.2015.11.356

Khwaldeh, S. M., Al-Hadid, I., Masa'deh, R. e., & Alrowwad, A. (2017). The Association between E-Services Web Portals Information Quality and ICT Competence in the Jordanian Universities. *Asian Social Science*, *13*(3), 156. doi:10.5539/ass.v13n3p156

Kim, J., & Fesenmaier, D. R. (2015). Measuring emotions in real time: Implications for tourism experience design. *Journal of Travel Research*, *54*(4), 419–429. doi:10.1177/0047287514550100

Kim, M. (2008). Factors influencing the acceptance of e-learning courses for mainstream faculty in higher institutions. *International Journal of Instructional Technology and Distance Learning*, *5*(2), 29–44.

Kim-Prieto, C., Fujita, F., & Diener, E. (2004). *Culture and structure of emotional experience* (Unpublished manuscript). University of Illinois, Urbana-Champaign, IL.

Kishbaugh, T. L., Cessna, S., Horst, S. J., Leaman, L., Flanagan, T., Neufeld, D. G., & Siderhurst, M. (2012). Measuring beyond content: A rubric bank for assessing skills in authentic research assignments in the sciences. *Chemistry Education Research and Practice*, *13*(3), 268–276. doi:10.1039/C2RP00023G

Kizilkaya, G., & Askar, P. (2008). The effect of an embedded pedagogical agent on the students' science achievement. *Interactive Technology and Smart Education*, *5*(4), 208–216. doi:10.1108/17415650810930893

Knight, W. (2018). Here's how the U.S. needs to prepare for the age of artificial intelligence. *MIT Technology Review*. Retrieved from https://www.technologyreview.com/s/610379/heres-how-the-us-needs-to-prepare-for-the-age-of-artificial-intelligence/

Koedinger, K. R., McLaughlin, E. A., & Stamper, J. C. (2012). Automated student model improvement. In *Proceedings of the 5th International Conference of Educational Data Mining* (pp. 17-24). Worcester, MA: International Data Mining Society.

Kotsiantis, S. B. (2012). Use of machine learning techniques for educational proposes: A decision support system for forecasting students' grades. *Artificial Intelligence Review*, *37*(4), 331–344. doi:10.100710462-011-9234-x

Kruse, S. D., & Louis, K. S. (1993). *Developing Professional Community in New and Restructuring Urban Schools*. Academic Press.

Kruse, E., & Dai, F. (2001). Virtual Training Using Web and Interactive Visualisation. *Proc. of the IFAC International Conference: Telematics Applications in Automation and Robotics*, 517-522. 10.1016/S1474-6670(17)41704-6

Ku, H., Choi, J. J., Lee, S., Jang, S., & Do, W. (2018). Shelly, a Tortoise-Like Robot for One-to-Many Interaction with Children. *Companion of the 2018 ACM/IEEE International Conference on Human-Robot Interaction*, 353-354. 10.1145/3173386.3177824

Kulik, J. A., & Flecher, J. D. (2016). Effectiveness of intelligent tutoring systems: A meta-analytic review. *Review of Educational Research*, *86*(1), 42–78. doi:10.3102/0034654315581420

Kumar, A. (2017). *10 roles for Artificial Intelligence in education*. Retrieved from https://www.linkedin.com/pulse/10-roles-artificial-intelligence-education-anil-kumar

Kumar, D., Radhamani, R., Nizar, N., Achuthan, K., Nair, B., & Diwakar, S. (2018). *Virtual and remote laboratories augment self learning and interactions: Development, deployment and assessments with direct and online feedback*. Academic Press. doi:10.7287/peerj.preprints.26715v1

Kurth, M., Schleyer, C., & Feuser, D. (2016). Smart factory and education: An integrated automation concept. 2016 IEEE 11th Conference on Industrial Electronics and Applications (ICIEA), 1057–1061. 10.1109/ICIEA.2016.7603738

Lagud, M. C. V., & Rodrigo, M. M. T. (2010, June). The affective and learning profiles of students using an intelligent tutoring system for algebra. In *International Conference on Intelligent Tutoring Systems* (pp. 255-263). Berlin: Springer 10.1007/978-3-642-13388-6_30

Lai, D. T., Begg, R. K., & Palaniswami, M. (2009). Computational intelligence in gait research: A perspective on current applications and future challenges. *IEEE Transactions on Information Technology in Biomedicine*, *13*(5), 687–702. doi:10.1109/TITB.2009.2022913 PMID:19447724

Lambert, K. (2018). Could Artificial Intelligence replace our teachers? *Education World*. Retrieved from http://www.educationworld.com/could-artificial-intelligence-replace-our-teachers

Lan, Y. J., Sung, Y. T., & Chang, K. E. (2007). *A mobile-device-supported peer-assisted learning system for collaborative early EFL reading*. Academic Press.

Lancor, R. A. (2014). Using student-generated analogies to investigate conceptions of energy: A multidisciplinary study. *International Journal of Science Education*, *36*(1), 1–23. doi:10.1080/09500693.2012.714512

Landauer, T. K. (2006). Latent semantic analysis. In *Encyclopedia of Cognitive Science*. London: Wiley. doi:10.1002/0470018860.s00561

Landauer, T. K., Foltz, P. W., & Laham, D. (1998). An introduction to latent semantic analysis. *Discourse Processes*, *25*(2-3), 259–284. doi:10.1080/01638539809545028

Lang, M. (2017). Beyond Fitbit: A critical appraisal of optical heart rate monitoring wearables and apps, their current limitations and legal implications. *Alb. LJ Sci. & Tech.*, *28*, 39.

Lantos, G. P. (2001). The boundaries of strategic corporate social responsibility. *Journal of Consumer Marketing*, *18*(7), 595–632. doi:10.1108/07363760110410281

Lasquety-Reyes, J. (2016). In defense of hiya as a Filipino virtue. *Asian Philosophy*, *26*(1), 66–78. doi:10.1080/09552367.2015.1136203

Lasswell, H. D. (1948). The structure and function of communication in society. *The Communication of Ideas, 37*, 215-228.

Lawless, K. A., & Pellegrino, J. W. (2007). Professional development in integrating technology into teaching and learning: Knowns, unknowns, and ways to pursue better questions and answers. *Review of Educational Research*, *77*(4), 575–614. doi:10.3102/0034654307309921

Learner, R. A. (2006). Teacher As Researcher. Teachers Engaged in Research: Inquiry Into Mathematics Classrooms. *Grades*, *3-5*, 129.

Lee, K. (2018). Tech companies should stop pretending AI won't destroy jobs. *MIT Technology Review*. Retrieved from https://www.technologyreview.com/s/610298/tech-companies-should-stop-pretending-ai-wont-destroy-jobs/

Lee, J. G., Jun, S., Cho, Y. W., Lee, H., Kim, G. B., Seo, J. B., & Kim, N. (2017). Deep learning in medical imaging: General overview. *Korean Journal of Radiology*, *18*(4), 570–584. doi:10.3348/kjr.2017.18.4.570 PMID:28670152

Lee, J. I., & Brunskill, E. (2012). The impact on individualizing student models on necessary practice opportunities. In *Proceedings of the 5th International Conference of Educational Data Mining* (pp. 118-125). Worcester, MA: International Data Mining Society.

Lehtomäki, E., Moate, J., & Posti-Ahokas, H. (2016). Global connectedness in higher education: Student voices on the value of cross-cultural learning dialogue. *Studies in Higher Education*, *41*(11), 2011–2027. doi:10.1080/03075079.2015.1007943

Levinson, B. A. (1996). *The Cultural Production of the Educated Person. Critical Ethnographies of Schooling and Local Practice. SUNY Series, Power, Social Identity, and Education*. ERIC.

Levinson, B. U. (2001). *We are all equal: Student culture and identity at a Mexican secondary school, 1988–1998*. Duke University Press. doi:10.1215/9780822381075

Lickona, T. (1996). Eleven principles of effective character education. *Journal of Moral Education*, *25*(1), 93–100. doi:10.1080/0305724960250110

Li, Y., Humphreys, P. C., Mendoza, G. J., & Benjamin, S. C. (2015). Resource costs for fault-tolerant linear optical quantum computing. *Physical Review X*, *5*(4), 041007. doi:10.1103/PhysRevX.5.041007

Loehlin, J. C., & Beaujean, A. A. (2017). *Latent variable models: An introduction to factor, path, and structural equation analysis*. Taylor & Francis.

Luckin, R., Holmes, W., Griffiths, M., & Forcier, L. B. (2016). *Intelligence unleashed: An argument for AI in education*. London: Pearson.

Luckin, R., Holmes, W., Griffiths, M., & Forcier, L. B. (2017). *Intelligence unleashed: An argument for AI in Education*. Pearson.

Lumsakul, P., Sheldrick, L., & Rahimifard, S. (2018). The Sustainable Co-Design of Products and Production Systems. *Procedia Manufacturing*, *21*, 854–861. doi:10.1016/j.promfg.2018.02.193

Madda, M. J. (2017). *Educators on Artificial Intelligence: Here's the one thing it can't do well*. Retrieved from https://www.edsurge.com/news/2017-11-20-educators-on-artificial-intelligence-here-s-the-one-thing-it-can-t-do-well

Mahler, J., Liang, J., Niyaz, S., Laskey, M., Doan, R., Liu, X., . . . Goldberg, K. (2017). *Dex-net 2.0: Deep learning to plan robust grasps with synthetic point clouds and analytic grasp metrics*. arXiv preprint arXiv:1703.09312

Mahon, J., Bryant, B., Brown, B., & Kim, M. (2010). Using second life to enhance classroom management practice in teacher education. *Educational Media International, 47*(2), 121–134. doi:10.1080/09523987.2010.492677

Majadlawi, Y., Almarabeh, T., & Mohammad, H. (2014). Factors affecting students' usage of learning management system at The University of Jordan. *Life Science Journal, 11*(6), 666–671.

Majdalawi, Y. K., Almarabeh, T., & Mohammad, H. (2014). *Factors Affecting Students' Usage of Learning Management System at the University of Jordan*. Academic Press.

Maki, P. L. (2010). *Assessing for Learning: Building a Sustainable Commitment Across the Institution* (2nd ed.). Sterling, VA: Stylus Publishing.

Mallawaarachchi, V. (2017). *Living with robots – the good, the bad and the ugly on humanity*. Retrieved from https://becominghuman.ai/living-with-robots-the-good-the-bad-and-the-ugly-on-humanity-1097f524f936

Malone, J. J., Lovell, R., Varley, M. C., & Coutts, A. J. (2017). Unpacking the black box: Applications and considerations for using GPS devices in sport. *International Journal of Sports Physiology and Performance, 12*(s2), S2–S18. doi:10.1123/ijspp.2016-0236 PMID:27736244

Mandela, N. (2014). Education is the most powerful weapon which you can use to change the world. *Computer, 8*.

Mannino, A., Althaus, D., Erhardt, J., Gloor, L., Hutter, A., & Metzinger, T. (2015). Artificial Intelligence: Opportunities and risks. *Policy Paper by the Effective Altruism Foundation*, (2), 1-16.

Marcelino, E. P. (1990). Towards understanding the psychology of the Filipino. *Women & Therapy, 9*(1-2), 105–128. doi:10.1300/J015v09n01_07

Marginson, S. (2006). Dynamics of national and global competition in higher education. *Higher Education, 52*(1), 1–39. doi:10.100710734-004-7649-x

Marion, A. O., & Oluwafunmilayo, A. A. (2011). Design and development of an intelligent instructive system: Scholastic Tutor (St*). *Turkish Online Journal of Distance Education-TOJDE, 12*(4), 34–44.

Marsland, S. (2014). *Machine learning: an algorithmic perspective*. Taylor & Francis Inc. doi:10.1201/b17476

Martin, B., Mitrovic, A., Koedinger, K. R., & Mathan, S. (2011). Evaluating and improving adaptive educational systems with learning curves. *User Modeling and User-Adapted Interaction, 21*(3), 249–283. doi:10.100711257-010-9084-2

Martin, F. G. (2012). Will massive open online courses change how we teach? *Communications of the ACM, 55*(8), 26–28. doi:10.1145/2240236.2240246

Matsuda, N., Cohen, W. W., Koedinger, K. R., Keiser, V., Raizada, R., Yarzebinski, E., & Stylianides, G. (2012). Studying the effect of tutor learning using a teachable agent that asks the student tutor for explanations. In M. Sugimoto, V. Aleven, Y. S. Chee, & B. F. Manjon (Eds.), *Proceedings of the International Conference on Digital Game and Intelligent Toy Enhanced Learning (DIGITEL 2012)* (pp. 25–32). Takagawa, Japan: Conference Publishing Services. 10.1109/DIGITEL.2012.12

Matsuda, N., Cohen, W. W., Sewall, J., Lacerda, G., & Koedinger, K. R. (2007). Predicting students' performance with simstudent that learns cognitive skills from observation. In R. Luckin, K. R. Koedinger, & J. Greer (Eds.), *Proceedings of the International Conference on Artificial Intelligence in Education* (pp. 467-476). Amsterdam: IOS Press.

Matsuda, N., Sekar, V. P. C., & Wall, N. (2018, June). Metacognitive Scaffolding Amplifies the Effect of Learning by Teaching a Teachable Agent. In *Proceedings of the International Conference on Artificial Intelligence in Education* (pp. 311-323). Cham: Springer. 10.1007/978-3-319-93843-1_23

Matsuda, N., Yarzebinski, E., Keiser, V., Raizada, R., Cohen, W. W., Stylianides, G. J., & Koedinger, K. R. (2013). Cognitive anatomy of tutor learning: Lessons learned with SimStudent. *Journal of Educational Psychology*, *105*(4), 1152–1163. doi:10.1037/a0031955

Ma, W., Adesope, O. O., Nesbit, J. C., & Liu, Q. (2014). Intelligent tutoring systems and learning outcomes: A meta-analysis. *Journal of Educational Psychology*, *106*(4), 901–918. doi:10.1037/a0037123

McArthur, D., Lewis, M., & Bishay, M. (2005). The role of Artificial Intelligence in education: Current progress and future prospects. *I-manager's Journal of Educational Technology*, *1*(4), 42–80.

McCarthy, J. (2006). *The philosophy of AI and the AI of philosophy*. Retrieved from http://jmc.stanford.edu/articles/aiphil2.html

McCarthy, J. (2007). *What is Artificial Intelligence?* Retrieved from http://jmc.stanford.edu/artificial-intelligence/index.html

McCarthy, J., Minsky, M. L., Rochester, N., & Shannon, C. E. (2006). A proposal for the Dartmouth summer research project on Artificial Intelligence. *AI Magazine*, *27*(4), 12–14. Retrieved from http://jmc.stanford.edu/articles/dartmouth.html

McClure, P. K. (2018). "You're fired," says the robot: The rise of automation in the workplace, technophobes, and fears of unemployment. *Social Science Computer Review*, *36*(2), 139–156. doi:10.1177/0894439317698637

McDaniel, R., Fanfarelli, J. R., & Lindgren, R. (2017). Creative Content Management: Importance, Novelty, and Affect as Design Heuristics for Learning Management Systems. *IEEE Transactions on Professional Communication*, *60*(2), 183–200. doi:10.1109/TPC.2017.2656578

McIntosh, J., & Torres, M. I. (2014). *Learning Management Systems: Revisiting Learning Management Systems at the University Level*. The University of Tampa.

Merchant, Z., Goetz, E. T., Cifuentes, L., Keeney-Kennicutt, W., & Davis, T. J. (2014). Effectiveness of virtual reality-based instruction on students' learning outcomes in K-12 and higher education: A meta-analysis. *Computers & Education*, *70*, 29–40. doi:10.1016/j.compedu.2013.07.033

Meredith, J. P. (2010). Combating cyberbullying: Emphasizing education over criminalization. *Fed. Comm. LJ*, *63*, 311.

Mesurado, B., Richaud, M. C., & Mateo, N. J. (2016). Engagement, flow, self-efficacy, and eustress of university students: A cross-national comparison between the Philippines and Argentina. *The Journal of Psychology*, *150*(3), 281–299. doi:10.1080/00223980.2015.1024595 PMID:25915707

Metzler, M. (2017). *Instructional models in physical education*. Routledge. doi:10.4324/9781315213521

Michalski, R. S., Carbonell, J. G., & Mitchell, T. M. (2013). *Machine learning: An artificial intelligence approach*. Springer Science & Business Media.

Missingham, D., Shah, S., & Sabir, F. (2018). Student Engineers Optimising Problem Solving and Research Skills. *Journal of University Teaching & Learning Practice*, *15*(4), 1–17.

Mitrovic, A., Williamson, C., Bebbington, A., Mathews, M., Suraweera, P., Martin, B., ... Holland, J. (2011). Thermo-Tutor: An intelligent tutoring system for thermodynamics. In *Proceedings of the IEEE Global Engineering Education Conference (EDUCON)* (pp. 378-385). Piscataway, NJ: IEEE.

Mitrovic, A., Koedinger, K. R., & Martin, B. (2003). A comparative analysis of cognitive tutoring and constraint-based modeling. In *Proceedings of the International Conference on User Modeling* (pp. 313-322). Berlin: Springer. 10.1007/3-540-44963-9_42

Mitrovic, A., Martin, B., & Suraweera, P. (2007). Intelligent tutors for all: Constraint-based modeling methodology, systems and authoring. *IEEE Intelligent Systems*, *22*(4), 38–45. doi:10.1109/MIS.2007.74

Mkhize, P., Mtsweni, E. S., & Buthelezi, P. (2016). Diffusion of Innovations Approach to the Evaluation of Learning Management System Usage in an Open Distance Learning Institution. *The International Review of Research in Open and Distributed Learning*, *17*(3). doi:10.19173/irrodl.v17i3.2191

Moallem, P., Mousavi, B. S., & Naghibzadeh, S. S. (2015). Fuzzy Inference System Optimized by Genetic Algorithm for Robust Face and Pose Detection. *International Journal of Artificial Intelligence*, *13*(2), 73–88.

Mohammed, P., & Mohan, P. (2015). Dynamic cultural contextualisation of educational content in intelligent learning environments using ICON. *International Journal of Artificial Intelligence in Education*, *25*(2), 249–270. doi:10.100740593-014-0033-9

Morey, A. I. (2000). Changing higher education curricula for a global and multicultural world. *Higher Education in Europe*, *25*(1), 25–39. doi:10.1080/03797720050002170

Morey, A. I. (2004). Globalization and the emergence of for-profit higher education. *Higher Education, 48*(1), 131–150. doi:10.1023/B:HIGH.0000033768.76084.a0

Morikawa, M. (2017). Firms' expectations about the impact of ai and robotics: Evidence from a survey. *Economic Inquiry, 55*(2), 1054–1063. doi:10.1111/ecin.12412

Morreale, S. P., & Pearson, J. C. (2008). Why communication education is important: The centrality of the discipline in the 21st century. *Communication Education, 57*(2), 224–240. doi:10.1080/03634520701861713

Morri, A. (1997). *Bright Future for Distance Learning: One Touch/Hughes Alliance Promotes Interactive 'E-learning' Service.* Telephony Online - Chicago, Telephony Penton Media.

Mostafavi, B., Zhou, G., Lynch, C., Chi, M., & Barnes, T. (2015). Data-driven worked examples improve retention and completion in a logic tutor. In *Proceedings of the International Conference on Artificial Intelligence in Education* (pp. 726-729). Cham: Springer. 10.1007/978-3-319-19773-9_102

Moughamir, S., Manamanni, N., Zaytoon, J., & Afilal, L. (2001). Control law implementation for Multi-Iso: a training machine for lower limbs. *Engineering in Medicine and Biology Society, 2001. Proceedings of the 23rd Annual International Conference of the IEEE*, 2, 1477-1480. 10.1109/IEMBS.2001.1020484

Moughamir, S., Zaytoon, J., Manamanni, N., & Afilal, L. (2002). A system approach for control development of lower-limbs training machines. *Control Engineering Practice, 10*(3), 287–299. doi:10.1016/S0967-0661(01)00155-1

Murphy, R., Murphy, R. R., & Arkin, R. C. (2000). *Introduction to AI robotics.* MIT press.

Murray, S. (2011). Secondary students' descriptions of "good" mathematics teachers. *Australian Mathematics Teacher, 67*(4), 14–21.

Murray, T. (1999). Authoring intelligent tutoring systems: An analysis of the state of the art. *International Journal of Artificial Intelligence in Education, 10*, 98–129.

Nandi, A., & Mandernach, M. (2016). Hackathons as an informal learning platform. *Proceedings of the 47th ACM Technical Symposium on Computing Science Education.*

Neji, M., & Ben Ammar, M. (2007). Agent-based Collaborative Affective e-Learning Framework. *Electronic Journal of e-Learning, 5*(2), 123-134.

Neville, A. J. (2009). Problem-based learning and medical education forty years on. *Medical Principles and Practice, 18*(1), 1–9. doi:10.1159/000163038 PMID:19060483

Nicaud, J. F., Bouhineau, D., Mezerette, S., Andre, N. (2007). Aplusix II [Computer software].

Nicaud, J. F., Bouhineau, D., & Chaachoua, H. (2004). Mixing microworld and CAS features in building computer systems that help student learn algebra. *International Journal of Computers for Mathematical Learning, 9*(2), 169–211. doi:10.1023/B:IJCO.0000040890.20374.37

Nilsson, J., & Klügl, F. (2015). Human-in-the-Loop Simulation of a Virtual Classroom. In *Multi-Agent Systems and Agreement Technologies* (pp. 379–394). Cham: Springer.

Noddings, N. (2013). *Caring: A relational approach to ethics and moral education.* Univ of California Press.

Novak, E., Razzouk, R., & Johnson, T. E. (2012). The educational use of social annotation tools in higher education: A literature review. *The Internet and Higher Education, 15*(1), 39–49. doi:10.1016/j.iheduc.2011.09.002

Novatchkov, H., & Baca, A. (2013). Fuzzy Logic in Sports: A Review and an Illustrative Case Study in the Field of Strength Training. *International Journal of Computers and Applications, 71*(6), 8–14. doi:10.5120/12360-8675

Oblinger, D. G. (2018). Smart machines and human expertise: Challenges for higher education. *EDUCAUSE Review.* Retrieved from https://er.educause.edu/articles/2018/8/smart-machines-and-human-expertise-challenges-for-higher-education

Ogan, A., Walker, E., Baker, R., Rodrigo, M. M. T., Soriano, J. C., & Castro, M. J. (2015). Towards understanding how to assess help-seeking behavior across cultures. *International Journal of Artificial Intelligence in Education, 25*(2), 229–248. doi:10.100740593-014-0034-8

Ohler, J. (2011). Digital citizenship means character education for the digital age. *Kappa Delta Pi Record, 47*(sup1), 25-27.

Ordonez, R. V., & Gandeza, N. (2004). Integrating traditional beliefs and modern medicine: Filipino nurses' health beliefs, behaviors, and practices. *Home Health Care Management & Practice, 17*(1), 22–27. doi:10.1177/1084822304268152

Ortiz, A. M., & Shaunna, S. (2015). The power of educational robotics as an integrated STEM learning experience in teacher preparation programs. *Journal of College Science Teaching, 44*(5), 42–47. doi:10.2505/4/jcst15_044_05_42

Owens, R. G. (1995). *Organizational behavior in education.* Academic Press.

Page, R. M., & Zarco, E. P. (2001). Shyness, physical activity, and sports team participation among Philippine high school students. *Child Study Journal, 31*(3), 193–204.

Palensky, P., Meer, A. A. V. D., Lopez, C. D., Joseph, A., & Pan, K. (2017). Cosimulation of Intelligent Power Systems: Fundamentals, Software Architecture, Numerics, and Coupling. *IEEE Industrial Electronics Magazine, 11*(1), 34–50. doi:10.1109/MIE.2016.2639825

Panagidi, K., Kolomvatsos, K., & Hadjiefthymiades, S. (2014). An intelligent scheme for concurrent multi-issue negotiations. *International Journal of Artificial Intelligence, 12*(1), 129–149.

Pan, Y. (2016). Heading toward Artificial Intelligence 2.0. *Engineering, 2*(4), 409–413. doi:10.1016/J.ENG.2016.04.018

Pan, Z., Cheok, A. D., Yang, H., Zhu, J., & Shi, J. (2006). Virtual reality and mixed reality for virtual learning environments. *Computers & Graphics*, *30*(1), 20–28. doi:10.1016/j.cag.2005.10.004

Pardos, Z. A., & Heffernan, N. T. (2010). Modeling individualization in a Bayesian networks implementation of knowledge tracing. In *Proceedings of the International Conference on User Modeling, Adaptation, and Personalization* (pp. 255-266). Berlin: Springer. 10.1007/978-3-642-13470-8_24

Pardos, Z. A., & Heffernan, N. T. (2011). KT-IDEM: Introducing item difficulty to the knowledge tracing model. In *Proceedings of the International Conference on User Modeling, Adaptation, and Personalization* (pp. 243-254). Berlin: Springer. 10.1007/978-3-642-22362-4_21

Pareto, L. (2014). A teachable agent game engaging primary school children to learn arithmetic concepts and reasoning. *International Journal of Artificial Intelligence in Education*, *24*(3), 251–283. doi:10.100740593-014-0018-8

Pareto, L., Arvemo, T., Dahl, Y., Haake, M., & Gulz, A. (2011). A teachable-agent arithmetic game's effects on mathematics understanding, attitude and self-efficacy. In *Proceedings of the International Conference on Artificial Intelligence in Education* (pp. 247-255). Berlin: Springer. 10.1007/978-3-642-21869-9_33

Pătraşcu, A., Ungureanu, A., Pătraşcu, M., Drăgoicea, M., & Hanţiu, I. (2016). MOTION-AE: an Intelligent Mobile Application for Aerobic Endurance Training. *International Journal of Artificial Intelligence*, *14*(2), 42-59.

Pătraşcu, A., Pătraşcu, M., & Hanţiu, I. (2014). Nonlinear Fuzzy Control of Human Heart Rate During Aerobic Endurance Training with Respect to Significant Model Variations, *Proc. of the International Conference on System Theory, Control and Computing ICSTCC*, 311-316 10.1109/ICSTCC.2014.6982434

Patrizio, A. (2016). *Pros and cons of AI*. Retrieved from https://www.datamation.com/applications/pros-and-cons-of-artificial-intelligence.html

Pedregosa, F., Varoquaux, G., Gramfort, A., Michel, V., Thirion, B., Grisel, O., ... Vanderplas, J. (2011). Scikit-learn: Machine learning in Python. *Journal of Machine Learning Research*, *12*(Oct), 2825–2830.

Phillipo, J., & Krongard, S. (2012). *Learning Management System*. LMS.

Pipatsarun, P., & Vicheanpanya, J. (2010). Adaptive intelligent tutoring systems for e-learning systems. *Computer and Information Science*, *2*(2), 4064–4069.

Poincaré, H. (1984). La moral y la ciencia. In E. de Gortari (Ed.), *Filosofia De La Ciencia* (pp. 269–283). UNAM.

Ponce, P., Ibarra, L., Mata, O., & Molina, A. (2019). How to develop research skills among undergraduate engineering students to tackle current ongoing topics? A Smart-Grid case study. *International Journal of Electrical Engineering Education*; Advance online publication. doi:10.1177/0020720918816004

Popenici, S. A. D., & Kerr, S. (2017). Exploring the impact of Artificial Intelligence on teaching and learning in higher education. *Research and Practice in Technology Enhanced Learning, 12*(22), 1-13. Retrieved from https://telrp.springeropen.com/articles/10.1186/s41039-017-0062-8

Poth, R. D. (2018). *Artificial Intelligence: Implications for the future of education.* Retrieved from http://www.gettingsmart.com/2018/01/artificial-intelligence-implications-for-the-future-of-education/

Potkonjak, V., Gardner, M., Callaghan, V., Mattila, P., Guetl, C., Petrović, V. M., & Jovanović, K. (2016). Virtual laboratories for education in science, technology, and engineering: A review. *Computers & Education, 95*, 309–327. doi:10.1016/j.compedu.2016.02.002

Precup, R. E., Bojan-Dragos, C. A., Petriu, E. M., Radac, M. B., & Stinean, A. I. (2015). Results on Optimal Tuning of Fuzzy Models of Magnetic Levitation Systems. *International Journal of Artificial Intelligence, 13*(2), 57–72.

Quinn, C. A., & Dalal, D. B. (2017). Empowering the electronics industry: A power technology roadmap. *CPSS Transactions on Power Electronics and Applications, 2*(4), 306–319. doi:10.24295/CPSSTPEA.2017.00028

Rajaraman, V. (2014). John McCarthy – Father of Artificial Intelligence. *Resonance: Journal of Science Education.* Retrieved from https://www.ias.ac.in/article/fulltext/reso/019/03/0198-0207

Rajasingham, L. (2009). The impact of Artificial Intelligence systems on future university paradigms. *MERLOT Journal of Online Learning and Teaching, 5*(2), 386-394. Retrieved from http://jolt.merlot.org/vol5no2/rajasingham_0609.pdf

Raufelder, D., Nitsche, L., Breitmeyer, S., Keßler, S., Herrmann, E., & Regner, N. (2016). Students' perception of "good" and "bad" teachers-Results of a qualitative thematic analysis with German adolescent. *International Journal of Educational Research, 75*, 31–44. doi:10.1016/j.ijer.2015.11.004

Raybourn, E. M., & Waern, A. (2004). Social learning through gaming. In *CHI'04 Extended Abstracts on Human Factors in Computing Systems* (pp. 1733–1734). New York: ACM.

Redmon, J., Divvala, S., Girshick, R., & Farhadi, A. (2016). You only look once: Unified, real-time object detection. In *Proceedings of the IEEE conference on computer vision and pattern recognition* (pp. 779-788). IEEE. 10.1109/CVPR.2016.91

Richards, D., & Taylor, M. (2015). A Comparison of learning gains when using a 2D simulation tool versus a 3D virtual world: An experiment to find the right representation involving the Marginal Value Theorem. *Computers & Education, 86*, 157–171. doi:10.1016/j.compedu.2015.03.009

Richardson, D. B. (2013). Electric vehicles and the electric grid: A review of modeling approaches, Impacts, and renewable energy integration. *Renewable & Sustainable Energy Reviews, 19*, 247–254. doi:10.1016/j.rser.2012.11.042

Rieland, R. (2017). Is Artificial Intelligence the key to personalized education? *Smithsonian.com*. Retrieved from https://www.smithsonianmag.com/innovation/artificial-intelligence-key-personalized-education-180963172/

Ritter, S., Anderson, J. R., Koedinger, K. R., & Corbett, A. (2007). Cognitive tutor: Applied research in mathematics education. *Psychonomic Bulletin & Review*, *14*(2), 249–255. doi:10.3758/BF03194060 PMID:17694909

Rizzotto, L. (2017). *The future of education: How A.I. and immersive tech will reshape learning forever*. Retrieved from https://tfpodcast.io/2017/08/30/episode-36-the-future-of-education-how-a-i-and-immersive-tech-will-reshape-learning-forever/

Roblyer, M. D., & Doering, A. H. (2006). Integrating educational technology into teaching (Vol. 2). Pearson/Merrill Prentice Hall.

Roco, M. C., & Bainbridge, W. S. (2003). *Overview converging technologies for improving human performance. In Converging technologies for improving human performance* (pp. 1–27). Springer. doi:10.1007/978-94-017-0359-8

Rosenberg, M. J. (2001). *E-Learning: Strategies for Delivering Knowledge in the Digital Age*. New York: McGraw-Hill.

Rossett, A. (2001). *Beyond The Podium: Delivering Training and Performance to a Digital World*. San Francisco: Jossey-Bass/Pfeiffer.

Rudas, I. T. (2012). Risk and Uncertainties of Physiological Processes Handled by the Fuzzy Implementation. *WSEAS International Conference on System Science and Simulation in Engineering*, 37-43.

Rui, S. (2013). Identification method of sports throwing force based on fuzzy neural network. *Journal of Networks*, *8*(7), 1574.

Russell, S. J., & Norvig, P. (2016). *Artificial intelligence: a modern approach*. Pearson Education Limited.

Rus, V., Niraula, N., & Banjade, R. (2015, March). DeepTutor: an effective, online intelligent tutoring system that promotes deep learning. *Twenty-Ninth AAAI Conference on Artificial Intelligence*.

Saadé, R., & Bahli, B. (2005). The impact of cognitive absorption on perceived usefulness and perceived ease of use in on-line learning: An extension of the technology acceptance model. *Information & Management*, *42*(2), 317–327. doi:10.1016/j.im.2003.12.013

Sallis, E. (2014). *Total quality management in education*. Routledge. doi:10.4324/9780203417010

Samak, A., & Tawfik, Z. (2017). *Exploration of Jordanian English Language Teachers' Attitudes*. Skills, and Access as Indicator of Information and Communication Technology Integration in Jordan.

Santa, C. M., & Santa, J. L. (1995). Teacher as researcher. *Journal of Reading Behavior*, *27*(3), 439–451. doi:10.1080/10862969509547891

Santiago, C., & Enriquez, V. (1976). Tungo sa makapilipinong pananaliksik. *Sikolohiyang Pilipino: Mga Ulat at Balita*, *1*(4), 3–10.

Sao Pedro, M., Baker, R. S., Montalvo, O., Nakama, A., & Gobert, J. D. (2010). Using text replay tagging to produce detectors of systematic experimentation behavior patterns. In *Proceedings of the International Conference on Educational Data Mining 2010* (pp. 191-200). Worcester, MA: International Data Mining Society.

Saranya, D., & Phil, M. (2016). A study on Artificial Intelligence and its applications. *International Journal of Advanced Research in Computer and Communication Engineering.*, *5*(4), 313–315.

Saravanan, K., Sreedevi, E., & Subhamathi, V. (2017). A review of Artificial Intelligence systems. *International Journal of Advanced Research in Computer Science*, *8*(9), 418–420. doi:10.26483/ijarcs.v8i9.5095

Schroeder, N. L., Adesope, O. O., & Gilbert, R. B. (2013). How effective are pedagogical agents for learning?: A meta-analytic review. *Journal of Educational Computing Research*, *49*(1), 1–39. doi:10.2190/EC.49.1.a

Scollon, C. N., Diener, E., Oishi, S., & Biswas-Diener, R. (2004). Emotions across cultures and methods. *Journal of Cross-Cultural Psychology*, *35*(3), 304–326. doi:10.1177/0022022104264124

Scott, S. S., Mcguire, J. M., & Shaw, S. F. (2003). Universal design for instruction: A new paradigm for adult instruction in postsecondary education. *Remedial and Special Education*, *24*(6), 369–379. doi:10.1177/07419325030240060801

Seidman, I. (2013). *Interviewing as qualitative research: A guide for researchers in education and the social sciences*. Teachers College Press.

Self, J. (1990). Theoretical foundations for intelligent tutoring systems. *Journal of Artificial Intelligence in Education*, *1*(4), 3–14.

Self, J. (1998). The defining characteristics of intelligent tutoring systems research: ITSs care, precisely. *International Journal of Artificial Intelligence in Education*, *10*, 350–364.

Seligman, M. E., Ernst, R. M., Gillham, J., Reivich, K., & Linkins, M. (2009). Positive education: Positive psychology and classroom interventions. *Oxford Review of Education*, *35*(3), 293–311. doi:10.1080/03054980902934563

Selmer, J., & De Leon, C. (2001). Pinoy-style HRM: Human resource management in the Philippines. *Asia Pacific Business Review*, *8*(1), 127–144. doi:10.1080/713999124

Seneviratne, S., Hu, Y., Nguyen, T., Lan, G., Khalifa, S., Thilakarathna, K., & Seneviratne, A. (2017). A survey of wearable devices and challenges. *IEEE Communications Surveys and Tutorials*, *19*(4), 2573–2620. doi:10.1109/COMST.2017.2731979

Serra Toledo, R., Pérez, I. A., Herrera Rodríguez, R., Magalhães, D. S. F., Muramatsu, M., Soga, D., & Zottola Pareja, D. (2013). Physical contribution to the development of research skills in engineering students. *Revista Brasileira de Ensino de Física*, *35*(4), 1–8.

Shahidehpour, M. (2011, November). *Smart Grid Education and Workforce Training Center*. doi:10.1109/ISGT-Asia.2011.6167128

Shah, N. B., Hastings, D. E., & Rhodes, D. H. (2007). Systems of systems and emergent system context. *5th Conference on Systems Engineering Research.*

Sharp, R., Green, A., & Lewis, J. (2017). *Education and social control: A study in progressive primary education*. Routledge. doi:10.4324/9781315210179

Shaver, P. R., & Schwartz, J. C. (1992). Cross-cultural similarities and differences in emotion and its representation. In C. Z. Malatesta & C. Izard (Eds.), *Emotions in adult development* (pp. 319–338). Beverly Hills, CA: Sage.

Sheridan, T. B. (2016). Human–robot interaction: Status and challenges. *Human Factors*, *58*(4), 525–532. doi:10.1177/0018720816644364 PMID:27098262

Simic, B., & Heller, A. (2019). *Autonomes Fahren: Spur- und Schilderkennung mit einem LEGO-Fahrzeug unter Matlab und Simulink. Bochum University of Applied Sciences, Höseler Platz 2, D-42579 Heiligenhaus*. Project Documentation.

Singh, R., Gulwani, S., & Rajamani, S. K. (2012). Automatically generating algebra problems. In *Proceedings of the Twenty-Sixth AAAI Conference on Artificial Intelligence*. (pp.1620-1627). Menlo Park, CA: AAAI Press.

Sivakumar, S. C., Robertson, W., Artimy, M., & Aslam, N. (2005). A web-based remote interactive laboratory for Internetworking education. *IEEE Transactions on Education*, *48*(4), 586–598. doi:10.1109/TE.2005.858393

Skiba, D. J. (2017). Horizon report: Knowledge obsolescence, Artificial Intelligence, and rethinking the education role. *Nursing Education Perspectives*, *38*(3), 165–167. doi:10.1097/01.NEP.0000000000000154

Skrtic, T. M. (1991). *Behind special education: A critical analysis of professional culture and school organization*. Love Publishing Company.

Sleeman, D., & Brown, J. S. (1982). *Intelligent tutoring systems*. London: Academic Press.

Smith, N. B. (2002). *American reading instruction*. Newark, DE: International Reading Association.

Smith, S. C., & Piele, P. K. (2006). *School leadership: Handbook for excellence in student learning*. Corwin Press.

Spencer-Oatey, H. (2008). *Culturally speaking: Culture, communication and politeness theory* (2nd ed.). London: Continuum.

Stamper, J., Barnes, T., & Croy, M. (2011). Enhancing the automatic generation of hints with expert seeding. *International Journal of Artificial Intelligence in Education, 21*(1-2), 153–167.

Steenbergen-Hu, S., & Cooper, H. (2014). A meta-analysis of the effectiveness of intelligent tutoring systems on college students' academic learning. *Journal of Educational Psychology, 106*(2), 331–347. doi:10.1037/a0034752

Steinbrink, C., Lehnhoff, S., Rohjans, S., Strasser, T. I., Widl, E., Moyo, C., … Degefa, M. Z. (2017). *Simulation-based Validation of Smart Grids - Status Quo and Future Research Trends.* doi:10.1007/978-3-319-64635-0_13

Stocker, M. (1979). Desiring the bad: An essay in moral psychology. *The Journal of Philosophy, 76*(12), 738–753. doi:10.2307/2025856

Su, S. W., Wang, L., Celler, B. G., & Savkin, A. V. (2006). Heart rate control during treadmill exercise. *Engineering in Medicine and Biology Society, 2005. IEEE-EMBS 2005. 27th Annual International Conference of the,* 2471-2474.

Sugisaka, M., & Hazry, D. (2007). Development of a proportional control method for a mobile robot. *Applied Mathematics and Computation, 186*(1), 74–82. doi:10.1016/j.amc.2006.05.214

Suraweera, P., & Mitrovic, A. (2002). KERMIT: A constraint-based tutor for database modeling. In *Proceedings of the International Conference on Intelligent Tutoring Systems* (pp. 377-387). Berlin: Springer. 10.1007/3-540-47987-2_41

Szajna, B. (1996). Empirical evaluation of the revised technology acceptance model. *Management Science, 42*(1), 85–92. doi:10.1287/mnsc.42.1.85

Tan, S. C., Yeo, A. C. J., & Lim, W. Y. (2005). Changing epistemology of science learning through inquiry with computer-supported collaborative learning. *Journal of Computers in Mathematics and Science Teaching, 24*(4), 367–386.

Tatsuoka, K. K., & Tatsuoka, M. M. (1983). Spotting erroneous rules of operation by the individual consistency index. *Journal of Educational Measurement, 20*(3), 221–230. doi:10.1111/j.1745-3984.1983.tb00201.x

Tokic, M., & Ammar, H. B. (2012). Teaching reinforcement learning using a physical robot. *Proceedings of the ICML Workshop on Teaching Machine Learning.*

Tomkins, A., Zhang, M., & Heavlin, W. D. (2017). Reviewer bias in single- versus double-blind peer review. *Proceedings of the National Academy of Sciences of the United States of America, 114*(48), 12708–12713. doi:10.1073/pnas.1707323114 PMID:29138317

Toro, C., Barandiaran, I., & Posada, J. (2015). A perspective on Knowledge Based and Intelligent systems implementation in Industrie 4.0. *Procedia Computer Science, 60*, 362–370. doi:10.1016/j.procs.2015.08.143

Trow, M. (2007). *Reflections on the transition from elite to mass to universal access: Forms and phases of higher education in modern societies since WWII. In International handbook of higher education* (pp. 243–280). Springer.

Truong, H. M. (2016). Computers in Human Behavior Integrating Learning Styles and Adaptive E-Learning System: Current Developments, Problems and Opportunities. *Computers in Human Behavior, 55*, 1185–1193. doi:10.1016/j.chb.2015.02.014

Tuckman, B. W., & Harper, B. E. (2012). *Conducting educational research.* Rowman & Littlefield Publishers.

Umashankar, V., & Dutta, K. (2007). Balanced scorecards in managing higher education institutions: An Indian perspective. *International Journal of Educational Management, 21*(1), 54–67. doi:10.1108/09513540710716821

Upadhyaya, J., & Ahuja, N. J. (2017). Quality of service in cloud computing in higher education: A critical survey and innovative model. *I-SMAC (IoT in Social, Mobile, Analytics and Cloud) (I-SMAC), 2017 International Conference on,* 137-140 10.1109/I-SMAC.2017.8058324

Vallon, C., Ercan, Z., Carvalho, A., & Borrelli, F. (2017, June). A machine learning approach for personalized autonomous lane change initiation and control. In *2017 IEEE Intelligent Vehicles Symposium (IV)* (pp. 1590-1595). IEEE. 10.1109/IVS.2017.7995936

Van Dalen, A. (2012). The algorithms behind the headlines: How machine-written news redefines the core skills of human journalists. *Journalism Practice, 6*(5-6), 648–658. doi:10.1080/17512786.2012.667268

van der Rijst, R. (2017). The Transformative Nature of Research-Based Education: A Thematic Overview of the Literature. In *Research-Based Learning* (pp. 3–22). Case Studies from Maastricht University. doi:10.1007/978-3-319-50993-8_1

Van Gogh Museum. (2015). *App Touch Van Gogh.* Retrieved from: vangoghmuseum.nl/en/app-touch-van-gogh

van Otterlo, M. (2012). *Reinforcement learning: State-of-the-Art.* Springer Berlin Heidelberg.

Van Wyk, J. D., & Lee, F. C. (2013). On a Future for Power Electronics. *IEEE Journal of Emerging and Selected Topics in Power Electronics, 1*(2), 59–72. doi:10.1109/JESTPE.2013.2271499

VanLehn, K., Lynch, C., Schulze, K., Shapiro, J. A., Shelby, R., Taylor, L., ... Wintersgill, M. (2005). The Andes physics tutoring system: Lessons learned. *International Journal of Artificial Intelligence in Education, 15*(3), 147–204.

Varis, T., & Al-Agtash, S. (2008). *Ubiquitous ICT for sustainable education and cultural literacy.* Citeseer.

Vassileva, J., McCalla, G., & Greer, J. (2003). Multi-agent multi-user modeling in I-Help. *User Modeling and User-Adapted Interaction, 13*(1-2), 179–210. doi:10.1023/A:1024072706526

Venkatesh, V. (1999). Creation of favorable user perceptions: Exploring the role of intrinsic motivation. *Management Information Systems Quarterly*, *23*(2), 239–260. doi:10.2307/249753

Venkatesh, V., & Davis, F. D. (2000). A theoretical extension of the technology acceptance model: Four longitudinal field studies. *Management Science*, *46*(2), 186–204. doi:10.1287/mnsc.46.2.186.11926

Verma, A., Rathore, S., Vishwakarma, S., & Goswani, S. (2017). Multilevel Analysis of Student's Feedback Using Moodle Logs in Virtual Cloud Environment. *International Journal of Computer Science and Information Technology*, *9*(5), 15–28. doi:10.5121/ijcsit.2017.9502

Verschaffel, L., Greer, B., & De Corte, E. (2000). *Making sense of word problems*. Lisse, The Netherlands: Swets & Zeitlinger.

Von Glasersfeld, E. (1998). Cognition, construction of knowledge, and teaching. In Constructivism in science education (pp. 11-30). Springer.

Wagner, K. (2018). *A blended environment: The future of AI and education*. Retrieved from http://www.gettingsmart.com/2018/01/a-blended-environment-the-future-of-ai-and-education/

Wagner, E. (1998). Creating a Virtual University in a Traditional Environment. *Proceedings of the 7th European Distance Education Network.*

Wals, A. E., & Jickling, B. (2002). "Sustainability" in higher education: From doublethink and newspeak to critical thinking and meaningful learning. *International Journal of Sustainability in Higher Education*, *3*(3), 221–232. doi:10.1108/14676370210434688

Wang, M., Shen, R., Novak, D., & Pan, X. (2009). The impact of mobile learning on students' learning behaviours and performance: Report from a large blended classroom. *British Journal of Educational Technology*, *40*(4), 673–695. doi:10.1111/j.1467-8535.2008.00846.x

Wang, R., Wiesemes, R., & Gibbons, C. (2012). Developing digital fluency through ubiquitous mobile devices: Findings from a small-scale study. *Computers & Education*, *58*(1), 570–578. doi:10.1016/j.compedu.2011.04.013

Watson, G., McKeown, N., & Casado, M. (2006). *NetFPGA: A tool for network research and education.* Paper presented at the 2nd workshop on Architectural Research using FPGA Platforms (WARFP).

Weiss, G. (2013). *Multiagent Systems, ser.* EBSCO ebook academic collection.

Whitby, B. (2013). *Artificial Intelligence. In Encyclopedia of philosophy and the social sciences.* Thousand Oaks, CA: SAGE Publications, Inc.

Wiering, M., & Van Otterlo, M. (2012). *Reinforcement learning. Adaptation, learning, and optimization.* Academic Press.

Williams, P. (2002). The learning web: The development, implementation and evaluation of internet-based undergraduate materials for the teaching of key skills. *Active Learning in Higher Education, 3*(1), 40–53. doi:10.1177/1469787402003001004

Williams, P. (2019). Does competency-based education with blockchain signal a new mission for universities? *Journal of Higher Education Policy and Management, 41*(1), 104–117. doi:10.1080/1360080X.2018.1520491

Willison, J., & O'Regan, K. (2007). Commonly known, commonly not known, totally unknown: A framework for students becoming researchers. *Higher Education Research & Development, 26*(4), 393–409. doi:10.1080/07294360701658609

Wilson, H. J., Daugherty, P. R., & Morini-Bianzino, N. (2017). The jobs that Artificial Intelligence will create. *MIT Sloan Management Review, 58*(4), 14–16. Retrieved from http://ilp.mit.edu/media/news_articles/smr/2017/58416.pdf

Winne, P. H., Nesbit, J. C., Kumar, V., Hadwin, A. F., Lajoie, S. P., Azevedo, R., & Perry, N. E. (2006). Supporting self-regulated learning with gStudy software: The Learning Kit Project. *Technology Instruction Cognition and Learning, 3*(1/2), 105–113.

Wolf, B. P. (2009). *Building Intelligent Interactive Tutors: Student-Centered Strategies for Revolutionizing E-Learning*. Morgan Kaufmann Publishers.

Wollowski, M., Neller, T., & Boerkoel, J. (2017). Artificial Intelligence education. Association for the Advancement of Artificial Intelligence. *AI Magazine*.

Wood, D. F. (2003). Problem based learning. *BMJ (Clinical Research Ed.), 326*(7384), 328–330. doi:10.1136/bmj.326.7384.328 PMID:12574050

Woolf, B. P. (2015). AI and education: Celebrating 30 years of marriage. *AIED 2015 Workshop Proceedings, 4*, 38-47.

Woolf, B. P., Lane, H. C., Chaudhri, V. K., & Kolodner, J. I. (2013). AI grand challenges for education. *AI Magazine*. Retrieved from https://www.aaai.org/ojs/index.php/aimagazine/article/view/2490

Woolf, B. P., Lane, H. C., Chaudhri, V. K., & Kolodner, J. L. (2013). AI grand challenges for education. *AI Magazine, 34*(4), 66–84. doi:10.1609/aimag.v34i4.2490

World Economic Forum. (2018). *The 10 skills you need to thrive in the Fourth Industrial Revolution*. Retrieved December 14, 2018, from World Economic Forum website: https://www.weforum.org/agenda/2016/01/the-10-skills-you-need-to-thrive-in-the-fourth-industrial-revolution/

Wright, S. A., & Schultz, A. E. (2018). The rising tide of artificial intelligence and business automation: Developing an ethical framework. *Business Horizons, 61*(6), 823–832. doi:10.1016/j.bushor.2018.07.001

Yasuda, K. (2017). The future vision of industrial robot. 2017 29th International Symposium on Power Semiconductor Devices and IC's (ISPSD), 7–12. 10.23919/ISPSD.2017.7988979

Yin, R. K. (1981). The case study crisis: Some answers. *Administrative Science Quarterly*, *26*(1), 58–65. doi:10.2307/2392599

Young, P. A. (2011). The significance of the Culture Based Model in designing culturally aware tutoring systems. *AI & Society*, *26*(1), 35–47. doi:10.100700146-010-0282-6

Zhang, F., Zhang, X., Zhang, M., & Edmonds, A. S. E. (2016). Literature review of electric vehicle technology and its applications. 2016 5th International Conference on Computer Science and Network Technology (ICCSNT), 832–837. 10.1109/ICCSNT.2016.8070276

Zheng, B., Niiya, M., & Warschauer, M. (2015). Wikis and collaborative learning in higher education. *Technology, Pedagogy and Education*, *24*(3), 357–374. doi:10.1080/1475939X.2014.948041

Zipes, J. (2013). *When dreams came true: classical fairy tales and their tradition.* Routledge. doi:10.4324/9780203949672

About the Contributors

Maki Habib obtained Doctor of Eng. Sciences in Intelligent and Autonomous Robotics, Univ. of Tsukuba Japan. Selected research scientist at RIKEN Japan. Senior researcher at RISO-Labs Japan. Visiting researcher at EPFL, Switzerland. Visiting expert under ADB, Associate Prof. UTM, Malaysia. Senior Manager MCRIA Malaysia. Senior research scientist with GMD-Japan. Associate Prof. with Monash Univ. leading Mechatronics program. A full Prof. Robotics and Mechatronics at Swinburne Univ. Invited Prof. KAIST South Korea, Visiting Prof. at Saga Univ. Japan. Since Sept. 2007 he is full Professor of Robotics and Mechatronics at AUC. He also served consultant and technical adviser for Toyota group, ABB, etc. He published 10 books, 24 book chapters, more than 275 papers at international journals and intern. confs. His main research focus: Human and Friendly Mechatronics, Intelligent and Autonomous Robotics/Vehicles: Control, Mapping-Localization, Navigation and Learning. Service Robots for Humanitarian Demining, Biomimetic and Biomedical Robotics, Telecooperation Distributed Teleoperation, and Collaborative Control, Intelligent and Nonlinear Control, Wireless Sensor Networks, Industry 4, Flying Robots.

* * *

Rex P. Bringula is a professor at the University of the East (UE) College of Computer Studies and Systems. He received his BS Computer Science degree from UE as a Department of Science and Technology scholar. He received his Master in Information Technology and Ph.D. in Technology Management in Technological University of the Philippines. He is currently taking up PhD in Computer Science in Ateneo de Manila University. He is active in conducting school- and government-funded research projects, and in participating in local and international conferences. His research interests are in computer science/IT education, affective computing, Internet studies, cyber-behavior, web usability, and environmental issues.

Shweta Chauhan has completed her PhD from Shoolini University Solan. She is working on different problems related to Science and Social science to make the world a better place to live.

Jörg Frochte studied mathematics at the University of Essen with a focus on numerical simulation, cryptography and physics (until 2002). Dissertation (2005) in the field of computational fluid dynamics at the University of Duisburg-Essen. Until 2010 he was working in the software development department of the dSPACE GmbH in Paderborn as a technical expert and project coordinator in the field of real time simulation and physical modeling. Appointment as a full professor for Applied Computer Science at the Bochum University of Applied Sciences in 2010. Beyond this he is active in the Bergische Innovationsplattform für Künstliche Intelligenz, which promotes cooperation between scientists as well as companies in the local region and the "Interdisciplinary Center for Machine Learning and Data Analytics (IZMD)" of the University of Wuppertal.

Luis Ibarra was born in Mexico City, Mexico in 1989. He received the B.S. degree in mechatronics and the Ph.D. degree in engineering sciences, with specialization in intelligent control from Tecnólogico de Monterrey, Mexico City in 2011 and 2016 respectively. He currently holds an Assistant Professor and Researcher position at Tecnológico de Monterrey in Mexico City. He has coauthored 1 book, 17 research articles, 1 book chapter, and 2 inventions. His research interests include robust control and artificial intelligence, particularly applied to power systems and electric machinery. Dr. Ibarra is a member of the Mexican National Researchers System since 2018.

Varun Jaiswal received his M.Tech degree in computational and system biology from Jawaharlal Nehru University (JNU), New Delhi and further pursued his PhD in Bio-Informatics from Jaypee University of Information Technology, Solan. He has computational expertise in data analysis of various fields and enjoys solving important issues primarily with computational means. He has applied machine learning methods in diverse fields which include biology, chemistry, medicine, computer science, and social science. He has authored dozens of paper in reputed top tier journals of diverse fields. He worked as an Assistant Professor in Shoolini University, Solan, India. Number of students have successfully completed their PhD and Master degree under his able guidance. Currently, he is working as an Assistant Director in National Center for Disease Control, Delhi, India. He prefers to work with new and emerging technology to answer different challenging problems of the nation and the world. He strongly believe that artificial intelligence powered with machine learning will change the global scenario in favor of humanity in almost all the fields.

Markus Lemmen is Professor of Control and Vehicle Systems Engineering and has been appointed to the Velbert-Heiligenhaus Campus (CVH) in February 2012. Mr. Lemmen completed his doctorate at the University of Duisburg in the field of nonlinear system analysis at the Institute of Instrumentation and Control. This was followed by a postdoctoral phase in Duisburg and at the Technical University Eindhoven (NL) in the field of nonlinear control of dynamic systems, especially hydraulic cylinder drives. Mr. Lemmen then moved to industry for almost ten years and worked for Ford. Here he worked all the time in the field of Vehicle Dynamics. Initially this was done in the context of research and advance development at Global Vehicle Dynamics and then for about seven years in series product development at Vehicle Dynamics. Many are particularly familiar with the electromechanical steering (EPAS) of the current Ford Fiesta and the C-Max/Grand C-Max.

Arturo Molina was born in Oaxaca, Mexico in 1964. He received the B.Eng. degree in Computational Systems and the M.Eng. degree in Computational Sciences from Tecnológico de Monterrey, Monterrey, Mexico. Later, he received a Doctoral degree in Mechanics from the Budapest University in Technology and Economics, Hungary, and a Ph.D. in Manufacturing Systems from the Loughborough University of Technology in England. He currently works as Vice-president of Research and Technology Transfer for Tecnológico de Monterrey. He has coauthored more than 300 research articles and several inventions. His research interests include Concurrent Engineering, Sustainability, and Collaborative Engineering Technologies. Dr. Molina is a member of the Mexican National Researchers System.

Ana Oliveira Lima, Doctor (PhD) and Masters degrees in Electrical Engineering from Universidade Federal de Campina Grande (UFCG), Brazil. Ana has been working for 14 years in the conceptual design of Assistive Technologies and innovative technology products, as well as performing as a postgraduate lecturer in the areas of Electrical Engineering and Information Technology. Ana has been awarded the Santander Universities prize in the Science and Innovation category in 2015 and nominated as a finalist of the Sports Technology Awards 2017 in London. Ana coordinates the Centro de Inovacao em Controle e Automacao e Robotica Industrial (Innovation in Control and Automation and Industrial Robotics) - CICARI, which runs important research projects in Assistive Technologies funded by the Brazilian national scientific research center government agency (Centro Nacional de Pesquisa Cientifica).

Adrian Pătraşcu has received a Ph.D. in Sport Science in 2019 and is undergoing his doctoral studies in Sport Science and has received an M.A. in Training and Sport Performance in 2011 and a B.A. in Physical Education and Sport in 2009. Adrian Patrascu is a junior researcher at the Center of Interdisciplinary Research in Physical Education and Sport at the Faculty of Physical Education and Sport, Babeş-Bolyai Cluj-Napoca. Research interests include intelligent control systems, human balance, sport performance and instrument development in sport.

Monica Patrascu received a Ph.D. in Systems Engineering in 2012, an M.Sc. in Intelligent Control Systems in 2009 and a B.Sc. in Control Engineering in 2007. Dr. Patrascu is an Associate Professor at the Department of Automatic Control and Systems Engineering, University Politehnica of Bucharest. Research interests include intelligent control systems, evolutionary computing, large scale systems, heuristic optimization, emergent systems, multi-agent systems, and complex systems.

Pedro Ponce was born in Mexico City, Mexico in 1971. He received the B.Eng. degree in Automation and Control, the M.Sc. and Ph.D. degrees in Electric Engineering with concentration in Automatic Control from Instituto Politécnico Nacional in 1995, 1998, and 2002, respectively. He worked for more than 12 years as a field and design engineer of electric drives and automation systems. He has coauthored more than 50 research articles and 6 inventions. He currently works as Senior Researcher at Tecnologico de Monterrey, Mexico City, Mexico. His research interests include Mechatronics, Electric Engineering, and Artificial Intelligence, all of them mostly focused to the integration of power sources to the electric grid. Dr. Ponce is a member of the Mexican National Researchers System.

Kamaljeet Sandhu's teaching and research expertise are in Accounting, Information Systems & IT Adoption, Management Accounting and Corporate Governance Adoption, and E-Learning Acceptance at Universities. Dr. Sandhu is an active, experienced researcher & passionate about research in Digital Accounting Innovation & Strategy, Blockchain, Business Analytics, AI, IoT, Cryptocurrencies, IT Startups, FinTech, Cybersecurity, Corporate Social Responsibility, Supply Chain, ERP, EHealth, SMEs, & Entrepreneurship.

Marco Schmidt is Professor at Bochum University of Applied Sciences. He initiated the Robotics and Computer Technology group at the newly founded Campus Velbert Heiligenhaus. His research interests are intelligent systems in robotics and computer science related topics in space technology. Marco Schmidt studied computer science at the University of Würzburg. After finishing his Diploma degree in 2006, he started to work as scientific collaborator in the field of space technology.

He received his doctorate degree (Dr. rer. nat.) from the University of Würzburg in 2011. Before he was appointed at Bochum University of Applied Sciences, he worked as Professor for Telematics with focus on intelligent systems.

Kapil Sethi has perusing his Ph.D. in computer science under the Shoolini University Solan Himachal Pradesh, India. He has received the master degree in two different courses i.e. MSC.IT and MCA from Guru Nanak Dev University Amritsar, Punjab, and Punjab Technical University Jalandhar. During his Ph.D., he has published three research papers in different journals. He has two-year experience in UIIT Himachal Pradesh University, Shimla India as an Assistant Professor. He has another two-year Teaching experience in different Institutes. His field is computer science and he has love to learn more and more about computers. During his Ph.D., his research area is Machine Learning.

Ajay Sharma is M.Tech Computer Science student. He has obtained his B.tech Bioinformatics and got a certificate of merit from Shoolini University. He has a passion for computer science along with Biology. Before joining at Shoolini University he obtained his three-year Diploma in Computer Science Engineering From Lovely Professional University. Currently, he is working on deep learning and applying deep learning algorithm in medical image analysis. He has Passionate about Learning new things in Computer Science and apply these techniques in the field of biology. Ajay has presented three posters in the international conferences and one poster at AIIMS RISHIKESH. Along with his studies, Ajay is an Art of Living Volunteer and a yoga practitioner.

Libi Shen has a Ph.D. from University of Pittsburgh, PA. She started her college teaching career in 1989. She is an online faculty for University of Phoenix. Libi is a contributing author for twelve IGI Global books. Her research interests include artificial intelligence, cybersecurity, K-12 education, curriculum design, adult literacy, communication, leadership, online instruction and learning, Internet addiction, and instructional technology.

Luis Arturo Soriano was born in México in 1985. He received the B.Eng. degree in Industrial Robotic and the M.Sc. in Manufacturing Engineering from Instituto Politécnico Nacional. He obtained his Ph. D. in Automatic Control at the Centro de Investigación y de Estudios Avanzados from the same institution. He currently works as a full-time professor in Tecnológico de Estudios Superiores de Ixtapaluca. His research interests are control, mathematical modeling, renewable energy, education, and optimization methods. He is a member of the Mexican National Researchers System.

Anchi Su has an MS and a BS in Electrical Engineering from University of California, Los Angeles. She is a systems engineer for Northrop Grumman Corporation. She is an IEEE member and Society of Women Engineers member. Her research interests include robotics design, embedded systems, wireless communication systems design, computer architecture, computer networking, VLSI design, and circuits and systems design.

Stefka Tzanova is the Science Librarian at York College, CUNY. Her research interests include science literacy, STEM, OER, advanced technologies in education, history of science and technology, and scholarly communications. Professor Tzanova has a strong background in the hard sciences and holds Master's degrees in engineering and library science.

Index

I

J

L

M

O

P

R

S

T

U

V

www.ingramcontent.com/pod-product-compliance
Lightning Source LLC
LaVergne TN
LVHW081326300926
849161LV00008B/1889